American Contract Bridge League

# Introduction to Bridge

# "Defense"

by
Audrey Grant

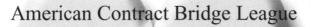

# ACBL BRIDGE SERIES

*Defense* is the third in the ACBL Bridge Series of texts written by Audrey Grant, world famous bridge teacher and author. There are five texts in all.

Volume One —
*Bidding – The Club Series*

Volume Two —
*Play of the Hand – The Diamond Series*

Volume Three —
*Defense – The Heart Series*

Volume Four —
*Commonly Used Conventions – The Spade Series*

Volume Five —
*More Commonly Used Conventions – The Notrump Series*

Trained teachers across North America offer bridge courses using these materials. Information on teachers in your area is available at the ACBL web site at www.acbl.org or by calling the ACBL Education Department in Memphis, Tennessee at 901–332–5586, extension 264.

Coordinated decks of E-Z Deal Cards which allow the reader to deal out the exercise deals at the end of each chapter are available for each bridge text. Social players can create a bridge party by dealing and playing the bridge hands and then looking in the text for information on the desired results.

The decks of cards can be ordered from the American Contract Bridge League online from the Product Catalog at www.acbl.org or by calling the ACBL Sales Department toll free at 1–800–264–2743 in the USA or at 1–800–264–8786 in Canada.

ISBN 0-943855-47-0

# INTRODUCTION

The American Contract Bridge League's *Defense* student text is the third in the ACBL Bridge Series of bridge books. The first book, *Bidding*, is followed by *Play of the Hand, Defense, Commonly Used Conventions,* and *More Commonly Used Conventions.* The books focus on introducing players to the game of bridge and helping them to advance.

This series of books is unusual in the field of bridge writing for several reasons. First, they were written by a professional educator, Audrey Grant, who also happens to be a bridge player. Accordingly these books encompass all of the sound principles that facilitate learning any subject and are built on the firm foundation of a basic understanding of the game of bridge.

Next, the technical approach to these books was determined by surveying a cross section of North American bridge teachers. This means that whether a student learns bridge from this book in Vancouver, British Columbia; St. Louis, Missouri; or Orlando, Florida, that student will be able to play bridge with virtually any other beginning bridge players in North America.

Third, the effectiveness of the teaching principles was field-tested in five cities prior to the publication of the first book in this series (*Bidding*), originally known as *The Club Series*, with more than 800 actual bridge students and at least 25 bridge teachers involved.

Finally, it is the first time in the more than 60-year history of ACBL that the sanctioning body for bridge in North America has produced its own series of bridge texts. The end result of the joint effort of Audrey Grant and the ACBL is this series which enables the reader to learn bridge or to review and improve bridge techniques in a logical and progressive fashion. More importantly, the reader will have fun while learning the fundamental concepts of good bridge bidding, play, defense, and use of conventions which will be beneficial for a lifetime.

# The American Contract Bridge League

The American Contract Bridge League (ACBL) is dedicated to the playing, teaching, and promotion of contract bridge. The membership of 170,000 includes a wide range of players — from the thousands who are just learning the joy of bridge to the most proficient players in North America.

ACBL offers a variety of services, including:

- **Tournament play.** Thousands of tournaments — North American Bridge Championships (three a year), as well as tournaments at the regional, sectional, local, and club levels — are sanctioned annually.

- **Two magazines.** The Bridge Bulletin, a monthly publication, offers articles on tournaments, card play, the Laws, personalities, special ACBL activities, and much more. A bi-monthly magazine, Play Bridge, is geared to the interests of new and advancing bridge players.

- **A ranking plan.** Each time a member does well in any ACBL event, whether at the club level or at a North American Bridge Championship, that member receives a masterpoint award. Players achieve rankings and prestige as a result of their cumulative masterpoint holdings.

- **A teaching program.** ACBL has trained more than 5,000 people through the Teacher Accreditation Program (TAP) to effectively teach beginning bridge lessons. You can find a teacher in your area at ACBL's web site at www.acbl.org.

- **A newcomer program.** ACBL offers special games and programs for players new to bridge and new to duplicate. The Intermediate/Newcomer (IN) Programs at the three North America Bridge Championships are very popular as is Easybridge!

- **Access to 3500 bridge clubs.** ACBL offers sanctioned bridge play at clubs across the United States, Canada, Mexico, Bermuda, on cruise ships, and even at a few foreign-based bridge clubs. You can locate a club in your area at ACBL's web site at www.acbl.org.

- **A charity program.** Each year the ACBL Charity Foundation selects a "Charity of the Year," which is the main beneficiary of ACBL charity games and general donations by the membership. All ACBL clubs participate to raise money for the charity.

- **A cooperative advertising program.** ACBL assists teachers, clubs, units, and districts by subsidizing costs incurred for advertising programs designed to recruit students, and promote bridge lessons and games.

- **An education program.** The ACBL Educational Foundation is dedicated to bringing the enjoyment of bridge to people of all ages and firmly believes this can be accomplished through bridge education. Grants are provided for special bridge projects.

- **A funded school lesson program.** ACBL and the ACBL Educational Foundation have joined together to provide materials and teachers for bridge lessons at all levels — elementary, secondary, and college.

- **A Junior program for players age 25 and under.** ACBL offers a funded teaching program, student membership, special events, and a newsletter, *The Grapevine.*

- **Products.** ACBL offers a wide variety of bridge supplies, books, clothing, and other bridge products for new players and teachers through the ACBL Sales Department. Visit ACBL's Internet shop on the web at www.acbl.org.

- **Membership in the World Bridge Federation.** Each year ACBL sends premiere players to compete in the world championships. ACBL's Junior team participates in the World Junior Team Championship in odd-numbered years.

- **Membership benefits**. Credit card programs, member discounts on product purchases, special hotel rates at tournaments, airline discounts for NABCs, an 800 line for member services, discounted entry fees at most tournament play, recognition for levels of achievement, discounted Hertz car rental, and supplemental insurance products are offered.

ACBL has long been the center of North American bridge activity. 1997 was our 60th anniversary. We invite you to join us in the excitement of organized bridge play. You can enjoy the fun, friendship, and competition of bridge with an ACBL membership!

# TABLE OF CONTENTS

## CHAPTER 4 — SECOND-HAND PLAY

## CHAPTER 5 — DEFENSIVE SIGNALS

## CHAPTER 6 — DEVELPING DEFENSIVE TRICKS

## CHAPTER 7 — INTERFERING WITH DECLARER

## CHAPTER 8 — MAKING A PLAN

## APPENDIX

# *Why play bridge?*

You may be a little confused — why is Martina Navratilova writing the introduction to a bridge book?

The answer is that I believe it takes a strong mind, as well as a strong body, to live life to its fullest.

Bridge is more than just a card game. *It's a cerebral sport.* Bridge teaches logic, reasoning, quick thinking, patience, concentration and partnership skills.

Once at Wimbledon, when we got rained out, I spent my time playing bridge to keep me sharp and on my toes. An evening of bridge at home with family and friends is so much more fulfilling than sitting around watching TV.

The American Contract Bridge League has commissioned one of the world's most successful bridge teachers, Audrey Grant, to write this book. Audrey has taken what many people consider a complex game and made it easy and fun to learn.

Bridge has meant a lot to me in my travels. No matter where I go, I can always make new friends at the bridge table.

You know, tennis is a sport for a lifetime, and bridge is a game for a lifetime. It can be enjoyed by young and old, male and female, weak and strong. It crosses all barriers!

Take this book home with you today. Start learning a game and a sport — to last a lifetime!

MARTINA NAVRATILOVA
World Tennis Champion

# CHAPTER 1

## Opening Leads against Notrump Contracts

# INTRODUCTION TO DEFENSE

Playing bridge is a combination of skill, luck, and your ability to communicate with your partner. Nowhere is partnership communication more important than on defense. When you are declarer, you can look at all 26 cards held by your side before making any decision about how to play. When you are a defender, you and your partner need to work as a team to try to defeat the contract, even though you can't see the cards in each other's hands. That's quite a challenge.

During the auction, you work with your partner to exchange information through your bids in order to reach a suitable contract. As defenders, you must give each other as much information as possible about your hands in order to achieve your goal of defeating the contract. This is done by means of the cards you choose to play on each trick. With each card played, the defenders get a clearer picture of each other's hands and can use this information to try to defeat the contract. The defenders are not only trying to take their tricks but are also trying to do what they can to prevent declarer from taking tricks.

After defending a deal, you and your partner may wonder, "Could we have defeated that contract?" In the *Defense* book, we will look at techniques for defeating contracts that declarer would make if we don't defend carefully. We start by looking at the guidelines for handling specific situations on defense: opening leads, third-hand play, second-hand play, and signals. We move on to look at how the defenders establish winners and take their sure tricks. Then we see how the defenders can interfere with declarer's plans to make the contract. Finally, we take a look at how the defenders formulate their plan and put it into action.

Let's start at the beginning, with the opening lead.

## THE OPENING LEAD

Declarer's objective is to make the contract. The defenders' objective is to defeat the contract. With the opening lead, the defenders get the first opportunity to choose the suit that seems to have the best potential for their side. Many of the greatest players in the game have said that opening leads alone can make the difference between winning and losing a world championship. In this chapter, we will look at how you can choose an effective lead when defending against a notrump contract. First, you have to consider which suit you should lead, then you have to decide which card in the suit you should lead.

## CHOOSING THE SUIT

There are many bridge sayings designed to guide you on defense. One of the best known is *lead the fourth highest from your longest and strongest suit against a notrump contract.* It's necessary to understand what this guideline means and when it applies so you can use it in the right place at the right time.

In a notrump contract, rarely do either the defenders or declarer start with enough winners to reach their objective. The defenders need to develop tricks in the same manner that declarer does. The most common method is by developing tricks from long suits. By repeatedly leading the suit until all of the high cards are gone, you can manufacture winners from low cards. The advantage of playing in notrump is that once your winners in a long suit have been established, there is no trump suit to stop you from taking them. It becomes a race to see which side can set up its *spot* (low) cards in time to make or break the contract.

Since a defender makes the opening lead, the defenders have a head start in the race to establish winners. The opening leader should start with the suit that offers the greatest potential for developing the winners needed to defeat the contract. This suit will usually be the longest combined suit in the defenders' hands. For example, compare the following notrump holdings:

| 1) | YOU | 2) | YOU |
|---|---|---|---|
| | A K 4 | | J 10 9 7 4 2 |
| | ■ | | ■ |
| | PARTNER | | PARTNER |
| | Q 8 3 | | Q 8 3 |

In the first case, you have the top three cards in the suit and can take three tricks. Leading this suit doesn't develop any further tricks for your side and will establish at least one long-card winner for declarer. In the second holding, you have less high card strength, but because of the length of the suit you may be able to establish four tricks by driving out declarer's ace and king. The length of the suit rather than the location of the high cards tends to determine the best suit to attack.

When making the opening lead, you have to choose the suit without seeing partner's hand. Usually the bidding helps you to make the best decision. At other times, the decision has to come from examining only the cards held in your hand.

## Partner's Suit

If partner has opened the bidding or overcalled in a suit, lead partner's suit unless you clearly have a better alternative. Partner normally opens the bidding or overcalls in the longest suit in the hand. Even if you have only one or two small cards, partner's suit may well be your longest combined suit. When partner opens the bidding or overcalls, partner will usually have the majority of strength for your side and is the player most likely to have an entry to a suit once that suit is established. Even if your suit is longer, you may have no way to regain the lead and take your winners, so it's a good idea to lead partner's suit in the interest of the ongoing harmony of the partnership.

For example, consider the following hand. You're on lead against 3NT after partner has opened the bidding 1 ♠.

♠ Q 7
♥ 9 6 2
♦ J 9 6 4 3 2
♣ 10 4

Lead a spade, partner's suit, rather than a diamond, your long suit. Partner opened the bidding with 1 ♠ and should have length in spades as well as some high cards in the other suits. Partner should be able to get the lead once the low spades are established as winners. If you were to lead a diamond, you would probably not have an entry to the suit even if you could establish it.

## Your Suit

If there is no help from partner during the auction, you'll have to choose the suit to lead by looking at your own hand, taking into account any information you have from the opponents' bidding. The guideline is straightforward: with no information about the opponents' suits, choose your longest suit. This may not work out to be the best lead 100% of the time, but with nothing else to go on, it certainly gives your side the greatest potential to establish winners.

For example, suppose you are on lead against 3NT with the following hand and have no information from the auction:

♠ 9 5
♥ J 10 9 6 5 2
♦ A K 5
♣ 7 3

Lead a heart, your long suit, even though the diamonds contain more high cards. The heart suit provides the opportunity to establish tricks for your side while the diamonds are already winners. You want to keep the ♦ A and the ♦ K as entries to get to the heart suit.

If you have two suits of equal length, choose the stronger. It will usually require less help from partner to establish. For example, suppose you're on lead against 1NT with the following hand:

♠ K J 8 6 3        Lead a spade rather than a diamond. If partner has
♥ 7 4              the ♠A or the ♠Q, you may be able to establish
♦ J 9 6 4 2        winners in the suit quickly. On the other hand, even
♣ Q                if partner has the ♦ A or the ♦ Q, diamonds will take
                   longer to establish.

## The Unbid Suit

The opponents may have bid one or more suits before arriving at their final contract. It's usually best to avoid leading the opponents' suit when you have a reasonable alternative. If the opponents bid a suit, they will normally have some length and strength in it. For example, suppose the auction proceeds as follows:

| NORTH | EAST | SOUTH | WEST |
|---|---|---|---|
| (DUMMY) | (PARTNER) | (DECLARER) | **(YOU)** |
| 1 ♦ | Pass | 1 ♥ | Pass |
| 1 ♠ | Pass | 1NT | Pass |
| 3NT | Pass | Pass | Pass |

Here are three possible hands that you might hold:

| 1) ♠ Q 3 | 2) ♠ J 9 7 2 | 3) ♠ K Q J 10 8 |
|---|---|---|
| ♥ K J 8 3 | ♥ Q 7 4 3 | ♥ J 8 |
| ♦ Q 6 3 | ♦ Q 5 | ♦ J 7 2 |
| ♣ J 10 7 2 | ♣ 10 9 7 | ♣ A 8 4 |

In the first hand, your heart suit is stronger than your club suit. The opponent on your right, however, has bid hearts — this tends to make a heart lead unattractive. It isn't likely that your partner has much length or strength in the heart suit. You may even be helping declarer to establish tricks in the suit. Instead, lead a club, the unbid suit. Since the opponents have never bid clubs, it's reasonable to expect that partner will have some help in that suit.

In the second hand, your only long suits are spades and hearts, both of which have been bid by the opponents. Again, leading the unbid suit, clubs, is the most attractive alternative, even though you have only a three-card suit. Since the opponents didn't bid the suit, it's reasonable to expect that partner has some length and strength in this suit.

You don't always avoid leading the opponents' suit. In the third example, your spade suit is strong enough to lead even though it was bid by an opponent. You expect to drive out the ace and establish four winners, keeping the ♣A as an entry to your hand.

### Considering the Contract

The level of the contract is another factor that affects your choice of lead. Consider the following hand:

♠ 8 6         If you are leading against a contract of 1NT or 3NT
♥ J 10 9 7 3    with no help from the bidding, lead hearts, your long-
♦ A K        est suit. Keep the ♦ A and the ♦ K as entries to your
♣ 7 6 4 2     hand to help you establish and take your winners. If
the contract is 6NT, however, you would take your ♦ A and ♦ K right away since you need only two tricks to defeat the contract. If you lead a heart, the opponents may be able to take 12 tricks right away, giving you no second chance. Always keep your eye on the contract you are defending. If you see enough tricks to defeat it, take them.

## CHOOSING THE CARD

Once you have decided on the suit, the next decision is which card to lead. This is an important consideration for two reasons. First of all, since the defenders can't see each other's hand, every card they play sends a message, including the opening lead. Secondly, the card you choose can make it easier to take the tricks to which your side is entitled. Your choice of card depends on whether you are leading partner's suit or your own long suit. Let's take a look at each in turn.

## Leading Partner's Suit

When you are leading partner's suit rather than your own, you'll often be leading from a short suit. With a singleton, you have no choice of cards to lead, but with two or more cards use the following guideline:

*   Lead the top card from a doubleton *(e.g., 7–2, Q–5)*
*   Lead the top of touching honors *(e.g., Q–J–3, 10–9–5)*
*   Otherwise, lead low *(e.g., K–8–3, Q–9–4–2, 9–7–6\*)*

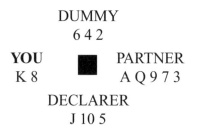

Let's see why these guidelines usually work well. Consider the following suit layout where you are on lead with a doubleton in partner's suit:

| | DUMMY | |
|---|---|---|
| | 6 4 2 | |
| **YOU** | | **PARTNER** |
| K 8 | | A Q 9 7 3 |
| | DECLARER | |
| | J 10 5 | |

If you lead the 8, rather than the king, partner would win the first trick and could then lead back to your king — but you would have no cards left to lead. Partner's winners would be stranded unless partner has an entry in another suit. The principle involved is *lead the high card from the short side first*. This situation is identical to the one where you are trying to establish the suit by driving out declarer's high cards.

Suppose this is the layout:

| | DUMMY | |
|---|---|---|
| | 9 8 3 | |
| **YOU** | | **PARTNER** |
| Q 5 | | K J 7 4 2 |
| | DECLARER | |
| | A 10 6 | |

If you lead the 5 and partner plays the king, declarer can win with the ace and the suit is *blocked*. If your side regains the lead, you have all of the winners in the suit. But, after winning a trick with your queen, you don't have any small cards left to get to partner's win-

---

\*From three small cards some partnerships, by agreement, prefer to lead the top card *(e.g., **9** 7 6)* or the middle card *(e.g., 9 **7** 6)*.

ners. Partner will need an entry in a side suit.

Alternatively, declarer may *hold up*, allowing partner to win the first trick with the king. When partner leads the suit again, declarer can hold up again, letting you win the trick with the queen. The suit still isn't established and you don't have a low card left to lead. Partner will need two entries to both establish the suit and get back in to take the winners. By leading the queen, high card from the short side, you avoid these problems.

Leading the top of touching high cards can be useful in *trapping* declarer's high cards. Consider the following layouts:

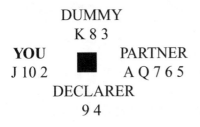

DUMMY
K 8 3
YOU
J 10 2
PARTNER
A Q 7 6 5
DECLARER
9 4

If you lead the 2 and declarer plays a low card from dummy, partner can win the first trick with the queen. Whether partner takes the ace now or leads a low card, partner can't lead the suit again without letting declarer win a trick with dummy's king. It's necessary to wait until you regain the lead if partner wants to trap dummy's king. If you lead the jack initially, top of your touching honors, declarer's king is trapped immediately. If declarer plays a low card from dummy, partner can play a low card and let you win the trick with the jack so you can lead the suit again. If declarer covers the jack with the king, your side takes all five tricks. If declarer held the king rather than dummy, it still wouldn't do any harm to lead the jack:

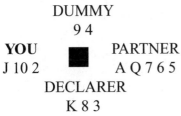

DUMMY
9 4
YOU
J 10 2
PARTNER
A Q 7 6 5
DECLARER
K 8 3

Declarer is entitled to one trick with the king whether or not you lead the jack. Once your jack has driven out declarer's king, your side's winners are ready to take.

When you have three or more cards without touching honors, the objective is also to trap one of declarer's high cards whenever possible. Consider this layout:

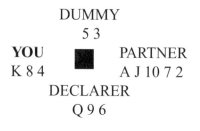

|              | DUMMY    |         |
|--------------|----------|---------|
|              | 5 3      |         |
| YOU          |          | PARTNER |
| K 8 4        |          | A J 10 7 2 |
|              | DECLARER |         |
|              | Q 9 6    |         |

If you lead the king and then a low card to partner's ace, declarer will win a trick with the queen. If you lead a low card to partner's ace instead, partner can lead back the jack, trapping declarer's queen. If declarer covers the jack with the queen, you can win the trick with the king and still have a low card left to lead over to partner's established tricks.

Here are some examples of leading partner's suit. The contract is 3NT and partner has bid diamonds:

♠ 8 7 5
♥ 10 8 3
♦ J 3
♣ K 8 6 5 2

Although your longest suit is clubs, lead partner's suit since the club suit isn't clearly a better choice. With a doubleton lead the top card, the ♦J.

♠ Q 10 8 4
♥ 9 2
♦ Q J 6
♣ J 10 8 3

Lead partner's suit rather than one of your own. With touching honors, lead the top card, the ♦Q.

♠ J 7 3
♥ 9 4 2
♦ Q 7 3
♣ Q 7 4 2

Once again you would lead partner's diamond suit rather than your meager club suit. With a three-card suit and no touching honors, lead a low card, the ♦3.

Here is an example of the effectiveness of leading partner's suit in a complete deal. The contract is 3NT and partner has overcalled 1 ♥.

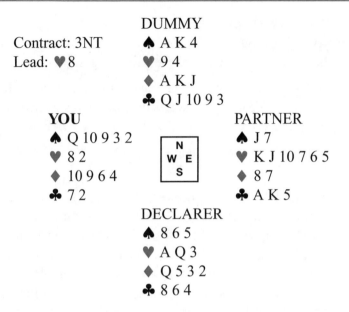

DUMMY
Contract: 3NT
Lead: ♥8

♠ A K 4
♥ 9 4
♦ A K J
♣ Q J 10 9 3

YOU
♠ Q 10 9 3 2
♥ 8 2
♦ 10 9 6 4
♣ 7 2

PARTNER
♠ J 7
♥ K J 10 7 6 5
♦ 8 7
♣ A K 5

DECLARER
♠ 8 6 5
♥ A Q 3
♦ Q 5 3 2
♣ 8 6 4

Although you have a long suit of your own, lead the suit partner overcalled. With a doubleton, lead the top card, the ♥ 8. Declarer can win partner's ♥ K with the ♥ A and still have the ♥ Q left as a second trick in the suit. However, declarer needs nine tricks. Together with the two heart tricks, declarer has two spade tricks and four diamond tricks for a total of eight. Declarer will have to lead clubs to establish a ninth trick. When declarer leads a club, partner can win the ♣ K and lead the ♥ J (or ♥ 10) to drive out declarer's ♥ Q. When declarer leads another club, partner can win the ♣ A and take the four established heart winners to defeat the contract by two tricks.

Notice what would happen if you led your long suit, spades. You may be able to drive out declarer's ♠ A and ♠ K, but you'll have no high card left as an entry to take your winners. In the meantime, declarer will drive out partner's high clubs and end up taking 10 tricks, making the contract with an overtrick!

## Leading Your Long Suit

When you're leading your own suit, you'll have four or more cards in the suit. In this case, you can use the following guideline:

- Lead the top of the touching honors from a three-card sequence, a broken sequence, or an interior sequence (*e.g.,* **K**–Q–J–3–2, **Q**–J–9–6–4, K–**J**–10–8)

- Otherwise, lead low (*e.g.,* Q–10–8–*3*, K–J–4–*2*, A–K–*7*–*5*)

There is a subtle difference between leading your suit and leading partner's suit when you have a suit headed by touching honors. When leading partner's suit, you lead the top of two touching honors. When leading your suit, lead the top of three touching honors but lead a low card when you have two touching honors. Let's look at why this usually works best. First, let's see why it is normally best to lead the top card from three or more touching honors. Consider the following suit layout:

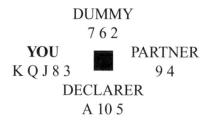

DUMMY
762
**YOU**          PARTNER
K Q J 8 3          9 4
DECLARER
A 10 5

If you were to lead a low card from this holding, declarer would win the first trick with the 10 and still have a second trick left, the ace. Declarer would get an undeserved trick, and your suit still wouldn't be established. By leading the king, the top of your three-card sequence, declarer gets only one trick, the ace, and the remainder of your cards are established as winners. The idea of leading high from such a strong sequence is to prevent declarer from winning a trick with a low card when partner doesn't have any help for you in the suit. If partner does have some help, so much the better.

Why the top card, rather than the queen or jack? While leading the top card from a sequence makes no difference to you, it provides information to partner about the other cards you hold. If you lead the queen from your long suit, for example, partner knows you have the next lower card, the jack, but not the next higher card, the king.

Leading from a suit headed by a three-card sequence can often lead to the rapid establishment of tricks for your side. Consider this layout:

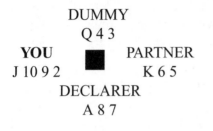

DUMMY
Q 4 3

YOU
J 10 9 2

PARTNER
K 6 5

DECLARER
A 8 7

If you lead the jack and it's covered by dummy's queen, partner's king, and declarer's ace, your 10 and 9 have been promoted into winners. Not only that but your 2 will be the last card in the suit and can also take a trick. You'll win three tricks from a suit headed by the jack.

Here is a complete deal that illustrates the value of leading a suit headed by a three-card sequence:

Contract: 3NT
Lead: ♥Q

DUMMY
♠ A 10 3
♥ A 5
♦ 10 9 7 6 2
♣ Q 9 6

YOU
♠ J 6 2
♥ Q J 10 7 2
♦ A K 4
♣ 8 4

PARTNER
♠ Q 8 7 5
♥ 6 4 3
♦ 3
♣ 10 7 5 3 2

DECLARER
♠ K 9 4
♥ K 9 8
♦ Q J 8 5
♣ A K J

Against a contract of 3NT, you (West) choose to lead your longest suit, hearts. With a three-card sequence, lead the top card, the ♥Q. Declarer needs nine tricks and has two sure tricks in spades, two in hearts, and three in clubs — for a total of seven. Two more tricks must be established, and they can come only from the diamond suit.

After winning a heart trick, declarer leads a high diamond to promote winners in that suit. When you win the diamond trick, lead another high heart to drive out declarer's remaining winner. Declarer wins the trick and leads another diamond. You win the race, however, taking your three heart winners and two diamond winners to defeat the contract.

If you originally lead a high diamond or any suit other than a heart, you would lose the race. Declarer would be able to establish the diamond winners before you could establish enough winners to defeat the contract. If you lead a low heart rather than a high heart, declarer will end up winning three heart tricks, and once again you wouldn't be able to defeat the contract.

A broken sequence is one in which you have the top two cards but are missing a card before the next highest card (*e.g.,* K–Q–10, Q–J–9, J–10–8). A suit headed by a broken sequence is treated in a similar fashion to a suit headed by a three-card sequence. Lead the top of the touching honors (*e.g., K*–Q–10–7–4, *Q*–J–9–4–3). The idea is to prevent declarer from winning a  trick with a small card.

For example, consider this layout:

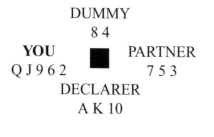

|  | DUMMY |  |
|---|---|---|
|  | 8 4 |  |
| **YOU** |  | PARTNER |
| Q J 9 6 2 |  | 7 5 3 |
|  | DECLARER |  |
|  | A K 10 |  |

If you lead a low card, declarer will win the first trick with the 10 since partner has no high cards in the suit to help out. Declarer ends up with three tricks in the suit. If you lead the top of your touching honors, the queen, declarer can win the trick with the king and the remaining cards will look like this:

DUMMY
8

YOU 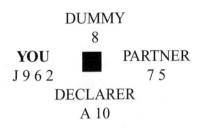 PARTNER
J 9 6 2              7 5

DECLARER
A 10

Declarer holds the ace and the 10. If partner gets the lead, partner can return the suit and declarer will end up with only two tricks no matter whether the 10 or the ace is played.

Notice that if you, rather than partner, lead the suit the second time, declarer will still get a trick with the 10. This is often the case when you lead from a broken sequence and partner doesn't have any help in the suit. Partner may have to lead the suit next if you want to trap the card missing from the broken sequence. On the other hand, if partner does have some help in the suit, it usually won't matter which defender leads the suit next.

An *interior sequence* is one in which the top card of the suit isn't part of the sequence (*e.g., K*–J–10, *Q*–10–9, *A*–10–9). Suits headed by an interior sequence are also treated in a similar fashion to suits headed by a three-card sequence. Lead the top of the touching honors (*e.g.,* K–*J*–10–8–4, Q–*10*–9–4–3, A–*J*–10–9). Again, the idea of leading one of your high cards is to avoid letting declarer win an undeserved trick with a low card. By not leading the highest card in the suit, however, you retain the possibility of trapping one of declarer's high cards when partner has some help in the suit.

For example, look at this layout:

DUMMY
Q 6 4

YOU 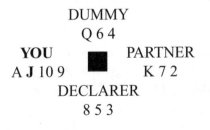 PARTNER
A J 10 9              K 7 2

DECLARER
8 5 3

When you lead the jack, top of the touching cards in your interior sequence, dummy's queen is trapped. If declarer covers the jack with the queen, partner wins the trick with the king and the rest of the tricks are yours. If declarer plays a low card from dummy, partner lets your jack win the trick and you can lead the suit again and take all of the tricks.

It wouldn't make any difference if declarer held the queen rather than dummy. You would still be able to trap it:

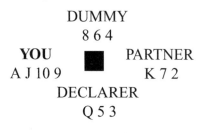

DUMMY
8 6 4
**YOU**     PARTNER
A J 10 9     K 7 2
DECLARER
Q 5 3

When you lead the jack and a low card is played from dummy, partner can win the trick with the king and lead a low card back to trap declarer's queen. Whether or not declarer plays the queen, your side takes all four tricks.

This shows the value of not leading the highest card when you have an interior sequence. If you start by leading the ace and then play a card over to partner's king, declarer will get a trick with the queen.

How does partner know to play the king when you lead the jack and there are only low cards in the dummy? Since you always lead the top of your touching honors, partner knows you don't have the queen when you lead the jack. If partner plays a low card, declarer will win the trick with the queen. By playing the king, partner will be able to trap declarer's queen if you are leading from an interior sequence. Of course, you may be leading the top of a three-card sequence:

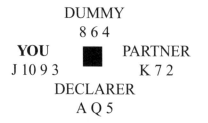

DUMMY
8 6 4
**YOU**     PARTNER
J 10 9 3     K 7 2
DECLARER
A Q 5

If this is the case, it still doesn't harm partner to play the king on your jack. Declarer is always entitled to two tricks in the suit no matter what your side does.

When your suit is not headed by a three-card sequence or a broken or interior sequence, the guideline is to lead a small card. The idea behind this is that, since you don't have a strong holding of high cards in the suit, you're probably going to need some help from partner. You want to preserve your high cards to help trap any high cards in declarer's hand and to use them as entries to your suit once it's established. Here's a typical example:

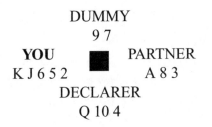

```
        DUMMY
          9 7
YOU      ■      PARTNER
K J 6 5 2        A 8 3
      DECLARER
        Q 10 4
```

When you lead a low card, partner wins the trick with the ace and leads the suit back, trapping declarer's high cards. Whether declarer plays the queen or the 10, you win the trick and can take all five tricks in the suit.

If you start by leading one of your high cards, the king or the jack, declarer will get a trick. If partner held the queen rather than the ace, leading a low card would still be effective. Partner would play the queen to help drive out the ace and establish the suit. But what if declarer holds both the ace and queen?

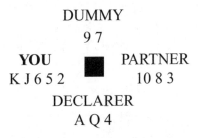

```
        DUMMY
          9 7
YOU      ■      PARTNER
K J 6 5 2        10 8 3
      DECLARER
        A Q 4
```

When you lead a low card, the best partner can contribute is the 10 and declarer wins with the queen. All is not lost, however. When you regain the lead, you can drive out declarer's ace and establish three winners in the suit.

Notice that you *sacrificed* a trick by leading a card into declarer's ace and queen. If you didn't lead the suit, declarer would get only one trick, the ace. If, for example, declarer led the suit from dummy and tried a finesse by playing the queen, you would win the trick with your king.

The objective of leading your long suit originally, however, is to try to establish enough winners to set the contract. In the above layout, you sacrifice one trick by leading the suit but are rewarded by eventually establishing three tricks in the suit. Since the contract is notrump, you can take all of your winners once you get the opportunity. If you sit back and don't lead your long suit, declarer can go about establishing long suits without having to worry about giving up the lead while doing it.

It may seem odd to be leading a low card when you have a suit such as A–K–8–6–3. After all, declarer may well win a trick with the queen or jack. Let's see why it usually works out best. First, suppose this is the layout of the entire suit:

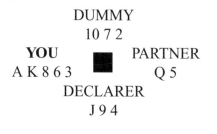

|          | DUMMY<br>10 7 2 |          |
|----------|:---------------:|----------|
| **YOU**  |                 | PARTNER  |
| A K 8 6 3|                 | Q 5      |
|          | DECLARER<br>J 9 4 |        |

If you were to start by leading the ace and king, partner's queen would have to be played on the second trick, and declarer would end up getting a trick with the jack. Even if you played only one high card and then led a low card to partner's queen, your remaining winners would be stranded. Unless you had an entry in another suit, your side would once again end up taking only two tricks. By leading a low card over to partner's queen, partner can win the trick and lead the 5 back to your winners. You'll end up taking all five tricks in the suit. Notice that the way you take or establish your winners in a suit is similar to the way declarer does. You're following the principle of *playing the high card from the short side first*.

Suppose, instead, the complete layout looked like this:

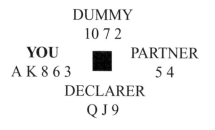

|          | DUMMY<br>10 7 2 |          |
|----------|:---------------:|----------|
| **YOU**  |                 | PARTNER  |
| A K 8 6 3|                 | 5 4      |
|          | DECLARER<br>Q J 9 |        |

If you lead the ace, king, and then a low card to establish your remaining cards as winners, declarer wins the third round of the suit with the queen. Your winners are stranded once again unless you have an entry in another suit. However, if you start by leading a low card, declarer wins the first trick with the 9 (or queen or jack), but partner still has a low card left in the suit. If *either* you **or partner** regains the lead, your side will be able to take four tricks in the suit. Leading a low card preserves the *link* to partner's hand. You are *taking your losses early* (ducking a trick to preserve an entry).

Let's look at an example of leading low from your long suit in a complete deal:

Contract: 3NT
Lead: ♠6

**DUMMY**
♠ 9 7 5
♥ 6 4 2
♦ A K 6 4
♣ K 8 3

**YOU**
♠ A Q 8 6 2
♥ 7 5
♦ 9 7
♣ J 10 7 4

**PARTNER**
♠ 4 3
♥ A 9 8 3
♦ 10 8 5 2
♣ Q 5 2

**DECLARER**
♠ K J 10
♥ K Q J 10
♦ Q J 3
♣ A 9 6

On lead against 3 NT, start by leading a low spade from your long suit (we will look at which low spade in a moment). It turns out that partner doesn't have much help in the suit and declarer wins the first trick with the 10. Declarer has four sure diamond tricks and two sure club tricks to go with the spade trick, but that's only a total of seven. To make the contract, declarer will have to establish tricks in the heart suit. When declarer leads a high heart to drive out the ♥ A, partner wins the trick and still has a low spade to lead back. Declarer's remaining ♠K and ♠J are trapped. Whichever one declarer plays, you'll win with the next higher card and take the rest of the spade tricks. You give declarer a spade trick early but end up taking a heart trick and four spade tricks to defeat the contract.

If you didn't lead a spade at all, declarer would make the contract by driving out partner's ♥ A before your side has established enough tricks to defeat the contract. Also, if you started by leading one of your high spades, you would no longer be able to trap declarer's ♠K later on to defeat the contract. Now let's take a look at which low spade you should choose when leading from your long suit.

## Fourth Highest

When leading a low card from a long suit, most players traditionally lead their fourth highest ranking card in the suit. The fourth highest (fourth best) card is determined by counting down from the top. For example, you would lead the card in bold type from each of the following holdings: Q–8–7–**5**–3–2, A–Q–8–**6**–2, K–10–5–**4**.

So we finally come to the source of the saying, *lead the fourth highest from your longest and strongest suit against notrump contracts.* Against a notrump contract, you generally lead from your longest suit and, with a choice of suits, pick your strongest suit. When leading a low card, you choose your fourth highest. This saying puts it all together, but notice, however, that it must be used in context. You don't necessarily lead from your longest suit if partner has bid another suit, and you don't necessarily lead your fourth highest card if you have a suit headed by a three-card sequence.

It may not appear to make any difference which low card you lead, but remember with every card you play you are trying to give partner as much information as possible. When you lead the fourth highest card, partner may be able to glean some extra information.

For example, if you lead the 2 from K–J–6–2, partner can figure out that you have only four cards in the suit since there are no lower cards you could hold if the 2 is the fourth card down from the top. If you lead a 5 and later follow suit with a lower card such as the 3, partner can figure out that you started with at least five cards in the suit (*e.g.,* K–10–8–5–3). Another reason for leading fourth best has to do with the *rule of eleven* which is discussed in *The Finer Points.*

Putting everything together, let's see what you would lead from each of the following hands against a contract of 3NT when you don't have any help from the bidding:

♠ A J 6 4 3
♥ K 9 2
♦ 7 5
♣ J 4 2

Start by picking your longest suit, spades. With no three–card sequence to lead from, lead the fourth highest card, the ♠4.

♠ 8 3
♥ K Q J 4
♦ K J 8 2
♣ 9 4 3

With a choice of suits, pick the stronger, hearts. With a three-card sequence, lead the top card, the ♥ K.

♠ 9 2
♥ Q 7 5
♦ A 10 9 8 4
♣ J 6 2

Your longest suit is diamonds. With an interior sequence, lead the top of your touching cards, the ♦ 10.

♠ Q 7 4
♥ J 9
♦ 10 8 2
♣ Q J 9 7 6

With a broken sequence lead the top of your touching cards, the ♣Q.

♠ K Q
♥ Q 10 6 4 2
♦ A 7 3
♣ 8 5 2

Your longest suit is hearts. With nothing else to go on, you would lead one. With no sequence to lead from, lead the ♥ 4, your fourth highest.

Here is a final example of leading against a notrump contract with a complete deal. First, the auction:

| NORTH (DUMMY) | EAST (PARTNER) | SOUTH (DECLARER) | WEST (YOU) |
|---|---|---|---|
| | | 1 ♥ | Pass |
| 2 ♦ | Pass | 2NT | Pass |
| 3NT | Pass | Pass | Pass |

Next, your hand:           ♠ A J 10 7
                           ♥ A Q 6 2
                           ♦ 5 2
                           ♣ 9 7 3

Would you pick the ♠ J? Here's the complete deal:

                           DUMMY
Contract: 3NT              ♠ 8 5
Lead: ♠ J                  ♥ 5 3
                           ♦ K Q J 10 8 4
                           ♣ K Q 10

YOU                                        PARTNER
♠ A J 10 7              ┌─────────┐        ♠ 6 4 3 2
♥ A Q 6 2              │    N    │        ♥ 9 7
♦ 5 2                  │  W   E  │        ♦ A 7 3
♣ 9 7 3                │    S    │        ♣ 8 5 4 2
                       └─────────┘
                           DECLARER
                           ♠ K Q 9
                           ♥ K J 10 8 4
                           ♦ 9 6
                           ♣ A J 6

With two equally long suits, you would normally lead the stronger —
but always listen to the auction before making your decision. Declarer
has bid hearts, so partner is unlikely to have much help in that suit. Instead choose the unbid suit, spades. With an interior sequence, lead the
top of the touching cards, the ♠ J. Look at what happens.

Declarer can win the first trick with the ♠ Q (or ♠ K) but must now
lead diamonds to try to establish the tricks needed to make the contract.
When partner wins the ♦ A, partner can return your suit, trapping
declarer's remaining honor. You get three spade tricks and, together with
partner's ♦ A and your ♥ A, that's enough to defeat the contract. If you
lead a heart or any suit other than spades, declarer would make the contract. Also, if you lead the ♠ A or the ♠ 7, declarer would make the
contract. By leading the ♠ J, you don't have to worry about asking partner at the end of the deal, "Could we have defeated that contract?"

# BIDDING REVIEW

As a refresher, here is a review of some of the bidding concepts covered in the *Bidding* and *Play of the Hand* texts which may come in handy when bidding the practice hands.

## Opening the Bidding

When you have the first opportunity to bid in an auction, value your hand using a combination of high-card points (HCPs) and distribution (length) points to determine whether or not you have enough strength to open the bidding. When you do have sufficient strength, start describing your hand to partner by opening the bidding at an appropriate level and in an appropriate denomination. Here are the guidelines for opening the bidding:

| HAND VALUATION | | | |
|---|---|---|---|
| *High-card Points* | | *Distribution Points* | |
| Ace | 4 points | Five-card suit | 1 point |
| King | 3 points | Six-card suit | 2 points |
| Queen | 2 points | Seven-card suit | 3 points |
| Jack | 1 point | Eight-card suit | 4 points |

## Opening the Bidding at the One Level

- With fewer than 13 points, pass.
- With 16 to 18 points and a balanced hand, bid 1NT.
- With 13 to 21 points and an unbalanced hand:
    - With a five-card or longer suit:
        - Bid your longer suit
        - Bid the higher ranking of two five-card or six-card suits.
    - With no five-card or longer suit*.
        - Bid your longer minor suit.
        - Bid the higher ranking of two four-card minor suits or the lower ranking of two three-card minor suits.

## Opening the Bidding at the Two Level

- With an unbalanced hand of 22 or more points, open the bidding at the two level in your longest suit.

- With a balanced hand of 22 to 24 points, open the bidding 2NT.

- With a balanced hand of 25 to 27 points, open the bidding 3NT.

## Opening the Bidding at the Three Level

- An opening bid in a suit at the three level or higher (preempt) shows:

  - A long suit — usually seven or more cards with three of the top five cards in the suit and

  - A weak hand — less than the point count values for an opening bid.

---

*This applies only if you are playing a five-card major system. If you are playing a four-card major suit system

- With no five-card or longer suit:
  - Bid the lower ranking of two four-card suits.
  - Bid the middle ranking of three four-card suits.

*Take Note*

Here are some examples of opening the bidding:

♠ K 9 6 4
♥ A 3 2
♦ Q 8
♣ A J 8 4

With 14 HCPs, there's enough to open the bidding at the one level. With no five-card major suit, open the bidding in your longer minor suit, 1♣. (Playing a four-card-major system, you would also open 1♣, the lower ranking of two four-card suits.)

♠ A Q
♥ A K Q 9 3
♦ 4
♣ A K 10 8 2

With 22 HCPs plus 1 point for each of the five-card suits, there's enough strength to open the bidding at the two level. With two five-card suits, use the same guideline as you would for opening at the one level and bid the higher ranking suit. Open the bidding 2♥.

♠ K Q J 9 7 6 2
♥ 8
♦ 9 4 2
♣ J 3

There aren't enough points to open the bidding at the one level, but with a good seven-card suit, you can open the bidding at the three level, 3♠. This is a pre-emptive opening bid, describing your hand and, at the same time, making it difficult for the opponents to enter the auction.

# PLAY OF THE HAND REVIEW

Here is a review of some of the material from the *Play of the Hand* text that may be useful when you are playing some of the practice hands.

## Declarer's Plan

When you are declarer, always take the time to make a PLAN before you start to play the hand:

> 1. **P**ause to consider your objective
> 2. **L**ook at your winners and losers
> 3. **A**nalyze your alternatives
> 4. **N**ow put it all together

When playing in a notrump contract, consider your objective in terms of the number of tricks you must take in order to make the contract. For example, in a contract of 3NT, you need nine winners. Look at the number of sure tricks you have — the tricks you can take without giving up the lead to the opponents. If you don't have enough *sure tricks*, examine each suit to see what alternatives you have for developing the extra tricks you need. Tricks can be developed in notrump contracts with the help of *promotion, long suits, and finesses*. Finally, put your plan together by choosing the best alternative. Make sure to keep track of your *entries* between the two hands, and watch out for the opponents if you are going to have to give up the lead.

# SUMMARY

When you are on lead against a notrump contract, use the following guideline:

- If partner has bid a suit, lead it:
    - Lead the top card from a doubleton (*e.g.*, 7–2, **Q**–5).
    - Lead the top of touching honors (*e.g.*, **Q**–J–3, **10**–9–5).
    - With no sequence, lead low (*e.g.*, K–8–**3**, Q–9–4–**2**, 9–7–**6**).
- Otherwise, lead your longest suit (unless bid by the opponents):
    - Lead the top of touching honors from a three-card sequence, a broken sequence, or an interior sequence (*e.g.*, **K**–Q–J–3–2, **Q**–J–9–6–4, K–**J**–10–8).
    - With no sequence, lead fourth highest (*e.g.*, Q–10–8–**3**, K–J–6–**5**–4, A–9–7–**6**–4–3).
- With a choice of suits:
    - Lead the stronger.
    - Lead the unbid suit.

# THE FINER POINTS

## Disregarding the Guidelines

Your objective as a defender is to defeat the contract. The guidelines on opening lead are there to help only when you are unsure what to do. If you see a better alternative, don't blindly follow the guideline. For example, suppose you're on lead against 3NT with the following hand:

♠ J 8 6 4 3
♥ Q J 10 9
♦ A K
♣ A 5

Your longest suit is spades, but leading a heart will give you the best chance to defeat the contract. By leading the ♥ Q, you will drive out declarer's ♥ K. When you regain the lead, you can lead another heart to drive out declarer's ♥ A. This will establish two sure heart tricks to go along with your club trick and two diamond tricks to defeat the contract. Leading a spade is much less likely to succeed since you will need considerable help from partner to establish the suit.

## Rule of Eleven

If your partner leads the fourth highest card against a notrump contract, you can get some additional information about the cards in declarer's hand by using the rule of eleven. Subtracting the number of the card led by partner from 11 tells you how many higher cards there are in the other three hands. Since you will be able to see the number of higher cards in your hand and the dummy, you can determine the number of higher cards held by declarer. Let's see how this could be useful. Suppose partner leads the ♥ 7 against a notrump contract and you see the following cards:

Subtracting partner's card from 11 tells you that there are four (11– 7 = 4) higher cards in the other three hands. You can see two of them in dummy, the ♥Q and the ♥8, and two in your hand, the ♥K and the ♥10. That means there aren't any higher than the ♥7 in declarer's hand. Suppose declarer plays dummy's ♥8. You can confidently play the ♥10 to win the trick, rather than expending the ♥K. The complete layout of the suit must be something like this:

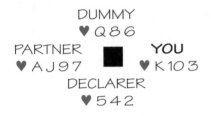

If you played the ♥K rather than the ♥10, declarer would eventually get a trick with dummy's ♥Q. Using the rule of eleven helped you make the right decision.

**Exercise One** — Choosing the Suit

You are on lead against a notrump contract with the following hand:

♠ 10 9 7 6 2
♥ 8 6
♦ A 9 4 3
♣ K Q

Which suit would you lead under each of these conditions:

1) The contract is 3NT and your partner overcalled in hearts.

2) The contract is 1NT with no bidding from your side.

3) The contract is 3NT after one of the opponents opened the bidding 1♠.

4) The contract is 6NT.

1) ___H 8___    2)___10 5___    3)___3 0___    4) ___K C___

---

**Exercise One** — Choosing the Suit

1) Heart     2) Spade     3) Diamond     4) Club

## Exercise Two — Choosing the Card in Partner's Suit

In each of the following examples, you're leading partner's suit. Which is the best card to lead? Why?

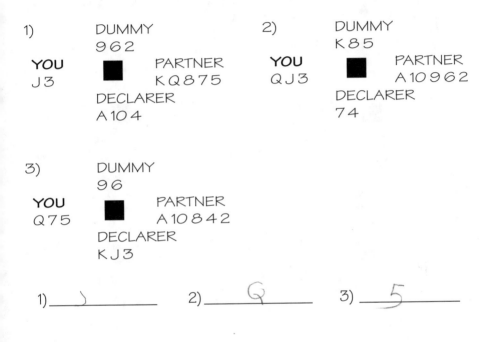

1)
DUMMY
9 6 2
YOU
J 3
PARTNER
K Q 8 7 5
DECLARER
A 10 4

2)
DUMMY
K 8 5
YOU
Q J 3
PARTNER
A 10 9 6 2
DECLARER
7 4

3)
DUMMY
9 6
YOU
Q 7 5
PARTNER
A 10 8 4 2
DECLARER
K J 3

1) _____J_____     2) _____Q_____     3) _____5_____

## Exercise Two — Choosing the Card in Partner's Suit

1) Jack, the top of a doubleton

2) Queen, top of a sequence

3) Five, low from three cards not headed by touching high cards

## Exercise Three — Leading the Top of a Sequence

You're leading your own suit against a notrump contract. Which is the best card to lead (a)? How many tricks can your side develop from the suit (b)? What must the defenders do to ensure that they take all of the tricks they have coming (c)?

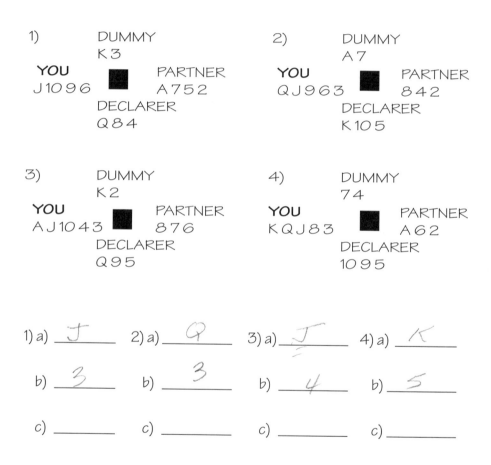

1)           DUMMY
             K 3
   **YOU**              PARTNER
   J 10 9 6 ■           A 7 5 2
             DECLARER
             Q 8 4

2)           DUMMY
             A 7
   **YOU**              PARTNER
   Q J 9 6 3 ■          8 4 2
             DECLARER
             K 10 5

3)           DUMMY
             K 2
   **YOU**              PARTNER
   A J 10 4 3 ■         8 7 6
             DECLARER
             Q 9 5

4)           DUMMY
             7 4
   **YOU**              PARTNER
   K Q J 8 3 ■          A 6 2
             DECLARER
             10 9 5

1) a) _J_        2) a) _Q_        3) a) _J_        4) a) _K_

   b) _3_           b) _3_           b) _4_           b) _5_

   c) ___           c) ___           c) ___           c) ___

**Exercise Three** — Leading the Top of a Sequence

1)  a)  Jack, top of a three-card sequence.

    b)  You expect to take three tricks.

    c)  Partner plays the ace only when dummy's king is played.

2)  a)  Queen, top of a broken sequence.

    b)  You expect to take three tricks.

    c)  The suit has to be led by partner the second time in order to trap declarer's 10.

3)  a)  Jack, top of an interior sequence.

    b)  You expect to take four tricks.

    c)  If dummy's king wins the first trick, the suit has to be led by partner the second time in order to trap declarer's queen.

4)  a)  King, top of a three-card sequence.

    b)  You expect to take five tricks.

    c)  Partner has to overtake your king with the ace (or overtake your queen with the ace on trick two) and lead back the suit.

## Exercise Four — Leading a Low Card

You're leading your own suit against a notrump contract. Which is the best card to lead (a)? How many tricks can your side develop from the suit (b)? What must the defenders do to ensure that they take all of the tricks they have coming (c)?

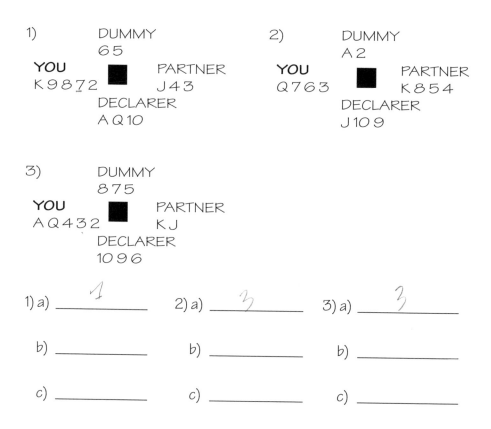

1)
```
            DUMMY
             65
YOU                   PARTNER
K9872     ■            J43
            DECLARER
             AQ10
```

2)
```
            DUMMY
             A2
YOU                   PARTNER
Q763      ■            K854
            DECLARER
             J109
```

3)
```
            DUMMY
             875
YOU                   PARTNER
AQ432     ■            KJ
            DECLARER
             1096
```

1) a) ___1___     2) a) ___3___     3) a) ___3___

b) _____     b) _____     b) _____

c) _____     c) _____     c) _____

**Exercise Four** — Leading a Low Card

1) a) The 7 (or 2).

   b) You expect to take three tricks.

   c) The suit has to be led by East the second time in order to trap declarer's 10.

2) a) The 3.

   b) You expect to take three tricks.

   c) Partner has to return the suit.

3) a) The 3 (or 2).

   b) You expect to take five tricks.

   c) You must overtake partner's honor card in order to take the lead and play the rest of your winners in the suit.

## Exercise Five — Leading against a Notrump Contract

The opening bid is 1NT by the opponent on your right and everybody passes. Which card do you lead from each of the following hands?

1) ♠ A K
   ♥ Q 10 8 4 3
   ♦ J 9 5
   ♣ 7 4 2

2) ♠ J 9 6 3
   ♥ Q 4
   ♦ Q J 10 5
   ♣ K 8 3

3) ♠ A J 8 6 5 2
   ♥ K 8 3
   ♦ 8 4
   ♣ 9 2

1)_____4♥_____   2)_____QD_____   3)_____6S_____

## Exercise Six — Listening to the Bidding

You are on lead against a contract of 3NT after this auction:

| NORTH (DUMMY) | EAST (PARTNER) | SOUTH (DECLARER) | WEST (YOU) |
|---|---|---|---|
|  |  | 1♥ | Pass |
| 1♠ | Pass | 2♣ | Pass |
| 3♠ | Pass | 3NT | Pass |
| Pass | Pass |  |  |

Which card do you lead from each of the following hands?

1) ♠ 7 4
   ♥ K Q 8 3
   ♦ K J 6 2
   ♣ 9 8 5

2) ♠ Q 6 5 2
   ♥ Q 8 4
   ♦ J 10 9
   ♣ J 8 3

3) ♠ 6 3
   ♥ J 9 4 2
   ♦ Q 8 3
   ♣ K Q J 10

1)_____2D_____   2)_____J_____   3)_____KC_____

**Exercise Five** — Leading against a Notrump Contract

   1) ♥4       2) ♦Q      3) ♠6

**Exercise Six** — Listening to the Bidding

   1) ♦2       2) ♦J      3) ♣K

## Exercise Seven — Review of Opening the Bidding

What would your opening bid be with each of the following hands?

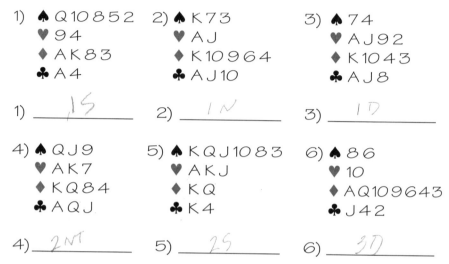

1) ♠ Q 10 8 5 2
♥ 9 4
♦ A K 8 3
♣ A 4

2) ♠ K 7 3
♥ A J
♦ K 10 9 6 4
♣ A J 10

3) ♠ 7 4
♥ A J 9 2
♦ K 10 4 3
♣ A J 8

1) _____ 1S _____   2) _____ 1N _____   3) _____ 1D _____

4) ♠ Q J 9
♥ A K 7
♦ K Q 8 4
♣ A Q J

5) ♠ K Q J 10 8 3
♥ A K J
♦ K Q
♣ K 4

6) ♠ 8 6
♥ 10
♦ A Q 10 9 6 4 3
♣ J 4 2

4) _____ 2NT _____   5) _____ 2S _____   6) _____ 3D _____

## Exercise Eight — Review of Declarer's Plan

Go through the four steps of declarer's PLAN to decide how to play the following deal in a contract of 3NT after the opening lead of the ♣Q.

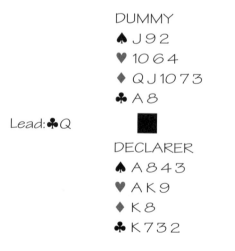

DUMMY
♠ J 9 2
♥ 10 6 4
♦ Q J 10 7 3
♣ A 8

Lead: ♣Q

DECLARER
♠ A 8 4 3
♥ A K 9
♦ K 8
♣ K 7 3 2

**Exercise Seven** — *Review of Opening the Bidding*

1) 1♠        2) 1NT        3) 1♦

4) 2NT        5) 2♠        6) 3♦

**Exercise Eight** — *Review of Declarer's Plan*

Declarer needs nine tricks and has five. Four more tricks can be promoted in diamonds. Declarer has to make sure to leave the ♣A in the dummy as an entry to the diamonds once they are established. Declarer also has to play the ♦K first, high card from the short side.

## Exercise Nine — Leading Partner's Suit
### (E-Z Deal Cards: #1, Hand 1 — Dealer, North)

Turn up all of the cards from the first pre-dealt deal. Put each hand dummy-style at the edge of the table in front of each player.

### The Bidding

What would North open the bidding? How can East describe the hand? South passes. How many points does West have? At what level does the partnership belong? Is there a Golden Fit? What does West respond? How does the auction proceed from there? What is the contract? Who is the declarer?

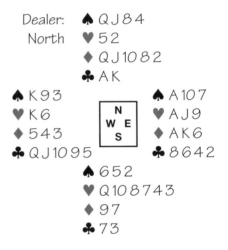

Dealer: ♠ Q J 8 4
North ♥ 5 2
♦ Q J 10 8 2
♣ A K

♠ K 9 3　♠ A 10 7
♥ K 6　♥ A J 9
♦ 5 4 3　♦ A K 6
♣ Q J 10 9 5　♣ 8 6 4 2

♠ 6 5 2
♥ Q 10 8 7 4 3
♦ 9 7
♣ 7 3

### The Defense

Which player makes the opening lead? What would the opening lead be? Why? How does North plan to defeat the contract?

### The Play

Review the steps in declarer's PLAN. How does declarer plan to make the contract?

## Exercise Nine — Leading Partner's Suit

### The Bidding

- North opens the bidding 1♦.

- East bids 1 NT and South passes.

- West has 10 total points — 9 HCPs plus 1 for the five-card suit.

- The partnership belongs in game.

- There is no Golden Fit, so West responds 3NT.

- All players pass and the contract is 3NT.

- East is the declarer.

### The Defense

- South leads partner's suit, the ♦9.

- North plans to drive out declarer's ♦A and ♦K and take three promoted diamond tricks along with the two club winners, to defeat the contract.

### The Play

- Declarer needs nine winners and has six sure tricks. Declarer plans to promote the club suit into three winners by driving out the ♣A and the ♣K, hoping the defenders don't collect their diamond tricks before declarer has a chance to follow through with this plan.

## Exercise Ten — Leading from a Sequence
### (E-Z Deal Cards: #1, Hand 2 — Dealer, East)

Turn up all of the cards from the second pre-dealt deal. Put each hand dummy-style at the edge of the table in front of each player.

### The Bidding

East and West pass throughout the auction. What would South open the bidding? What does North respond? How does South finish describing this balanced hand? At what level does the partnership belong? Is there a Golden Fit? What does North rebid? How does the auction proceed from there? What is the contract? Who is the declarer?

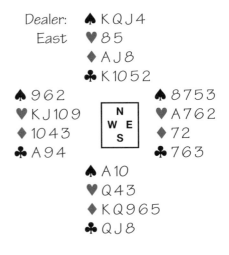

Dealer: ♠ K Q J 4
East    ♥ 8 5
        ♦ A J 8
        ♣ K 10 5 2

♠ 9 6 2              ♠ 8 7 5 3
♥ K J 10 9       ♥ A 7 6 2
♦ 10 4 3         ♦ 7 2
♣ A 9 4           ♣ 7 6 3

        ♠ A 10
        ♥ Q 4 3
        ♦ K Q 9 6 5
        ♣ Q J 8

### The Defense

Which player makes the opening lead? What would the opening lead be? Why? From the opening lead, which card does East know that declarer has? How do the defenders plan to defeat the contract?

### The Play

Review the steps in declarer's PLAN. How does declarer plan to make the contract?

**Exercise Ten** — Leading from a Sequence

## The Bidding

- South opens with 1♦ and North responds 1♠.
- South rebids 1NT, showing a balanced, minimum hand.
- The partnership belongs in game and, since there is no Golden Fit, North rebids 3NT.
- All players pass and South is the declarer.

## The Defense

- West leads the ♥J, the top of touching honors from an interior sequence.
- East knows declarer has the ♥Q because of West's lead of the ♥J.
- East has to play the ♥A on the ♥J and return a heart so that declarer's ♥Q is trapped. The defenders take four heart tricks and the ♣A.

## The Play

- Declarer needs nine tricks. There are four spade tricks and five diamond tricks to take as soon as declarer gets the lead. The defenders, however, may take four heart tricks and a club trick before declarer gets a chance.

## Exercise Eleven — Fourth Highest

### (E-Z Deal Cards: #1, Hand 3 — Dealer, South)

Turn up all of the cards from the third pre-dealt deal. Put each hand dummy-style at the edge of the table in front of each player.

### The Bidding

South passes. With a balanced hand and 22 HCPs, what is West's opening bid? North passes. Knowing that partner has 22 to 24 points, what does East respond? How does the auction proceed from there? What is the contract? Who is the declarer?

Dealer:   ♠ 10 7 6 2
South    ♥ A K 9 6 2
        ♦ 10 4
        ♣ 6 3

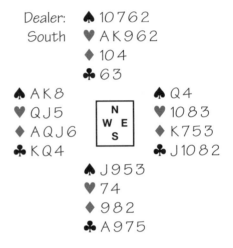

♠ A K 8            ♠ Q 4
♥ Q J 5    [N W E S]   ♥ 10 8 3
♦ A Q J 6         ♦ K 7 5 3
♣ K Q 4          ♣ J 10 8 2

        ♠ J 9 5 3
        ♥ 7 4
        ♦ 9 8 2
        ♣ A 9 7 5

### The Defense

Which player makes the opening lead? What would the opening lead be? Why? After the opening lead, which cards must North and South be careful to hold on to if declarer starts winning a lot of tricks?

### The Play

Review the steps in declarer's PLAN. How does declarer plan to make the contract?

## Exercise Eleven — Fourth Highest

### The Bidding

- West opens 2NT.

- East responds 3NT.

- Everyone passes. 3NT is the final contract and West is the declarer.

### The Defense

- Without a three-card or longer sequence, North leads a low heart.

- The defenders lose the first trick but have four heart winners and a club winner ready to take. Eventually declarer has to give South the lead with the ♣A. South will need to keep a heart to have an entry back to North's winners and North will need to keep all of the heart cards in order to take enough tricks to defeat the contract.

### The Play

- After taking the first heart trick, declarer has eight tricks and needs to promote a club in order to make the contract. Unfortunately the defenders get the lead and take their heart tricks before declarer can promote enough winners in the club suit.

# Exercise Twelve — Listening to the Opponents
## (E-Z Deal Cards: #1, Hand 4 — Dealer, West)

Turn up all of the cards from the fourth pre-dealt deal. Put each hand dummy-style at the edge of the table in front of each player.

## The Bidding

West passes. What is North's opening bid? Why can East not overcall or make a takeout double? What does East do? Which suit does South bid at the one level? West passes. How does North describe this balanced hand? East passes. At what level and in what denomination does the contract belong? What does South bid? How does the auction proceed from there? What is the contract? Who is the declarer?

Dealer:    ♠ K Q J
West     ♥ 9 6
          ♦ K J 9 4 3
          ♣ A 7 6

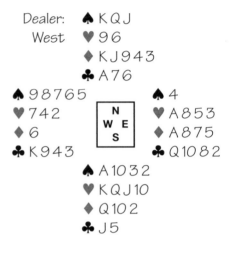

♠ 9 8 7 6 5          ♠ 4
♥ 7 4 2             ♥ A 8 5 3
♦ 6                  ♦ A 8 7 5
♣ K 9 4 3           ♣ Q 10 8 2

          ♠ A 10 3 2
          ♥ K Q J 10
          ♦ Q 10 2
          ♣ J 5

## The Defense

Which player makes the opening lead? After listening to the auction, which suit should that player choose? Which card? What would happen if a different suit were chosen?

## The Play

Review the steps in declarer's PLAN. How does declarer plan to make the contract?

## Exercise Twelve — Listening to the Opponents

### The Bidding

- North opens the bidding 1♦.

- East doesn't have any five-card suits to overcall and can't make a takeout double without support for the unbid suits and passes.

- South bids 1♥.

- North bids 1NT.

- The contract belongs in a game, so South bids 3NT.

- All pass and North is the declarer in 3NT.

### The Defense

- East leads the ♣2, the unbid suit.

- If a different suit were chosen, declarer would win the trick and have time to drive out the ♦A to make the contract.

### The Play

- Declarer starts with five tricks and plans to promote four winners in the diamond suit before the defenders establish enough club tricks to defeat the contract.

# CHAPTER 2

## Opening Leads against Suit Contracts

The presence of a trump suit influences both the way declarer plays and the way the defenders try to defeat the contract. Starting with the opening lead, the defenders must take a different approach in choosing the suit to attack and in choosing the specific card to lead. In this chapter, we will look at where the differences arise and we'll come up with guidelines for making the opening lead against a suit (trump) contract.

## CHOOSING THE SUIT

"When in doubt lead trumps" is a popular saying to guide you when it is your lead. There are many situations where you are "in doubt" as to what is the best lead, but in only a few of these cases will leading a trump be the most effective defense. To help remove some of the doubt, let's start by looking at the major difference between a suit contract and a notrump contract.

When defending against a notrump contact, you look to your long suit as a potential source of tricks when you don't have enough sure tricks to defeat the contract. You're often willing to sacrifice a trick if it will help establish some winners in your long suit. When you eventually regain the lead, you can take your winners without interference from declarer.

All of this changes when there is a trump suit. Even if you can establish your low cards as winners, it's unlikely you'll be able to take many tricks with them. Why? Because declarer will be able to ruff your winners once declarer or dummy runs out of the suit. For example, consider the layout of the following suit:

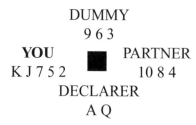

DUMMY
9 6 3
**YOU**      PARTNER
K J 7 5 2      10 8 4
DECLARER
A Q

Against a notrump contract, leading this suit will often be effective. Although declarer can win the first two tricks, you are compensated by eventually establishing three winners in the suit. If you can regain the lead, declarer can do nothing to stop you from taking your winners.

Against a suit contract, leading this suit from your side is unlikely to be successful. Declarer can win the first two tricks, and then use trump cards to prevent you from taking any tricks in the suit. Declarer ends up with no losers in the suit. If you bide your time and wait for declarer or partner to lead the suit, you'll be able to win a trick with the king.

The trump suit, therefore, shifts the defenders' focus away from their length toward their strength. Of course, the trump suit itself is a double-edged sword. Whereas declarer can use trumps to *ruff* (trump) your winners, the trump suit also presents the defenders with an opportunity to ruff some of declarer's winners.

## Partner's Suit

If partner has bid a suit during the auction, that's a good place to look for tricks for your side. As when leading against notrump contracts, lead partner's suit unless you clearly have something better to do. It's often important to establish your side's tricks before declarer has an opportunity to discard some losers. For example, suppose your partner opens the bidding 1♥ and the opponents, undaunted, bid all the way up to 6♠. It's your lead from the following hand:

♠ 8
♥ 7 4
♦ 9 6 3 2
♣ 10 9 8 7 4 3

Your hand is so weak that you may think it doesn't matter what you lead, but you're the player in the key position. Lead your partner's suit, hearts. Whatever tricks your side has coming are likely to come from the suit bid by partner. Even if partner can't win the first trick, you may help your side establish winners. This could be the complete deal:

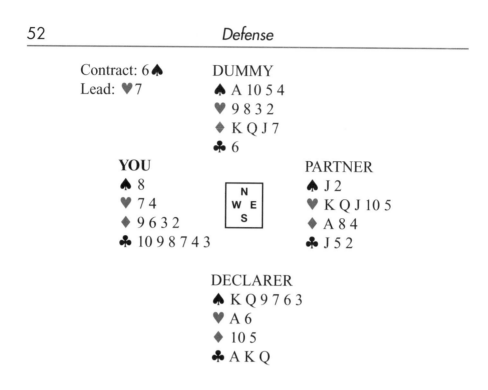

Contract: 6♠        DUMMY
Lead: ♥7            ♠ A 10 5 4
                   ♥ 9 8 3 2
                   ◆ K Q J 7
                   ♣ 6

YOU                                PARTNER
♠ 8                                ♠ J 2
♥ 7 4                              ♥ K Q J 10 5
◆ 9 6 3 2                          ◆ A 8 4
♣ 10 9 8 7 4 3                     ♣ J 5 2

                   DECLARER
                   ♠ K Q 9 7 6 3
                   ♥ A 6
                   ◆ 10 5
                   ♣ A K Q

When you lead a heart, declarer can win the trick with the ♥A, but eventually has to lead diamonds to drive out partner's ◆A. Partner can then take a heart trick to defeat the slam. If you lead anything other than partner's suit, declarer can make the slam. After drawing trumps, declarer loses a trick to partner's ◆A. When partner leads a heart, declarer wins the ♥A and discards the ♥6 on dummy's extra diamond winner.

## Your Suits

When leading a suit of your own, the best choice of suits is usually one in which you have a sequence of high cards. For example, suppose the opponents bid only spades during the auction and you are on lead against 4♠ with the following hand:

♠ 8
♥ Q 10 6 4 2
♦ K Q J
♣ K 8 6 3

Although both the heart and club suits are longer, leading from the strong sequence in diamonds is likely to work out best against a spade contract. By leading the ♦ K you should be able to drive out declarer's ♦ A and establish both the ♦ Q and the ♦ J as winners. Because you have only three diamonds, declarer is less likely to have a singleton or doubleton. You should be able to take both your winners. Notice that you don't need any help from partner to establish winners in the suit. If partner has the ♦ A, so much the better. If not, it should still work out well.

On the other hand, if you lead a heart, you'll need some help from partner, either the ♥ A, the ♥ K, or the ♥ J. If partner doesn't have any of these cards, leading a heart may well give up a trick for your side. The full layout of the heart suit might be something like this:

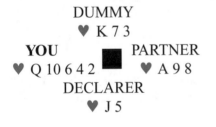

| | DUMMY | |
| | ♥ K 7 3 | |
| YOU | | PARTNER |
| ♥ Q 10 6 4 2 | | ♥ A 9 8 |
| | DECLARER | |
| | ♥ J 5 | |

When you lead a low heart, declarer can play a low heart from dummy and win the first trick with the ♥ J. After drawing trumps, the ♥ A and the ♥ K will also be winners. If you don't lead a heart, declarer has a loser in the suit. It's better to wait until partner can lead through declarer's high cards, or

until declarer plays the suit. Leading a heart could cost a trick even in situations where partner has some cards that will help and declarer's holding isn't as strong. Consider this layout:

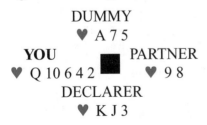

| | DUMMY | |
| | ♥ A 7 5 | |
| YOU | | PARTNER |
| ♥ Q 10 6 4 2 | | ♥ 9 8 |
| | DECLARER | |
| | ♥ K J 3 | |

When you lead a low heart, declarer will play a low heart from dummy. Partner will have to win the trick with the ♥ A to avoid letting declarer win the trick with the ♥ J. Now dummy's ♥ K is a winner. If you don't lead a heart, your side will get two heart tricks. If, for example, declarer were to lead the ♥J, you could cover with the ♥Q and partner would win dummy's ♥K with the ♥A. Now your side has the remaining high hearts.

Leading a club from the example hand could have equally unfortunate results if partner has no help in the suit. The complete layout of the suit might look like this:

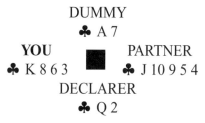

DUMMY
♣ A 7
YOU       PARTNER
♣ K 8 6 3      ♣ J 10 9 5 4
DECLARER
♣ Q 2

If you lead a low club, declarer can play a low club from dummy and win the trick with the ♣Q, ending up with no losers in the suit. If you don't lead a club, declarer has a loser in the suit.

It's often best against a trump contract to lead a suit containing a sequence even if it's not the longest suit in your hand. A suit with a strong two-card sequence has good potential for developing tricks for your side. For example, leading a suit such as K–Q–4 will work very well if partner has either the ace or jack. Even when declarer holds both of these cards, you can develop one trick.

If you have bid a suit which partner has supported, it's safe to lead it even when it's not headed by touching high cards. For example, your suit is K–J–8–6–3 and partner has raised it during the auction. It's likely that partner holds either the ace or the queen. It's usually important to lead your suit as soon as possible, before declarer has an opportunity to discard any losers in the suit.

## The Unbid Suits

On many deals, when it's your turn to lead, partner will not have bid and there won't be a strong sequence in your hand. As when leading against notrump contracts, it's usually preferable to lead an unbid suit. The fact that the opponents haven't bid the suit increases the probability that partner will have some strength there. For example, suppose the auction proceeds in this manner:

| NORTH | EAST | SOUTH | WEST |
|-------|------|-------|------|
| (DUMMY) | (PARTNER) | (DECLARER) | **(YOU)** |
| | | 1♠ | Pass |
| 2♦ | Pass | 3♦ | Pass |
| 3♠ | Pass | 4♠ | Pass |
| Pass | Pass | | |

You have to choose a lead from the following hand:

♠ 8 4
♥ K 7 6 3
♦ J 10 9
♣ K 8 7 5

You have a safe-looking sequence in diamonds, but that's one of the opponents' suits. It's better to choose one of the unbid suits. Which one? With no help from partner during the auction, it's difficult to say. Yet it's reasonable to hope that partner will have some strength in whichever suit you choose since both of the opponents have bid spades and diamonds.

The complete deal might look like this:

Contract: 4♠
Lead: ♥3 or ♣5

DUMMY
♠ Q 9 3
♥ Q 5 4
♦ A Q 7 5 3
♣ J 10

YOU
♠ 8 4
♥ K 7 6 3
♦ J 10 9
♣ K 8 7 5

```
   N
 W   E
   S
```

PARTNER
♠ 10 6 2
♥ A 10 9 2
♦ 6
♣ A 9 4 3 2

DECLARER
♠ A K J 7 5
♥ J 8
♦ K 8 4 2
♣ Q 6

It turns out that either lead is effective and allows you to take the first four tricks: the ♥A, the ♥K, the ♣A, and the ♣K. If you lead one of the opponents' suits, declarer can draw trumps and discard a loser on dummy's extra diamond trick to make the contract. If the opponents have bid and supported two suits during the auction, lead one of the unbid suits quickly in order to take or establish your winners before they disappear.

## Leading a Short Suit

Leading a short suit — a singleton or sometimes a doubleton — can be an effective way to get tricks. The idea is to get declarer's trump suit to work for you. You hope to be able to ruff declarer's high cards when the suit is led again. For the lead of a short suit to work, one or both of the following conditions must be present:

- Partner must be able to win a trick in the suit and then lead the suit back so that you can ruff it. This is a reasonable expectation if partner has bid the suit or if it's an unbid suit and the auction indicates that partner has some strength. If the opponents stop in a contract of 4♠ and you have only a couple of points, assume partner has some strength, but if you have a lot of points, assume partner has very little.

- If partner can't win an early trick in the suit, partner will need to regain the lead before declarer draws all of your trumps. This might be the case if partner has an early winner in the trump suit (the ace or, perhaps, the king), or if you have an early winner in the trump suit and can find an entry to partner's hand in another suit.

Without being able to look into partner's hand, the lead of a singleton carries some risk. You may help declarer establish a suit, and your trumps may be drawn before you get an opportunity to use them. Nonetheless, the situation occasionally merits taking the chance. Suppose the auction proceeds as follows:

| NORTH | EAST | SOUTH | WEST |
|-------|------|-------|------|
| (DUMMY) | (PARTNER) | (DECLARER) | **(YOU)** |
| | | 1 ♥ | Pass |
| 1 ♠ | Pass | 1NT | Pass |
| 4 ♥ | Pass | Pass | Pass |

This is your hand:

♠ 8  
♥ 6 5 2  
♦ J 9 7 6 5 2  
♣ 10 8 3

You don't have much high card strength. Partner is marked with some strength, however, because the opponents would probably be in a slam contract otherwise. Lead your singleton spade and see what develops. The complete layout may be something like this:

Contract: 4 ♥  
Lead: ♠ 8

DUMMY  
♠ K Q J 4  
♥ Q 9 8 3  
♦ A K  
♣ 6 5 4

YOU  
♠ 8  
♥ 6 5 2  
♦ J 9 7 6 5 2  
♣ 10 8 3

```
     N
  W     E
     S
```

PARTNER  
♠ A 10 7 5 3  
♥ 10  
♦ Q 4 3  
♣ A 9 7 2

DECLARER  
♠ 9 6 2  
♥ A K J 7 4  
♦ 10 8  
♣ K Q J

When you lead the ♠8, partner wins the trick with the ♠A and leads back a spade for you to ruff. Since the diamond suit doesn't look attractive, you now lead a club. (We'll see in a later chapter how partner may be able to help out in this situation.) Partner wins the ♣A and leads another spade for you to ruff. All of a sudden, your side has four tricks, despite the fact that the opponents started with 29 HCPs.

Of course, there is one more ingredient to making your lead of a single-ton effective. Partner has to visualize the opportunity for you to ruff declarer's winners and must cooperate by leading back the suit for you to ruff. Hopefully you'll do the same when partner leads a singleton.

Leading a short suit is not a good idea when you're likely to get tricks with your trumps anyway. For example, if your holding in the trump suit is Q–J–10–9, you'll get two trump tricks even if declarer has both the ace and the king. If you lead a singleton and partner returns the suit for you to ruff, you've gained nothing. You were entitled to your trump tricks any-way. In the meantime, you may be helping declarer establish winners. If you hold natural trump tricks (*i.e.*, likely winners in the trump suit), it's better to try to establish winners in other suits.

## Leading a Long Suit

It's not always advantageous to lead your long suit against a trump contract since declarer will often be able to ruff it. Leading from your long suit can be an effective defense, however, when either you or part-ner holds four or more trumps. Consider the following deal:

```
                          DUMMY
Contract: 4♠             ♠ 8 7 4
Lead: ♣K                 ♥ Q 9 3
                         ♦ K 10 9 2
                         ♣ A 6 5
        YOU                              PARTNER
     ♠ 10 5 3 2        ┌─────────┐      ♠ 9
     ♥ A 8 5           │   N     │      ♥ 10 6 4 2
     ♦ 4               │ W   E   │      ♦ A 8 6 3
     ♣ K Q J 10 8      │   S     │      ♣ 9 7 4 2
                       └─────────┘
                         DECLARER
                         ♠ A K Q J 6
                         ♥ K J 7
                         ♦ Q J 7 5
                         ♣ 3
```

If you start by leading the ♣K, declarer can win the ♣A and draw all of your trumps. Since you have four of them, declarer is left with only one trump. When declarer leads a diamond to drive out your partner's ♦A, your partner can lead another club and force declarer to play the last trump. Declarer can take three diamond tricks while you discard your small hearts and a club. When declarer leads a heart, you can win the ♥A and take your remaining two club tricks. Declarer, with no trump left, is powerless to stop you.

By continuing to lead the club suit at every opportunity, you force declarer to use trumps. This is called a forcing defense. The idea is to run declarer out of trumps so that you can take all of your established winners when you regain the lead. If this happens, declarer will lose control of the hand.

Notice what would happen if you led your singleton diamond. Your partner can win the ♦A and lead one back for you to ruff. You have two tricks and can see one more with the ♥A. Now if you lead a club to promote a fourth winner, declarer takes the trick, draws your three remaining trumps, and leads a heart to drive out the ♥A. With two trumps left and your partner's ♦A gone, declarer is firmly in control. Declarer has the rest of the tricks no matter what you do. When you have long trumps, leading your long suit to make declarer ruff is often more effective than leading a singleton.

## Leading a Trump

Leading the trump suit may be effective when declarer is planning to ruff some losers with dummy's trumps. With a limited supply of trumps, however, declarer can't always afford to draw trumps and still have enough left in the dummy for all of the losers. In such cases, declarer wants to delay drawing trumps until the losers have been ruffed. By leading trumps whenever you get the opportunity, you may be able to thwart declarer's plan.

How do you know when declarer is planning to ruff losers in the dummy? You have to listen carefully to the auction and try to visualize the distribution of both declarer's and dummy's hands. If it sounds as though dummy has shortness in one of declarer's long suits, it's likely that declarer will make use of dummy's shortness to ruff some long suit losers. In order to protect your side's winners in that suit, it may be the right time to lead a trump. For example, suppose the auction proceeds as follows:

| NORTH (DUMMY) | EAST (PARTNER) | SOUTH (DECLARER) | WEST (YOU) |
|---|---|---|---|
| Pass | Pass | 1 ♠ | Pass |
| 1NT | Pass | 2 ♥ | Pass |
| 2 ♠ | Pass | Pass | Pass |

You are on lead with:

♠ 8 4 3
♥ A K J 10
♦ K 10 7 5
♣ 9 3

What do you know about declarer's hand? Declarer has opened the bidding 1 ♠ and then bid hearts. Declarer probably has at least five spades and four hearts. What do you know about dummy's hand? Dummy didn't raise declarer's spades right away but preferred to play with spades as trump rather than hearts. Therefore, dummy is quite likely short in hearts. Looking at the potential heart winners in your hand, it looks as though declarer will have some heart losers to ruff in dummy. It's time to lead a trump in order to spoil declarer's plan.

The complete deal might look like this:

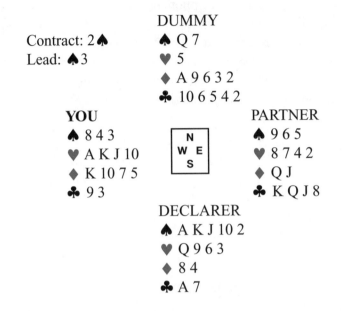

DUMMY
Contract: 2♠
Lead: ♠3
♠ Q 7
♥ 5
♦ A 9 6 3 2
♣ 10 6 5 4 2

YOU
♠ 8 4 3
♥ A K J 10
♦ K 10 7 5
♣ 9 3

PARTNER
♠ 9 6 5
♥ 8 7 4 2
♦ Q J
♣ K Q J 8

DECLARER
♠ A K J 10 2
♥ Q 9 6 3
♦ 8 4
♣ A 7

With four heart losers, one diamond loser, and one club loser, declarer needs to ruff a heart loser in dummy. Declarer plans to lose one heart trick and then ruff a heart with one of dummy's trumps. By leading a trump, you spoil the plan. When declarer wins the trump lead and gives up a heart trick, you win the heart and lead another spade to remove dummy's remaining trump. If your partner returns a heart when on lead, declarer ends up losing all four heart tricks and is defeated. If your opening lead is anything except a trump, declarer has an opportunity to ruff at least one loser in dummy and will end up making the contract.

It's not always easy to tell from the auction whether a trump lead will be effective. Listening to the bidding, however, and trying to visualize the opponents' hands is always a useful exercise. When the dummy is actually put down, you get an opportunity to verify part of your prediction. Throughout the play, the more you know about declarer's distribution, the easier it will be to defend. With practice, you'll soon recognize some of the opportunities to lead trumps.

It's often a good idea to lead trumps when your side appears to have the majority of the high cards but the opponents end up playing the contract. They may have bid too much trying to prevent your side from getting the contract (*sacrificing*), and you may even have made a penalty double of the final contract. In such a situation, the opponents are hoping to use their trumps to ruff your winners. By leading a trump, you cut down their ability to do so. For example, suppose the auction goes this way:

| NORTH (DUMMY) | EAST (PARTNER) | SOUTH (DECLARER) | WEST (YOU) |
|---|---|---|---|
| Pass | 1♣ | 1♦ | 1♥ |
| 2♦ | 4♥ | 5♦ | Double |
| Pass | Pass | Pass | |

A trump lead will protect your high cards if the complete deal is something like this:

```
                        DUMMY
   Contract:            ♠ 6 4
   5♦ Doubled           ♥ Q 10 2
   Lead: ♦ 2            ♦ K J 5
                        ♣ 9 7 6 4 2
        YOU                                PARTNER
     ♠ Q 10 2          ┌─────────┐        ♠ A K 9 3
     ♥ K J 8 7 6       │    N    │        ♥ A 9 5 3
     ♦ 8 4 2           │  W   E  │        ♦ 7
     ♣ J 5             │    S    │        ♣ K Q 10 8
                       └─────────┘
                        DECLARER
                        ♠ J 8 7 5
                        ♥ 4
                        ♦ A Q 10 9 6 3
                        ♣ A 3
```

South bid to the five level because South assumed that your side can make 4♥ and that the penalty for going down in 5♦ will be less than the value of your game. Since you know your side has most of the high cards, you double and lead a trump. South has four spade losers, a heart loser, and a club loser. By leading a trump and continuing to lead trumps every time you gain the lead, you can prevent declarer from ruffing any spade losers in dummy. Declarer is defeated four tricks. If you never lead trumps, declarer would go down only two tricks for a relatively inexpensive sacrifice.

Another time when it's usually right to lead a trump is when you are truly "in doubt" as to what the best lead would be. Sometimes it will look like the lead of any other suit would be likely to give up a trick for your side. By making the passive lead of a trump, you are biding your time and leaving it up to declarer to play the other suits. For example, suppose the auction proceeds as follows:

| NORTH (DUMMY) | EAST (PARTNER) | SOUTH (DECLARER) | WEST (YOU) |
|---|---|---|---|
| 1 ♣ | Pass | 1 ♦ | Pass |
| 1 ♥ | Pass | 1 ♠ | Pass |
| 2 ♠ | Pass | 4 ♠ | Pass |
| Pass | Pass | | |

With the opponents having bid all four suits, you have to find a lead from this hand:

♠ 9 4 2
♥ Q 10 9
♦ K 10 8 2
♣ K 7 5

You have finally come to the situation where the saying "when in doubt, lead trumps" comes in handy. Lead a spade and let declarer play the other suits.

The complete deal might look like this:

DUMMY

Contract: 4♠
Lead: ♠2

♠ A Q 8 3
♥ K 7 4 2
♦ 7 4
♣ A 10 6

YOU

♠ 9 4 2
♥ Q 10 9
♦ K 10 8 2
♣ K 7 5

|  |
|---|
| N |
| W    E |
| S |

PARTNER

♠ 10 5
♥ A 8 6 3
♦ 9 5
♣ J 9 8 4 2

DECLARER

♠ K J 7 6
♥ J 5
♦ A Q J 6 3
♣ Q 3

If you lead anything other than a trump, it costs your side a trick. By making the passive lead of a trump, you don't give declarer any help. Declarer will eventually lose two heart tricks, a diamond trick, and a club trick — one too many.

Putting together the various options you have when leading against a suit contract, let's look at which suit you would lead from various hands after this auction:

| NORTH (DUMMY) | EAST (PARTNER) | SOUTH (DECLARER) | WEST (YOU) |
|---|---|---|---|
| 1♦ | Pass | 1♥ | Pass |
| 2♥ | Pass | 4♥ | Pass |
| Pass | Pass | | |

♠ K 8 4 2
♥ 7 3
♦ Q 9 4
♣ Q J 10 6

With no bidding from partner, you'll have to choose a suit to lead. Starting with one of the suits bid by the opponents is unlikely to be profitable, so pick an unbid suit. With a strong sequence in clubs, that suit is preferable to spades. If partner doesn't have any help in spades, leading a spade might cost a trick. Lead a **club.**

♠ 6
♥ A 8 3
♦ 10 9 6 2
♣ J 8 6 4 2

To establish the club suit will require a lot of help from partner. Even if partner has some help, it's unlikely you can get more than one or two tricks before declarer ruffs the suit. Instead, lead a **spade,** your singleton, hoping to get a ruff. Since you have the ♥A, declarer won't be able to draw all of your trumps right away even if partner can't win the first spade trick.

♠ 8
♥ J 10 7 3
♦ Q 6 2
♣ K Q J 9 8

Although you have a singleton, leading it is unlikely to work out best. You'll probably get a trump trick anyway, even if the opponents have the ♥A, the ♥K, and the ♥Q. Instead, lead a **club,** your long suit. Perhaps you can force declarer to ruff too often and lose control of the hand.

♠ K Q 3
♥ 9 7
♦ J 8 5
♣ A 10 8 6 3

Your touching honors in spades are more attractive than the long club suit. If partner has either the ♠A or the ♠J, a **spade** lead will work out well. Even if partner doesn't hold a high spade, you'll establish one spade winner in your own hand. Then you'll have the opportunity to lead a club if it seems necessary.

♠ K 10 5
♥ 8 7 4
♦ K J 8 7
♣ K J 3

Nothing looks particularly attractive here. You don't want to lead a diamond since the opponents bid that suit. You could guess whether partner has something in either spades or clubs, but maybe this is the time to lead a **trump** since you are in doubt.

# CHOOSING THE CARD

Once you've decided on the suit, picking the card is relatively straight-forward. With only a couple of exceptions, the guidelines are similar to those for leading against notrump contracts.

## Leading Partner's Suit

The card you choose to lead in a suit contract when you decide to lead partner's suit is identical to the one you would lead against notrump with the proviso that you don't lead a low card if you hold the ace. Why is it better to lead the ace against a suit contract rather than a low card? Consider the following layout:

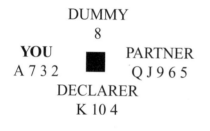

DUMMY
8
YOU                PARTNER
A 7 3 2            Q J 9 6 5
DECLARER
K 10 4

If you lead a low card away from the ace, declarer can win the first trick with the king. Defending against a notrump contract, this wouldn't be a problem. When your side regained the lead, you could take all of the established winners in the suit.

When defending against a suit contract, however, your side may never get a trick in the suit since declarer can ruff the remaining low cards in dummy. It's usually safer to lead an ace than to lead away from it.

In summary, when leading partner's suit:

- Lead the ace, if you have it (*e.g., A*–8–3, *A*–J–10–4)
- Lead the top card from a doubleton (*e.g., 7*–2, *Q*–5)
- Lead the top of touching honors (*e.g., Q*–J–3, *10*–9–5)
- With no sequence, lead low (*e.g.,* K–8–*3*, Q–9–4–*2*, 9–7–*6**)

---

* *From three small cards, some partnerships prefer to lead the top card* (e.g., **9** 7 6) *or the* **middle** *card* (e.g., 9 **7** 6).

## Leading Your Suit

When you're leading your own suit, the guidelines are similar to leading against a notrump contract with a couple of exceptions. First, if your suit is headed by the ace, lead the ace rather than a low card. The reason for not leading away from an ace, if you are leading the suit, is the same as when leading partner's suit. You don't want declarer to win the first trick with declarer's only card in the suit and find that declarer has no cards left in the suit when you later try to take your ace.

In a suit contract, you would lead the top of touching honors even if you have only a two-card sequence. Consider this layout:

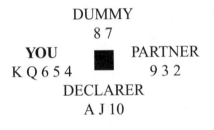

DUMMY
8 7
YOU          PARTNER
K Q 6 5 4          9 3 2
DECLARER
A J 10

Against a notrump contract, leading a low card from your holding won't usually cost a trick even though partner doesn't have any help in the suit. Declarer will win the first trick with the 10, but you can later drive out the ace and establish three winners in the suit. Declarer is always entitled to two tricks in the suit once you lead it, whether you lead a low card or the king. Against a suit contract, however, leading a low card doesn't work out well. Declarer could win the first trick with the 10, take the ace, and ruff the jack with one of dummy's trumps. You'd end up with no tricks in the suit. By leading the king, you ensure getting at least one trick even if partner has no help in the suit.

Leading a high card from a holding headed by the ace and the king can be very effective. You'll still be on lead after the first trick, so you'll be able to look at dummy before deciding whether or not to continue leading the suit. If you have a long suit headed by the ace and the king, you may even be able to make the trump suit work against the declarer. Take a look at this deal:

Contract: 4 ♥
Lead: ♦ A

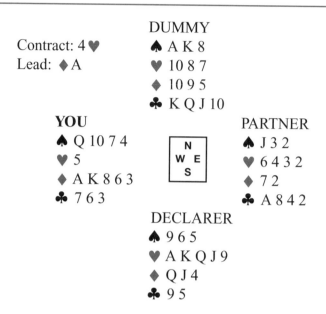

DUMMY
♠ A K 8
♥ 10 8 7
♦ 10 9 5
♣ K Q J 10

YOU
♠ Q 10 7 4
♥ 5
♦ A K 8 6 3
♣ 7 6 3

PARTNER
♠ J 3 2
♥ 6 4 3 2
♦ 7 2
♣ A 8 4 2

DECLARER
♠ 9 6 5
♥ A K Q J 9
♦ Q J 4
♣ 9 5

After leading the ♦ A and seeing dummy, no other suit looks particularly attractive — so continue with the ♦ K and another diamond. (We'll see how partner can help in this situation in a later chapter.) Partner can trump the third round of diamonds and take the ♣ A to defeat the contract. You can see the difference between leading from this holding in a suit contract and in notrump. If the opponents played this hand in 3NT, you'd have to lead a small diamond to defeat the contract. They would make it with any other lead.

When leading a low card from a suit of four cards or longer, lead the fourth highest, as you would against a notrump contract (*e.g.*, Q–8–7–5–3). The reasoning behind this is the same — you're trying to give information to partner about the number of cards you hold in the suit. This may help partner decide how many winners there are to take before declarer can trump. Against a suit contract, you also lead your lowest card from a three-card suit. Partner won't always be able to figure out exactly how many cards you have in the suit you started with, but partner will know you have at least three.

In summary, when leading against a suit contract:

- Lead the ace, if you have it (*e.g., A*–9–7–3, *A*–Q–J–8–3)
- Lead the top of touching honors from a sequence (*e.g., K*–Q–8–3–2, *Q*–J–9–3, K–*J*–10–8)
- With no sequence, lead low or fourth highest (*e.g.,* J–8–*4*, Q–10–8–*3*, K–J–7–*5*–2)

Let's put everything together and see which card you would lead from each of the following hands. The auction proceeds:

| NORTH (DUMMY) | EAST (PARTNER) | SOUTH (DECLARER) | WEST (YOU) |
|---|---|---|---|
| 1♣ | Pass | 1♠ | Pass |
| 3♠ | Pass | 4♠ | Pass |
| Pass | Pass | | |

♠ J 8 2
♥ K Q 4
♦ J 9 6 3 2
♣ Q 5

Rather than lead one of the opponents' suits, pick an unbid suit. The strong sequence in the heart suit offers better prospects than the diamond suit. Lead the top of touching honors, the ♥ K.

♠ 6 4
♥ K 9 3 2
♦ A K 6 5
♣ 10 8 4

The diamonds look like the best bet. Lead the top of the touching honors, the ♦ A. After seeing the dummy, you can change your mind and switch to another suit if that looks like a good idea.

♠ Q 3
♥ Q 9 6 4
♦ Q 8 5 3
♣ J 8 2

None of your choices is particularly attractive. It's probably best to pick one of the unbid suits. With no touching honors, lead a low card, either the ♥ 4 or the ♦ 3.

♠ J 2
♥ A J 9 8
♦ A 10 6 4
♣ Q 6 4

You'd like to avoid leading the opponents' suit if possible. If you have to pick one of the unbid suits, don't lead away from an ace. Choose either the ♥A or the ♦A, rather than a low card. After seeing the dummy, you'll have a better idea of what to lead next.

# BIDDING REVIEW

## Responding to Opening Bids of One in a Suit

When partner starts describing the hand by opening the bidding at the one level in a suit, responder, as *captain*, doesn't have enough information yet to determine the final level and denomination of the contract. Instead, responder categorizes the strength of the hand and responds using the following guideline:

## Responses to Opening Bids of One in a Suit

0 to 5    • Pass

6 to 10    **Responding to a major suit**

• Raise to the two level with three-card support.

• Bid a new suit at the one level.

• Bid 1NT.

**Responding to a minor suit**

• Bid a new suit at the one level.

• Raise to the two level with five-card support.

• Bid 1NT.

11 or 12    **Responding to a major suit**

• Raise to the three level with three-card or longer support.

• Bid a new suit.

**Responding to a minor suit**

• Bid a new suit.

• Raise to the three level with five-card or longer support.

13 or more    **Responding to a major suit**

• Jump to 2NT with a balanced hand.

• Bid a new suit.

**Responding to a minor suit**

• Bid a new suit.

• Jump to 2NT with a balanced hand.

## Responding to Opening Bids of Two in a Suit

A two-level opening bid is a forcing bid. Responder must bid again until game is reached. With a weak hand of 0 to 5 points, responder makes a *conventional (artificial)* response of 2NT to keep the bidding going. Use the following guideline when responding to a *strong two-bid*:

### Responses to Opening Bids of Two in a Suit

| | |
|---|---|
| 0 to 5 points | • Bid 2NT (conventional). |
| 6 or more points | • Raise to the three level with three-card or longer support. |
| | • Bid a new suit. |
| | • Bid 3NT with a balanced hand. |

## Responding to Opening Bids of Three in a Suit

When partner starts the bidding at the three level or higher in a suit, partner is making a *preemptive opening bid*. It shows a seven-card or longer suit and less than the values for an opening bid at the one level. Since partner has a weak hand, one that is likely of value only if played with partner's suit as trump, responder must proceed cautiously. Use the following guideline when responding:

### Responses to Opening Bids of Three in a Suit

| | |
|---|---|
| 0 to 15 points | • Pass. |
| 16 or more points | • Raise partner to game in partner's suit. |
| | • Bid a new suit (forcing if below game level). |
| | • Bid 3NT. |

# PLAY OF THE HAND REVIEW

## Declarer's Plan

When you're declarer in a suit contract, you go through the same four planning steps as you do when playing in a notrump contract:

1. **P**ause to consider your objective
2. **L**ook at your winners and losers
3. **A**nalyze your alternatives
4. **N**ow put it all together

In a suit contract, consider your objective in terms of the number of **losers** you can afford and still make the contract. For example, in a contract of 2♥, you can afford five losers. Then look at the number of losers you have — the cards in your hand which may not win tricks even with the help of dummy's high cards. If you don't have more losers than you can afford, start by **drawing trumps**. You want to make sure that the opponents don't ruff any of your winners.

If you have too many losers, look at each suit to see how the losers can be eliminated. In addition to the techniques available in a notrump contract — **promotion, long suits,** and **finesses** — there are techniques for eliminating losers which are unique to suit contracts — **ruffing losers** in the dummy and **discarding losers** on dummy's extra winners. Finally, put your plan together by choosing the best alternative. Decide whether you can draw trumps right away or whether you have to delay drawing trumps until you have eliminated some losers.

# SUMMARY

Use the following guidelines when choosing a suit to lead against a trump contract:

- Lead partner's suit.
- Lead a strong sequence rather than low from an honor.
- Lead an unbid suit.
- Lead a short suit when partner is likely to be able to give you a ruff before the trumps are drawn.
- Lead a trump when declarer is likely to want to ruff losers in dummy or when all other leads are unattractive.
- Lead a long suit when you, or perhaps partner, have four or more trumps.

When choosing the card to lead:

- Lead the top card from a doubleton (*e.g.*, *7*-2, *Q*-5).
- Lead the top of touching honors (*e.g.*, *K*-Q-8-3-2, *Q*-J-3).
- With no sequence, lead low (fourth highest) (*e.g.*, K-8-*3*, Q-9-4-*2*, K-J-7-*5*-2).
- Lead the ace, if you have it (*e.g.*, *A*-8-3, *A*-Q-J-9-4).

# THE FINER POINTS

### Leading from Three Small Cards

When leading from a three-card suit with no honor card, some partnerships prefer leading the top card (*e.g.*, *8*-6-2) rather than the lowest card. This is referred to as leading the *top of nothing*. There is an advantage to making this kind of lead. When you lead the highest of three small cards, partner knows that you don't hold an honor card. When you lead a low card, partner can assume that you have at least one honor in the suit.

This may be helpful when partner has to decide what to lead next. The disadvantage is that you also lead the top card when you have a doubleton (*e.g.*, *8*-6). So, when you lead the top card, partner can't tell whether you have two or three cards in the suit (or even a singleton).

Some partnerships prefer to get around the problem by leading the middle of three low cards (*e.g.,* 8–**6**–2). By not leading a low card, they're not promising an honor in the suit and, when the suit is played again, they can play a higher card (*i.e.,* the 8 from the remaining 8–2), so that partner won't think they have a doubleton. Because the idea is to lead the **M**iddle card, then play a higher card (**U**p), and finally the low card (**D**own), this is referred to as leading **MUD** (middle, up, down) from three small. While this has some advantages, partner will have to wait until the second or third round of the suit before being able to interpret your exact holding. By then, it may be too late to be of much use.

Rather than add a new guideline for leading from three low cards, it's easier to continue to lead low from three or more cards, whether or not you have an honor in the suit. Although partner may not know if you have an honor, neither will declarer, so you won't be giving any helpful information to the declarer.

## Leading from the Ace and the King

When leading from a suit headed by the ace and the king, the guideline recommends leading the top of touching honors, the ace. This is consistent with the lead from other touching honor combinations. Some partnerships, however, prefer to lead the **king from the ace and the king** against a suit contract. The reasoning behind this is that, since you don't want to lead away from an ace against a suit contract, you'll sometimes lead an ace when you don't have the king. By always leading the king when you have both the ace and the king, partner will know when you lead an ace that you **don't have the king** and can plan the defense accordingly. The disadvantage of this method is that since you also lead the king when you have both the king and the queen, partner won't know when you lead a king whether you also have the ace or the queen.

Again you want to be aware of variations such as this when playing with a new partner who might have come from a different school of thought. Until you have a regular partner with whom to discuss such variations, however, be consistent and always lead the ace when you have both the ace and the king.

## Exercise One — Strength Versus Length

Compare what would happen if you led each of the following suits against a notrump contract and against a suit contract (assuming another suit is trump). Would you normally lead the suit against a notrump contract, a suit contract, or both?

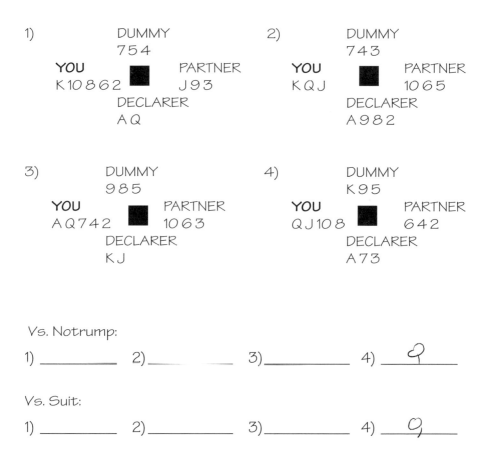

Vs. Notrump:

1) _____ 2)_____ 3)_____ 4) ___Q___

Vs. Suit:

1) _____ 2)_____ 3)_____ 4) ___Q___

**Exercise One** — Strength Versus Length

1) Against a notrump contract, you sacrifice one trick but develop three winners in the process. Against a suit contract, the trick is sacrificed in vain.

2) Against a notrump contract, you promote two tricks for your side, but at the same time declarer also gets two tricks. In a way, you are helping declarer develop an extra trick. Against a suit contract, it's a good idea to lead the suit to get the tricks that are coming to you.

3) You give up a trick by leading the suit, but against notrump you have a chance of developing four tricks in return. Against a suit contract, you give up a trick that declarer couldn't get without help and you gain nothing.

4) You hope to develop two tricks against a notrump contract and one trick against a suit contract. This type of suit is a good choice to lead against either notrump or a suit.

## Exercise Two — Utilizing the Trump Suit

You are defending a contract of 4♠ with no other suits bid during the auction. What would the advantage be of leading a diamond rather than a club on each of the following hands?

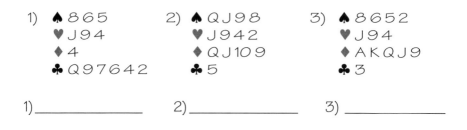

1) ♠ 8 6 5
   ♥ J 9 4
   ♦ 4
   ♣ Q 9 7 6 4 2

2) ♠ Q J 9 8
   ♥ J 9 4 2
   ♦ Q J 10 9
   ♣ 5

3) ♠ 8 6 5 2
   ♥ J 9 4
   ♦ A K Q J 9
   ♣ 3

1)_____     2)_____     3) _____

**Exercise Two** — Utilizing the Trump Suit

1)  You're hoping to ruff one or more diamonds.

2)  You have natural trump tricks, so leading the club for a ruff would gain nothing. Leading the ♦ Q could promote a diamond trick for your side.

3)  By leading a diamond, you could force declarer to use trumps. One of your trumps could be promoted into a winner if you end up with more trumps than declarer.

## Exercise Three — Leading Trumps

For each of the following auctions put down a possible suit distribution for both declarer's hand and dummy's hand (using X's to represent the cards). On which auctions might leading a trump prevent declarer from ruffing losers in the dummy?

1)
| NORTH (DUMMY) | EAST (PARTNER) | SOUTH (DECLARER) | WEST (YOU) |
|---|---|---|---|
| Pass | Pass | 1♥ | Pass |
| 1NT | Pass | 2♦ | Pass |
| Pass | Pass | | |

2)
| NORTH (DUMMY) | EAST (PARTNER) | SOUTH (DECLARER) | WEST (YOU) |
|---|---|---|---|
| 1♦ | Pass | 1♠ | Pass |
| 2♣ | Pass | 2♥ | Pass |
| 3♥ | Pass | 4♥ | Pass |
| Pass | Pass | | |

3)
| NORTH (DUMMY) | EAST (PARTNER) | SOUTH (DECLARER) | WEST (YOU) |
|---|---|---|---|
| | | 1♠ | Pass |
| 2♣ | Pass | 3♣ | Pass |
| 3♠ | Pass | 4♠ | Pass |
| Pass | Pass | | |

| 1) DUMMY | 2) DUMMY | 3) DUMMY |
|---|---|---|
| ♠ ♥ ♦ ♣ | ♠ ♥ ♦ ♣ | ♠ ♥ ♦ ♣ |
| DECLARER | DECLARER | DECLARER |
| ♠ ♥ ♦ ♣ | ♠ ♥ ♦ ♣ | ♠ ♥ ♦ ♣ |

Lead trump? _____ _____ _____

## Exercise Three — Leading Trumps

Possible suit distribution for dummy and declarer might be:

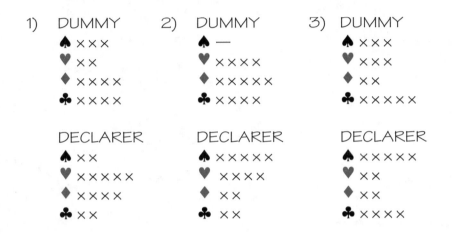

1)  DUMMY
♠ x x x
♥ x x
♦ x x x x
♣ x x x x

DECLARER
♠ x x
♥ x x x x x
♦ x x x x
♣ x x

2)  DUMMY
♠ —
♥ x x x x
♦ x x x x x
♣ x x x x

DECLARER
♠ x x x x x
♥ x x x x
♦ x x
♣ x x

3)  DUMMY
♠ x x x
♥ x x x
♦ x x
♣ x x x x x

DECLARER
♠ x x x x x
♥ x x
♦ x x
♣ x x x x

On the first two hands, a trump lead is a good idea. On the third hand, it would be better to find another lead.

*don't underlead an Ace on the suit contr...*

**EXERCISES**

## **Exercise Four** — Choosing the Suit

You're on lead against 4 ♥ with the following hand:

Which suit would you lead under each of these conditions:

♠ Q 9 2
♥ 8 6 3
♦ K Q 8 2
♣ Q 7 2

1)  Your partner overcalled in clubs during the auction.

2)  The only suit bid during the auction was hearts.

3)  The opponents bid all four suits during the auction.

4)  The opponents bid hearts and diamonds during the auction.

1) __2 C__    2) __K ♦__    3) __Trump 3H__    4) __25 (either black suit)__

## **Exercise Five** — Choosing the Card

In each of the following examples, which would be the best card to lead from the suit against a notrump contract? Which would be the best card against a suit contract?

1)          DUMMY
            7 5 3
  **YOU**          PARTNER
  A K 8 4 2          10 6
            DECLARER
            Q J 9

2)          DUMMY
            8
  **YOU**          PARTNER
  A J 10 9 3          7 5 4 2
            DECLARER
            K Q 6

3)          DUMMY
            6 4
  **YOU**          PARTNER
  K Q 9 7 3          10 5
            DECLARER
            A J 8 2

Notrump:    1) _____    2) __J__    3) __7__

Suit:              _____    _____    __K__

**Exercise Four** — Choosing the Suit

   1) Club     2) Diamond    3) Heart    4) Club or Spade

**Exercise Five** — Choosing the Card

1)  Lead low against a notrump contract and the ace against a suit contract.

2)  Lead the jack against a notrump contract. If you decide to lead the suit against a suit contract, the ace is safer.

3)  Lead low against a notrump contract and the king against a suit contract.

**Exercise Six** — Putting It All Together

The auction proceeds:

| NORTH (DUMMY) | EAST (PARTNER) | SOUTH (DECLARER) | WEST (YOU) |
|---|---|---|---|
| | | 1♣ | Pass |
| 1♥ | Pass | 1♠ | Pass |
| 2♠ | Pass | 4♠ | Pass |
| Pass | Pass | | |

Which card would you lead from each of the following hands?

1) ♠ Q74
   ♥ J83
   ♦ QJ62
   ♣ J108

1) _____

2) ♠ J92
   ♥ J75
   ♦ AJ975
   ♣ Q4

2) _____

3) ♠ K8
   ♥ Q97
   ♦ Q10832
   ♣ Q54

3) _____

4) ♠ A93
   ♥ 108532
   ♦ 6
   ♣ J865

4) _____

5) ♠ 864
   ♥ J932
   ♦ K5
   ♣ Q874

5) _____

6) ♠ 753
   ♥ A105
   ♦ AQ10
   ♣ K1042

6) _____

**Exercise Six** — Putting It All Together

| | | |
|---|---|---|
| 1) ♦ Q | 2) ♦ A | 3) ♦ 3 |
| 4) ♦ 6 | 5) ♦ K | 6) ♠ 3 |

**Exercise Seven** — Review of Responses to Opening Bids
in a Suit

What would you respond with each of the following hands if
partner opened 1 ♥? If partner opened 2 ♥? If partner opened 3 ♥?

1) ♠ Q 7 6 4 3     2) ♠ K Q 7 6 5     3) ♠ A J 8 3
      ♥ 8 5              ♥ Q 8               ♥ Q 8 6 2
      ♦ 7 4 2           ♦ J 9 2           ♦ Q J 9
      ♣ J 8 6           ♣ 10 6 4         ♣ J 6

1 ♥:    1)_____    2)_____    3)_____

2 ♥:    1)_____    2)_____    3)_____

3 ♥:    1)_____    2)_____    3)_____


**Exercise Eight** — Review of Declarer's Plan

Go through the four steps of declarer's PLAN to decide how
to play the following hands in a contract of 4 ♥ after the opening
lead of the ♣K.

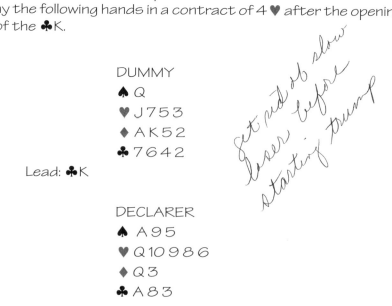

DUMMY
♠ Q
♥ J 7 5 3
♦ A K 5 2
♣ 7 6 4 2

Lead: ♣K

*Get rid of slow
loser before
starting trump*

DECLARER
♠ A 9 5
♥ Q 10 9 8 6
♦ Q 3
♣ A 8 3

## Exercise Seven — Review of Responses to Opening Bids in a Suit

1) 1♥ — Pass; 2♥ — 2 NT; 3♥ — Pass.

2) 1♥ — 1♠; 2♥ — 2♠; 3♥ — Pass.

3) 1♥ — 3♥; 2♥ — 3♥; 3♥ — Pass.

## Exercise Eight — Review of Declarer's Plan

You can afford three losers and have six. Two spade losers can be ruffed in the dummy and one of the club losers can be discarded on the extra diamond winner in dummy. Declarer can't draw trumps before getting rid of the losers since declarer would have to give up the lead, and the defenders would take enough tricks to defeat the contract. Win the ♣A, cash the ♠A, ruff a spade, cross to the ♦Q, ruff a second spade, and cash the ♦A and the ♦K, discarding a losing club.

## Exercise Nine — Leading Partner's Suit

### (E-Z Deal Cards: #2, Hand 1 — Dealer, North)

Turn up the cards from the first pre-dealt deal. Put each hand dummy-style at the edge of the table in front of each player.

### The Bidding

What would North open the bidding? How can East describe this hand? What does South bid? West passes. What rebid does North make to show support for partner's suit? East passes. How many points does South have? At what level does the partnership belong? Is there a Golden Fit? What does South rebid? How does the auction proceed from there? What is the contract? Who is the declarer?

Dealer:  ♠ Q 7 6 2
North    ♥ K J 5
        ♦ Q J 10 8
        ♣ A 6

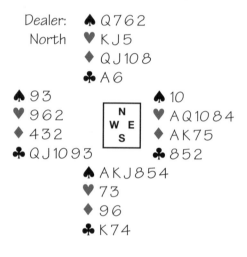

♠ 9 3                  ♠ 10
♥ 9 6 2             ♥ A Q 10 8 4
♦ 4 3 2             ♦ A K 7 5
♣ Q J 10 9 3      ♣ 8 5 2

        ♠ A K J 8 5 4
        ♥ 7 3
        ♦ 9 6
        ♣ K 7 4

### The Defense

Which player makes the opening lead? What would the opening lead be? Why? How does East plan to defeat the contract?

### The Play

Review the steps in declarer's PLAN. How does declarer plan to make the contract?

## Exercise Nine — Leading Partner's Suit

### The Bidding

- North opens the bidding 1♦.
- East overcalls by bidding 1♥.
- South bids 1♠ and North rebids 2♠ to show support.
- With 13 points, South knows the partnership belongs in game.
- Since there is a Golden Fit, South rebids 4♠.
- All players pass and South is the declarer in 4♠.

### The Defense

- West leads the ♥2, partner's suit.
- East plans to take two heart tricks and two diamond tricks to defeat the contract.

### The Play

- Declarer has two too many losers. Decarer can try the heart finesse and/or plan to promote an extra diamond winner in dummy on which to discard a heart loser. The club loser can be ruffed in dummy. After the heart lead, however, the defenders can take four tricks, giving declarer no opportunity to try to make the contract.

## Exercise Ten — Leading from a Sequence
### (E-Z Deal Cards: #2, Hand 2 — Dealer, East)

Turn up the cards from the second pre-dealt deal. Put each hand dummy-style at the edge of the table in front of each player.

### The Bidding

North and South pass throughout the auction. What would East open the bidding? How does West show trump support and the strength of the hand? What does East rebid? How does the auction proceed from there? What's the contract? Who is the declarer?

Dealer: ♠ J 7 6
East ♥ 9 7
♦ 9 8 6 3
♣ Q J 9 3

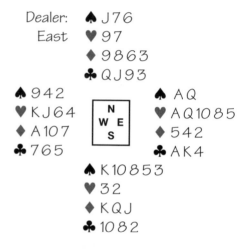

♠ 9 4 2          ♠ A Q
♥ K J 6 4        ♥ A Q 10 8 5
♦ A 10 7         ♦ 5 4 2
♣ 7 6 5          ♣ A K 4

♠ K 10 8 5 3
♥ 3 2
♦ K Q J
♣ 10 8 2

### The Defense

Which player makes the opening lead? What would the opening lead be? Why? What would happen if South led a spade?

### The Play

Review the steps in declarer's PLAN. How does declarer plan to make the contract?

## Exercise Ten — Leading from a Sequence

### The Bidding

- East opens the bidding 1 ♥.
- West raises to 2 ♥, showing 6 to 10 points.
- East rebids 4 ♥, showing maximum values.
- All players pass and East is the declarer in 4 ♥.

### The Defense

- South leads the ♦K, top of a strong sequence.
- If South chose the longest suit, spades, it would give up a trick since declarer would no longer have a spade loser and would make the contract.

### The Play

- Declarer has an extra loser. Declarer could take the spade finesse, hoping to eliminate the spade loser.

# Exercise Eleven — Leading a Trump

## (E-Z Deal Cards: #2, Hand 3 — Dealer, South)

Turn up the cards from the third pre-dealt deal. Put each hand dummy-style at the edge of the table in front of each player.

### The Bidding

South and West pass. What is North's opening bid? East passes. Without support for partner's suit and no suit that can be bid at the one level, what does South respond? West passes. Can North conveniently show a second suit? East passes. Which suit does South prefer? What does South do? What's the contract? Who is the declarer?

Dealer:   ♠ K 9 8 6 5
South   ♥ K J 10 6
          ♦ K 8 3
          ♣ A

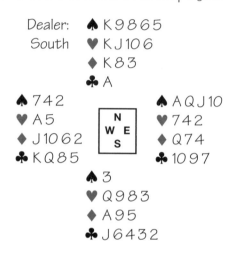

♠ 7 4 2        ♠ A Q J 10
♥ A 5          ♥ 7 4 2
♦ J 10 6 2     ♦ Q 7 4
♣ K Q 8 5      ♣ 10 9 7

          ♠ 3
          ♥ Q 9 8 3
          ♦ A 9 5
          ♣ J 6 4 3 2

### The Defense

Which player makes the opening lead? After listening to the auction, what would the opening lead be? Why? What does East plan to do when back in the lead? How can West help?

### The Play

Review the steps in declarer's PLAN. How does declarer plan to make the contract?

## Exercise Eleven — Leading a Trump

### The Bidding

- North opens the bidding 1♠.
- South responds 1NT.
- North rebids the second suit, 2♥, which South prefers.
- All players pass and North is the declarer in 2♥.

### The Defense

- East leads a trump because dummy is likely short in spades. It's also likely that declarer will want to ruff the spade losers in the dummy. When gaining the lead, East plans to lead another trump. West can help by leading a trump after winning the ♥A.

### The Play

- Declarer, with two losers to eliminate, plans to give up a spade trick and ruff two spade losers in the dummy.

## Exercise Twelve — Leading a Short Suit
### (E-Z Deal Cards: #2, Hand 4 — Dealer, West)

Turn up the cards from the fourth pre-dealt deal. Put each hand dummy-style at the edge of the table in front of each player.

### The Bidding

What is West's opening bid? North passes. What does East respond? South passes. What does West rebid? What's the contract? Who is the declarer?

### The Defense

Which player makes the opening lead? What hope is there to defeat the contract? What does North lead? How can South cooperate?

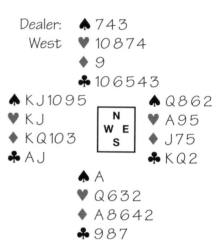

Dealer: ♠ 7 4 3
West    ♥ 10 8 7 4
        ♦ 9
        ♣ 10 6 5 4 3

♠ K J 10 9 5       ♠ Q 8 6 2
♥ K J             ♥ A 9 5
♦ K Q 10 3        ♦ J 7 5
♣ A J             ♣ K Q 2

        ♠ A
        ♥ Q 6 3 2
        ♦ A 8 6 4 2
        ♣ 9 8 7

### The Play

Review the steps in declarer's PLAN. How does declarer plan to make the contract? How many losers does declarer expect to have when the dummy goes down? What can go wrong?

## Exercise Twelve — Leading a Short Suit

### The Bidding

- West opens the bidding 1♠.
- East responds 3♠, a limit raise.
- West rebids 4♠.
- All players pass and West is the declarer in 4♠.

### The Defense

- North leads the ♦9, hoping that South has some strength, can win the trick, and return another diamond to allow North to ruff.
- South wins the ♦A and leads a diamond back for North to ruff. South leads another diamond after gaining the lead with the ♠A.

### The Play

- After driving out the ♠A, declarer plans to draw trumps and then promote the diamond suit by driving out the ♦A. At first, declarer expects to lose the ♠A and ♦A. If, however, trumps can't be drawn quickly enough, the defenders may ruff some of declarer's winners.

# CHAPTER 3
## *Third-Hand Play*

When your partner leads, you're in a position referred to as *third hand* because you are contributing the third card to the trick. As third hand, you have a special role to perform since it's your side's last opportunity to play to the trick. You are the third player to play to the first trick when partner makes the opening lead and dummy is put down on your right. This is true any time partner has the lead. The card you choose to play depends not only on the cards you hold in the suit but also on the card partner has led and the second card played to the trick. In this chapter, we'll look at guidelines for choosing the card to play when you are third hand.

## THIRD HAND HIGH

A common piece of advice handed down from the days of whist, a predecessor of the game of bridge, is *third hand high*. This implies that you should contribute your highest card to the trick when in third position. Let's see where this advice came from and how to apply it in the appropriate situation.

### When Partner Leads a Low Card

Suppose partner's opening lead is the 2. After dummy is put down, you can see the following cards in the suit:

|  | DUMMY | |
|---|---|---|
|  | 7 6 5 | |
| PARTNER | ■ | YOU |
| 2 |  | A 4 3 |

When a low card is played from dummy, you are third hand to play. This is the last opportunity for your side to play to the trick. Play your ace, *third hand high*, in order to win the trick for your side.

But will you always be able to play a card that's high enough to win the trick for your side?

Suppose we change your holding slightly:

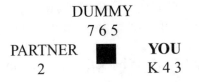

DUMMY
7 6 5
PARTNER YOU
2 K 4 3

Once again you are in third seat and the last to play for your side. The king will win the trick if partner has the ace.

Suppose, however, declarer has the ace and the complete layout looks like this:

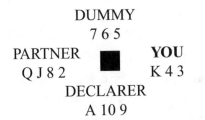

DUMMY
7 6 5
PARTNER YOU
Q J 8 2 K 4 3
DECLARER
A 10 9

When you play the king, third hand high, declarer can win the trick with the ace. All is not lost, however. By playing the king and driving out declarer's ace, you've helped promote partner's queen and jack into winners.

If you played a small card instead of the king, declarer would win the trick with the 9 (or 10) and still have the ace left. Your side would still not have established any winners in the suit. By playing third hand high, you are trying to win the trick for your side. Even if you can't win the trick, you're hoping to promote eventual winners for your side.

How high should you play? Suppose this is the layout you see after partner's lead:

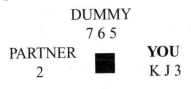

DUMMY
7 6 5
PARTNER YOU
2 K J 3

Should you play the king or the jack? If partner has the queen and declarer the ace, it won't matter which high card you play — either one will force declarer to play the ace to win the trick.

Suppose, however, this is the layout:

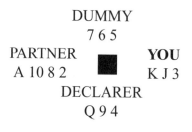

DUMMY
7 6 5
PARTNER     YOU
A 10 8 2     K J 3
DECLARER
Q 9 4

If you play the jack, declarer will win the trick with the queen. This can be prevented by playing the king, the highest card you can afford, rather than the jack. The king wins the trick, and you can lead back the jack to trap declarer's queen. Your side ends up taking all of the tricks in the suit, no matter which card declarer plays. The guideline in such situations is to play as high a card as you can afford when trying to win the trick.

It wouldn't do any harm to play the king even if declarer held both the ace and the queen. For example:

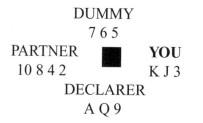

DUMMY
7 6 5
PARTNER     YOU
10 8 4 2     K J 3
DECLARER
A Q 9

Playing the king will force declarer to play the ace. Later, your jack can be used to drive out the queen and partner's 10 is promoted into a winner.

Playing "as high as you can afford to play" also applies in the following situation:

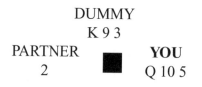

DUMMY
K 9 3
PARTNER     YOU
2     Q 10 5

If a low card is played from dummy, play the queen, the highest card you can afford, in order to try to win the trick. If declarer has the ace, your queen will drive it out.

If declarer doesn't have the ace and the layout is something like this, you'll save a trick for your side by playing the queen, rather than the 10:

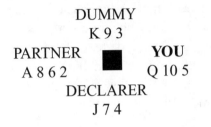

|              | DUMMY      |              |
|--------------|------------|--------------|
|              | K 9 3      |              |
| PARTNER      |            | YOU          |
| A 8 6 2      |            | Q 10 5       |
|              | DECLARER   |              |
|              | J 7 4      |              |

If you were to play the 10, declarer would win with the jack. Since your partner has the ace, declarer would later get a second trick in the suit with dummy's king. By playing the queen, you win the trick and can lead back to partner's ace. Declarer will get only one trick in the suit, with dummy's king. If dummy's king is played, there's no need to play third hand high since you can't win the trick.

Here is an example of third hand high in action:

Contract: 1NT
Lead: ♥6

DUMMY
♠ K J 2
♥ 7 4
♦ Q J 10 8 4
♣ Q 10 7

PARTNER
♠ 10 7 5
♥ K 10 8 6 2
♦ 5 3
♣ A 9 6

```
  N
W   E
  S
```

YOU
♠ 9 8 4 3
♥ Q 9 5
♦ A K 7
♣ J 4 2

DECLARER
♠ A Q 6
♥ A J 3
♦ 9 6 2
♣ K 8 5 3

Partner leads the ♥6, fourth best against declarer's 1NT contract, and a low heart is played from dummy. Play third hand high, the ♥Q. Declarer wins the trick with the ♥A and, needing to establish some diamond tricks to make the contract, leads a diamond. On winning the ♦K, you lead back a heart, trapping declarer's ♥J. Your side takes four heart tricks. Together with your two diamond tricks and the ♣A, that's enough to defeat the 1NT contract. If you played the ♥9 or the ♥5 on the first trick, declarer would win with the ♥J and make the contract.

## Using the Guideline

Here are a couple of examples of using the guideline *third hand high*:

|          | DUMMY |     |
|----------|-------|-----|
|          | 8 6 3 |     |
| PARTNER  | ■     | YOU |
| 5        |       | J 9 4 |

Partner leads the 5 and the 3 is played from dummy. Play the **jack**, third hand high. You want to make the best effort to win the trick for your side. Even though the jack is unlikely to win the trick, it may help promote some winners for partner.

|          | DUMMY |       |
|----------|-------|-------|
|          | A 7 5 |       |
| PARTNER  | ■     | YOU   |
| 3        |       | Q 10 2 |

When partner leads the 3 and the 5 is played from dummy, play the **queen**, the highest card you can afford, not the 10. If declarer had played the ace from dummy, you wouldn't need to play third hand high.

# THIRD HAND NOT SO HIGH

When you are trying to win the trick by playing third hand high, you want to play as high a card as you can afford, but you only need to play as high a card as is necessary.

## Touching Cards

Consider the following situation where partner leads the 4 and dummy plays the 3:

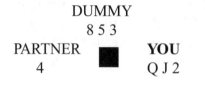

DUMMY
8 5 3

PARTNER
4

YOU
Q J 2

You want to play third hand high to try to win the trick for your side. Your queen and jack in this situation are equals. In such cases, play only as high a card as necessary, the jack, rather than the queen. It may seem odd to play the lower of touching honors in third hand since you play the higher of touching honors when leading to a trick. By playing the lowest card necessary to try to win the trick, however, you give valuable information to your partner.

For example, suppose you are defending a notrump contract and this is the complete layout of the suit:

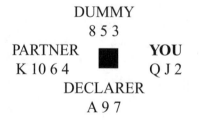

DUMMY
8 5 3

PARTNER
K 10 6 4

YOU
Q J 2

DECLARER
A 9 7

When the 4 is led and you play the jack, declarer has to play the ace to win the trick. Partner can now figure out that you have the queen. If declarer held the queen, declarer would use it to win the first trick, keeping the ace as a second trick. If partner regains the lead, partner can safely lead the suit again, knowing your side has all of the remaining high cards in the suit.

What difference would it make if you played the queen rather than the jack? Partner might think the complete layout of the suit was like this:

DUMMY
8 5 3
PARTNER        ■        YOU
K 10 6 4                      Q 7 2
DECLARER
A J 9

When partner leads the 4, you have to play the queen to force out declarer's ace since you don't have a choice of equal cards. If partner regains the lead, it would be a mistake to lead the suit again from partner's side since declarer would get a trick with the jack. Partner will want to wait until you can lead the suit, trapping declarer's jack. By playing the lower of touching cards as third hand, you can help partner distinguish between the different situations. For example, if you play third hand "high" with the 10, partner knows you don't have the next lower card, the 9, but may have the next higher card, the jack, and perhaps the queen as well.

Let's look at this in a complete deal:

DUMMY

Contract: 3NT           ♠ 6 3
Lead: ♠4                ♥ 9 4 2
                        ♦ Q J 7 2
                        ♣ A Q J 8

PARTNER                              YOU
♠ K 9 7 4 2        ┌─────────┐      ♠ Q J 10
♥ Q 7 5 3          │ N       │      ♥ K 10 8 6
♦ A                │ W   E   │      ♦ 9 5 4
♣ 9 7 3            │   S     │      ♣ 10 4 2
                   └─────────┘
                   DECLARER
                   ♠ A 8 5
                   ♥ A J
                   ♦ K 10 8 6 3
                   ♣ K 6 5

When partner leads the ♠4 and a low card is played from dummy, you play the ♠10, third hand high — but only as high as necessary. When declarer wins this trick with the ♠A, partner knows you have the

♠ J and the ♠ Q since declarer would have won the trick with one of those cards rather than winning with the ♠ A. When declarer leads a small diamond toward dummy, planning to establish some diamond winners, partner wins the ♦ A. Now partner can lead a low spade over to your ♠ J since partner knows you have that card. You lead back the ♠ Q, and partner can overtake it with the ♠ K and take the remaining spade winners to defeat the contract. What if you played the ♠ Q rather than the ♠ 10 on the first trick? Now partner might think the complete hand looked something like this:

Contract: 3NT
Lead: ♠ 4

DUMMY
♠ 6 3
♥ 9 4 2
♦ Q J 7 2
♣ A Q J 8

PARTNER
♠ K 9 7 4 2
♥ Q 7 5 3
♦ A
♣ 9 7 3

```
   N
 W   E
   S
```

YOU
♠ Q 10 5
♥ J 10 8 6
♦ K 9 4
♣ 10 4 2

DECLARER
♠ A J 8
♥ A K
♦ 10 8 6 5 3
♣ K 6 5

When partner leads the ♠ 4, you're forced to play the ♠ Q, the highest card you can afford, to stop declarer from winning the first trick with the ♠ J. When a diamond is led and partner wins the ♦ A, partner doesn't want to lead another spade and let declarer win the trick with the ♠ J. Instead, partner wants to wait until you get the lead and can lead back the ♠ 10, trapping declarer's ♠ J. By playing the ♠ 10 on the first spade lead and the ♠ Q on the second spade lead, you help partner decide what to do in each case.

### Finessing against Dummy

Another situation in which you play only as high a card as necessary is the following:

DUMMY
Q 5
PARTNER          YOU
3       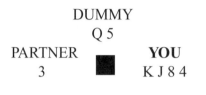      K J 8 4

If partner leads the 3 and the queen is played from dummy, you would try to win the trick for your side by playing the king. If the 5 is played from dummy rather than the queen, however, there's no need to play the king. Playing the jack is all that's necessary. If partner has the ace, the jack will win the trick. If declarer has the ace, the jack will force declarer to play it in order to win the trick, and dummy's queen is still trapped by your king. For example, the complete layout might be:

DUMMY
Q 5
PARTNER          YOU
9 7 6 3 2  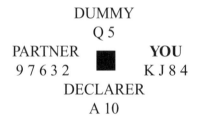  K J 8 4
DECLARER
A 10

If you were to play the king when dummy plays the 5, declarer would win with the ace and have the queen left as a second trick. By playing the jack, only as high a card as necessary, you restrict declarer to one trick in the suit. Your king and jack effectively trap dummy's queen. This is similar to the way declarer takes a finesse. The difference here is that you can see the cards on your right but you can't see partner's remaining cards. Being able to visualize what partner might hold comes in handy if we change the situation slightly:

DUMMY
Q 7 3
PARTNER          YOU
5            K 10 4

Again, partner leads a low card and a low card is played from dummy. You want to play third hand high, but only as high as necessary. How high is it necessary to play? That depends on which of the other players holds the ace and which player holds the jack.

If partner holds them both, then playing the 10 will be sufficient and it will also let you keep dummy's queen trapped with your king. Partner might have the jack and declarer the ace. This would be a likely situation if you were defending against a suit contract since, as you saw in the last chapter, partner wouldn't lead away from the ace.

The complete layout might be something like this:

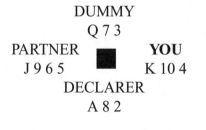

DUMMY
Q 7 3
PARTNER          YOU
J 9 6 5          K 10 4
DECLARER
A 8 2

Again, playing the 10 works better than playing the king. If you play the king, declarer wins with the ace and gets a second trick with dummy's queen. If you play the 10, declarer can win with the ace, but dummy's queen remains trapped by your king. Declarer gets only one trick in the suit.

Partner might have the ace and declarer the jack. This might be the case when you are defending against a notrump contract.

Suppose this is the layout:

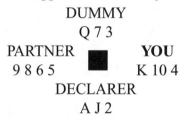

DUMMY
Q 7 3
PARTNER          YOU
9 8 6 5          K 10 4
DECLARER
A J 2

If you play the 10 on the first trick, declarer wins with the jack, but has any harm been done? Declarer is entitled to one trick in the suit anyway. Your side will still be able to take your three winners when you regain the lead. If you had won the first trick with the king, declarer would eventually get a trick with dummy's queen. Nothing is lost by playing the 10.

Finally, suppose declarer has both the ace and the jack:

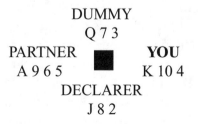

DUMMY
Q 7 3
PARTNER          YOU
A 9 6 5          K 10 4
DECLARER
J 8 2

If you play the king, declarer will get three tricks in the suit — the ace, the jack, and the queen. If you play the 10, declarer can win the first trick with the jack. Declarer will still have the ace left as a second trick, but dummy's queen remains trapped by your king. Declarer will get only two tricks in the suit.

In conclusion, playing the 10 works out best in most situations, even though declarer may win the first trick with the jack. The objective in all cases is to try to keep dummy's queen trapped by your king. This is the general idea when trying to decide how high a card it's necessary to play as third hand. You want to keep the opponents' high cards trapped whenever possible.

Here's an example in a complete deal:

|  | DUMMY |
|---|---|
| Contract: 3NT | ♠ K 10 5 |
| Lead: ♥ 2 | ♥ K 8 4 |
|  | ♦ K 5 |
|  | ♣ Q J 10 6 2 |

| PARTNER | | YOU |
|---|---|---|
| ♠ J 8 4 | N | ♠ Q 7 6 2 |
| ♥ J 7 6 2 | W  E | ♥ A 10 9 |
| ♦ 10 4 2 | S | ♦ 9 8 6 3 |
| ♣ A K 8 | | ♣ 7 5 |

DECLARER
♠ A 9 3
♥ Q 5 3
♦ A Q J 7
♣ 9 4 3

Partner leads the ♥ 2 and the ♥ 4 is played from dummy. Since you want to keep dummy's ♥ K trapped with your ♥ A, play the ♥ 9, the lower of your touching cards. The ♥ 9 will win the trick if partner has both the ♥ Q and the ♥ J. On the actual deal, declarer is able to win the trick with the ♥ Q. With only two spade tricks, the heart trick, and four diamond tricks, declarer needs to try to promote two extra tricks in clubs. Your partner wins a club trick and leads another heart. Dummy's ♥ K is trapped. If declarer plays a low card, you can win the trick with the ♥ 10 and take the ♥ A. Partner's other club winner and remaining heart will be enough to defeat the contract.

An analogous situation for trying to keep declarer's high cards trapped is the following. Suppose partner leads your suit against a notrump contract and this is the complete layout:

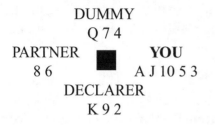

DUMMY
Q 7 4
PARTNER          YOU
8 6          A J 10 5 3
DECLARER
K 9 2

Partner leads the 8 and a low card is played from dummy. If you play the ace, dummy's queen is no longer trapped and declarer ends up with two tricks in the suit. Instead, play the 10, the lower of your touching high cards, and let declarer win the first trick with the king. When partner regains the lead and leads the suit again, dummy's queen is trapped by your remaining ace and jack. Whichever card declarer plays, you can't be prevented from taking the rest of the tricks in the suit.

Here are more third-hand situations:

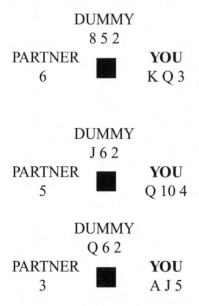

DUMMY
8 5 2
PARTNER          YOU
6          K Q 3

With touching high cards, play only as high as necessary, the queen. If declarer wins the trick with the ace, partner will know that you don't have the jack but may have the king.

DUMMY
J 6 2
PARTNER          YOU
5          Q 10 4

If a small card is played from dummy, play the 10, keeping dummy's jack trapped with your queen.

DUMMY
Q 6 2
PARTNER          YOU
3          A J 5

When a small card is played from dummy, play the jack. This will win the trick if partner has the king. If declarer has the king, dummy's queen will remain trapped by your ace.

## When Partner Leads a High Card

When partner leads a high card rather than a low card, you may not have to play third hand high in order to win the trick. Whether or not you need to play third hand high can depend on which high cards are in the dummy and which are in declarer's hand. You want to trap the missing high cards whenever possible.

Consider this situation where partner leads the queen:

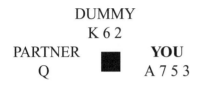

DUMMY
K 6 2
PARTNER                    YOU
Q                          A 7 5 3

Partner's lead of the queen looks to be from the top of a sequence headed by the queen and jack. If the king is played from dummy, you would win the trick with the ace and, unless you had something clearly better to do, lead the suit back to partner's winners. If a low card is played from dummy, however, there's no need for you to play the ace. Partner's queen will win the trick since you can see the king in dummy. If you were to automatically play third hand high and win the trick with the ace, you would establish dummy's king as a winner. Instead, you want to trap the king.

The complete layout might be something like this:

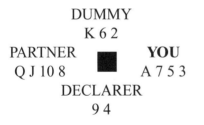

DUMMY
K 6 2
PARTNER                    YOU
Q J 10 8                   A 7 5 3
DECLARER
9 4

When you let partner's queen win the trick, partner can continue by leading the jack. Once again the king is trapped. Declarer can't get a trick with it no matter which card is played.

The situation is different if you can't see the high card you would like to trap and suspect that it's in declarer's hand:

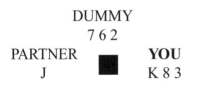

DUMMY
7 6 2
PARTNER                    YOU
J                          K 8 3

When partner leads the jack, you know declarer holds the queen. If you don't play the king, declarer will be able to win the trick with the queen. This may end up costing your side a trick if partner is leading from the top of an interior sequence and the complete layout is something like this:

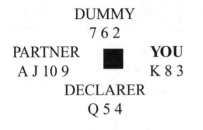

DUMMY
7 6 2
PARTNER          YOU
A J 10 9          K 8 3
DECLARER
Q 5 4

By winning the first trick with the king, you can lead the suit back and trap declarer's queen. Your side takes all four tricks in the suit. If it turned out that partner was leading the top of a sequence and that declarer held the ace as well as the queen, nothing would be lost by playing the king. Declarer is always entitled to two tricks.

You and your partner have to work together carefully to capture declarer's high cards when your side is missing two high cards. Consider this layout where partner has led the jack against a notrump contract and declarer plays a low card from the dummy:

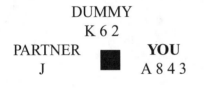

DUMMY
K 6 2
PARTNER          YOU
J                A 8 4 3

Partner's lead of the jack tells you that declarer has the queen. If you play a low card, declarer will be able to win the trick with the queen. You would have to play the ace to win the first trick for your side. Winning the first trick, however, may not be in the best long term interest for your side. Suppose the complete layout looks like this:

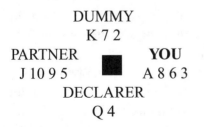

DUMMY
K 7 2
PARTNER          YOU
J 10 9 5          A 8 6 3
DECLARER
Q 4

If you play the ace on partner's jack, declarer will play the 4. Declarer will now get two tricks from the suit, one with the queen and one with the king. Your side hasn't trapped either of declarer's high cards. Since declarer is entitled to at least one trick in the suit, suppose you don't play third hand high but instead let declarer win the first trick with the queen. The remaining cards now look like this:

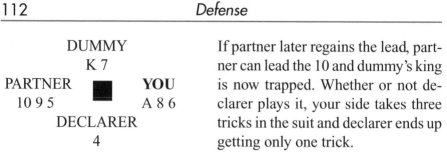

DUMMY
K 7

PARTNER          YOU
10 9 5           A 8 6

DECLARER
4

If partner later regains the lead, partner can lead the 10 and dummy's king is now trapped. Whether or not declarer plays it, your side takes three tricks in the suit and declarer ends up getting only one trick.

Let's look at this type of situation in a complete deal:

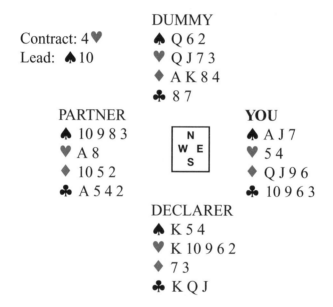

Contract: 4♥
Lead: ♠10

DUMMY
♠ Q 6 2
♥ Q J 7 3
♦ A K 8 4
♣ 8 7

PARTNER
♠ 10 9 8 3
♥ A 8
♦ 10 5 2
♣ A 5 4 2

YOU
♠ A J 7
♥ 5 4
♦ Q J 9 6
♣ 10 9 6 3

DECLARER
♠ K 5 4
♥ K 10 9 6 2
♦ 7 3
♣ K Q J

Your partner leads the ♠10 and declarer plays a low spade from dummy. Is this the time to play third hand high and win the trick with the ♠A? If declarer has the ♠K and you play the ♠A on the first trick, you won't trap either of declarer's high cards. Declarer will get two tricks in the suit. Instead, play the ♠7, letting declarer win the first trick with the ♠K but keeping dummy's ♠Q trapped. When partner later regains the lead, partner can lead another spade. Whichever card declarer plays from dummy, you can play a higher card to prevent declarer from getting a second trick. On the actual deal, you get two spade tricks to go along with partner's ♥A and ♣A to defeat the contract. If you play the ♠A on the first trick, your side gets only one spade trick and declarer makes the contract.

What if partner were leading from an interior sequence and held the ♠ K instead of declarer? The complete layout of the suit might have been this:

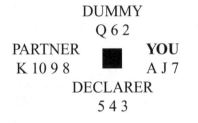

DUMMY
Q 6 2
PARTNER              YOU
K 10 9 8              A J 7
DECLARER
5 4 3

Again, you shouldn't play your ace on partner's 10. If partner has the king, the 10 will win the trick when you play the 7, and dummy's queen will remain trapped. If you were to play the ace on the first trick and lead back to partner's king, declarer would end up getting a trick with dummy's queen. In general, you don't want to play third hand high on the trick if it means giving up on trapping a high card held by the second hand.

Against a suit contract, you may be afraid that the complete layout is something like this:

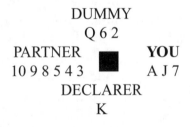

DUMMY
Q 6 2
PARTNER              YOU
10 9 8 5 4 3              A J 7
DECLARER
K

When partner leads the 10 and you play the 7, declarer wins the trick with the singleton king. Even though dummy's queen remains trapped, your side never gets a trick in the suit because declarer can trump the next time the suit is led. Nonetheless, it may not have cost your side a trick. Even if you were to guess to play the ace on the first trick while declarer had to follow suit with the king, dummy's queen would be established as a trick. Declarer might be able to use the queen for discarding a loser. You should still try to keep dummy's queen trapped unless you can clearly see that taking your ace on the first trick will result in defeating the contract.

Here are more examples of third-hand play when partner leads a high card:

DUMMY
Q 7 4

PARTNER 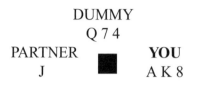 YOU
J                             A K 8

When partner leads the jack and a low card is played from dummy, there's no need for you to play third hand high. Play the **8**. Partner's jack will win the trick, and dummy's queen will remain trapped.

DUMMY
K 4

PARTNER  YOU
J                             A 7

Even though you know from partner's lead of the jack that declarer holds the queen, play the **7** and not the ace when a low card is played from dummy. Keep your ace to capture dummy's king to prevent declarer from getting two tricks in the suit.

DUMMY
6 5 4

PARTNER 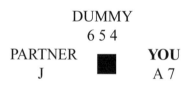 YOU
J                             A 7

This time there is nothing in dummy for your ace to capture. Partner's lead of the jack tells you that declarer has the queen, so you should win the first trick with the **ace** and return the 7. You may be able to trap declarer's queen if partner has led from an interior sequence and has a holding such as K–J–10–8–3.

## UNBLOCKING

Sometimes you have to play a high card from the third hand position even though it isn't needed to win the trick. This is called unblocking and it's used to avoid stranding partner's winners.

Consider the following layout of a suit where your partner leads the king against a notrump contract:

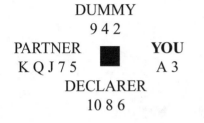

DUMMY
9 4 2
PARTNER            YOU
K Q J 7 5          A 3
DECLARER
10 8 6

Since your partner has led the king, it isn't necessary for you to play the ace in order to win the trick. If you play the 3, however, the suit becomes *blocked*. Your only remaining card is the ace. When partner leads the suit again, you can win with the ace but now partner's remaining winners in the suit are stranded. Unless partner has an entry in another suit, your side ends up with only two tricks. Instead, you must *overtake* partner's king with your ace so that you can lead back your low card and partner can take the established winners. By unblocking the suit, your side can take the first five tricks. This is really a variation of making sure you play the *high card from the short side first*.

Here is another example:

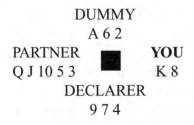

DUMMY
A 6 2
PARTNER            YOU
Q J 10 5 3         K 8
DECLARER
9 7 4

If partner leads the queen and a low card is played from dummy, you must overtake with the king to unblock the suit. Now you can lead the 8 back, and partner can drive out dummy's ace. If you let the queen win the first trick, you would win the second trick with the king when declarer holds up on playing dummy's ace again. You wouldn't have any low cards left, however, to help establish the suit by driving out dummy's ace. You would need two entries to partner's hand to both establish the suit and take the winners once they are established.

You must play the king even if declarer plays dummy's ace on the first trick and doesn't hold up. Otherwise, you'll be able to win a trick with the king when your side regains the lead, but once again partner's winners will be stranded.

Here is an example of unblocking in a complete deal:

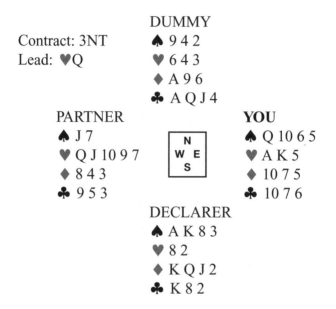

DUMMY

Contract: 3NT  ♠ 9 4 2
Lead: ♥Q      ♥ 6 4 3
              ♦ A 9 6
              ♣ A Q J 4

PARTNER                          YOU
♠ J 7                            ♠ Q 10 6 5
♥ Q J 10 9 7                     ♥ A K 5
♦ 8 4 3                          ♦ 10 7 5
♣ 9 5 3                          ♣ 10 7 6

DECLARER
♠ A K 8 3
♥ 8 2
♦ K Q J 2
♣ K 8 2

Partner leads the ♥Q. With both the ♥A and the ♥K, you could let partner's ♥Q win the first trick. However, when partner leads the suit again, your side ends up with only three tricks. Whatever you lead next, declarer wins and takes the rest of the tricks. Instead, unblock the suit by overtaking partner's ♥Q with the ♥K. Then cash the ♥A and lead the carefully preserved ♥5 back to partner's winners. Your side gets the first five heart tricks to defeat the contract.

# BIDDING REVIEW

We will summarize the responses to opening notrump bids as covered in the *Bidding* and *Play of the Hand* texts. We'll start by reviewing a useful conventional bid that most partnerships agree to play when responding to notrump opening bids.

## The Stayman Convention

The Stayman convention is an artificial response of 2♣ to an opening bid of 1NT. It's used to ask if opener has a four-card major suit. With a four-card (or longer) major suit, opener bids it at the two level. With no four-card major suit, opener makes the artificial rebid of 2♦.

The Stayman convention can also be used when responding to an opening bid of 2NT. In this case, 3♣ is used as the Stayman convention, and opener rebids 3♥ or 3♠ with a four-card or longer major suit. With no four-card major, opener rebids 3♦.

## Responding to 1NT Opening Bids

When partner opens 1NT, describing a balanced hand of 16 to 18 points, responder acts as captain and steers the partnership to the appropriate final contract using the following guidelines (we'll look at hands of 15 or more points under slam bidding):

## Responses to 1 NT Opening Bids

| 0 to 7 points | • Bid 2♦, 2♥, or 2♠ with a five-card or longer suit. |
| | • Otherwise pass. |
| 8 or 9 points | • Bid 2♣ (Stayman) with interest in a major suit. |
| | • Otherwise bid 2NT (invitational). |
| 10 to 14 points | • Bid 4♥ or 4♠ with a six-card or longer major suit. |
| | • Bid 3♥ or 3♠ (forcing) with a five-card major suit. |
| | • Bid 2♣ (Stayman) with a four-card major suit. |
| | • Otherwise bid 3NT. |

## Responding to 2NT Opening Bids

An opening bid of 2NT shows a balanced hand of 22 to 24 points. Use the following guidelines when responding (we will look at hands of 9 or more points under slam bidding):

## Responses to 2NT Opening Bids

0 to 2 points    • Pass.

3 to 8 points    • Bid 4 ♥ or 4 ♠ with a six-card or longer major suit.

• Bid 3 ♥ or 3 ♠ (forcing) with a five-card major suit.

• Bid 3 ♣ (Stayman) with one or both four-card major suits.

• Otherwise bid 3NT.

## Responding to 3NT Opening Bids

An opening bid of 3NT shows a balanced hand of 25 to 27 points. Responder doesn't have much room to explore. With a six-card or longer major, responder bids 4 ♥ or 4 ♠. Otherwise, responder passes. (We will look at slam bidding in a later chapter.)

# PLAY OF THE HAND REVIEW

## Developing Tricks in a Notrump Contract

When declarer needs extra tricks in a notrump contract, there are three ways in which tricks can be developed: through **promotion**; through **long suits**; and through **finesses**.

In promotion, declarer simply uses high cards to drive out the opponents' higher cards, keeping in mind to play the high card from the short side first. For example:

DUMMY

J 10 9 3

DECLARER

Q 5

Declarer can promote two tricks in this suit by driving out the opponents' ace and king. Declarer should start by playing the queen, high card from the short side.

To develop tricks from long suits, declarer keeps playing the suit until the opponents have no cards left, even if it means giving up tricks to the opponents. You can expect the missing cards in the opponents' hands to divide in the following manner:

- **An even number of missing cards will usually divide slightly unevenly.**
- **An odd number of missing cards will usually divide as evenly as possible.**

For example, suppose you have the following suit:

| | |
|---|---|
| DUMMY | There are five missing cards in the suit, an odd |
| K 8 4 2 | number, and you would expect them to divide |
|  | as evenly as possible, 3–2 (three in one opponent's hand, two in the other). By playing the |
| DECLARER | ace and the king and giving up a trick to the |
| A 7 6 3 | opponents, you can establish a trick through length since the opponents will have no cards left in the suit. |

...a of the finesse is to try and win a trick with one of ...n cards when the opponents have a higher card. You do ...y leading toward the high card which you are hoping will win a ...k. For example, consider the following suit:

DUMMY

K 3

■

DECLARER

6 4

In order to get a trick with the king, you must lead toward it from declarer's hand. If the ace is on declarer's left, the finesse will be successful. If the ace is played, declarer plays a small card from dummy, and the king takes a trick later. If the ace is not played, declarer plays the king and wins the trick. Of course, if the ace is on declarer's right, the finesse will not be successful and declarer can't get a trick in the suit.

If you are finessing for more than one missing card, lead toward the lower of your high cards first. Sometimes, you can afford to lead a high card to try to trap a missing card in an opponent's hand. Lead a high card only if you can afford to have the opponents cover it with a higher card.

For example:

DUMMY

A 7 3

■

DECLARER

Q J 10

Declarer can afford to lead the queen to try to trap the king on the left. If the queen is covered by the king, delcarer won't lose any tricks. If delcarer didn't have the jack, declarer couldn't afford to lead the queen but would have to lead toward it.

# SUMMARY

When your partner leads to a trick and you are the third person to play to the trick, a useful guideline is **third hand high**. When you are the last player on your side to contribute a card to a trick, you want to try to win the trick for your side if possible; otherwise you want to help promote winners in your partner's hand.

You need to play as high a card as necessary to try to win the trick. With a choice of equal (touching) cards, play the lowest. If partner leads a high card which will win the trick, you don't need to play a higher card unless you have to unblock the suit by overtaking partner's card.

When deciding how high a card it's necessary to play as third hand, try to keep the opponents' high cards trapped whenever possible. If the second hand has a high card which isn't played and you have both a higher card and a lower card which might win the trick, play the lower card.

## Exercise One — Third Hand High

In each of the following layouts, your partner leads the 5, and the 3 is played from dummy. Which card must you play as third hand to ensure that your side eventually takes the maximum number of tricks?

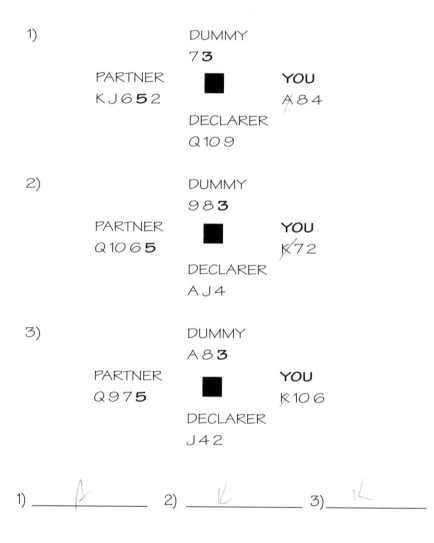

1)               DUMMY
              7 3

PARTNER      ■      **YOU**
K J 6 5 2             A 8 4

              DECLARER
              Q 10 9

2)               DUMMY
              9 8 3

PARTNER      ■      **YOU**
Q 10 6 5             K 7 2

              DECLARER
              A J 4

3)               DUMMY
              A 8 3

PARTNER      ■      **YOU**
Q 9 7 5             K 10 6

              DECLARER
              J 4 2

1) _____      2) _____      3) _____

**Exercise One** — Third Hand High

1) Ace        2) King        3) King

**Exercise Two —** Only as High as Necessary

Your partner leads the 5, and the 3 is played from dummy. Which card would you play (a)? What do you expect to happen (b)?

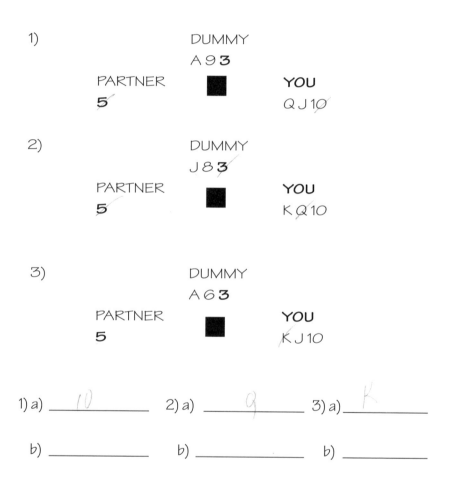

1)　　　　　　　　　　DUMMY
　　　　　　　　　　　A 9 **3**
　　　　PARTNER　　　■　　　　YOU
　　　　5　　　　　　　　　　　Q J 10

2)　　　　　　　　　　DUMMY
　　　　　　　　　　　J 8 **3**
　　　　PARTNER　　　■　　　　YOU
　　　　5　　　　　　　　　　　K Q 10

3)　　　　　　　　　　DUMMY
　　　　　　　　　　　A 6 **3**
　　　　PARTNER　　　■　　　　YOU
　　　　5　　　　　　　　　　　K J 10

1) a) ___10___　　2) a) ___Q___　　3) a) ___K___

　b) _____　　　b) _____　　　b) _____

## Exercise Two — Only as High as Necessary

1) a)  10, only as high as necessary.

   b)  If the 10 wins the trick, partner will know that you also have the queen and the jack. If declarer wins the trick with the king, partner might also suspect that you have the jack and perhaps the queen.

2) a)  10, trapping dummy's jack.

   b)  If partner has the ace, the 10 will win the trick. If declarer has the ace and wins the trick, your king and queen will have been promoted into winners.

3) a)  King, third hand high.

   b)  If you don't play third hand high, declarer may win the trick with the queen.

## Exercise Three — Trapping High Cards

In each of the following layouts, your partner leads the 5 and the 3 is played from dummy. Which card must you play to enable your side to eventually take the maximum number of tricks in the suit?

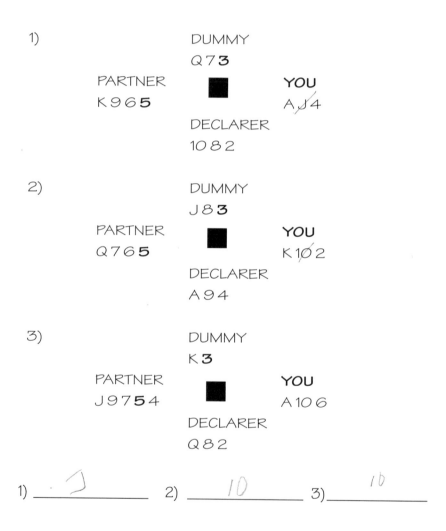

1)

DUMMY
Q 7 **3**

PARTNER        YOU
K 9 6 **5**        A J 4

DECLARER
10 8 2

2)

DUMMY
J 8 **3**

PARTNER        YOU
Q 7 6 **5**        K 10 2

DECLARER
A 9 4

3)

DUMMY
K **3**

PARTNER        YOU
J 9 7 **5** 4        A 10 6

DECLARER
Q 8 2

1) _____ J _____    2) _____ 10 _____    3) _____ 10 _____

**Exercise Three —** Trapping High Cards

    1) Jack      2) 10      3) 10

## Exercise Four — When Partner Leads a High Card

In each of the following layouts, your partner leads the jack, and the 4 is played from dummy. Which card must you play on the first trick (a)? How should the defenders play the suit to get all of the tricks to which they are entitled (b)?

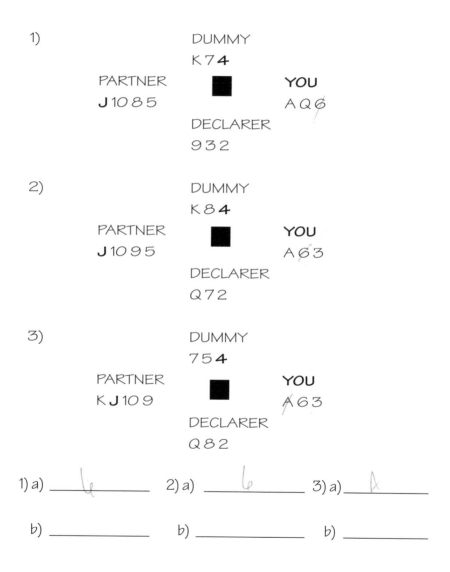

1)
                              DUMMY
                              K 7 **4**
PARTNER                     **YOU**
J 10 8 5                   A Q 6
                              DECLARER
                              9 3 2

2)
                                DUMMY
                              K 8 **4**
PARTNER                     **YOU**
J 10 9 5                   A 6 3
                              DECLARER
                              Q 7 2

3)
                                DUMMY
                              7 5 **4**
PARTNER                     **YOU**
K J 10 9                 A 6 3
                              DECLARER
                              Q 8 2

1) a) _____ 6 _____     2) a) _____ 6 _____     3) a) ___ A ___

b) _____     b) _____     b) _____

**Exercise Four** — When Partner Leads a High Card

1) a)  6, to let partner's jack win the trick.

   b)  Partner can lead the suit again and dummy's king remains trapped. The defenders get all of the tricks in the suit.

2) a)  6, keeping dummy's king trapped, even though you know declarer has the queen.

   b)  Partner will have to lead the suit again to trap dummy's king.

3) a)  Ace, to prevent declarer from getting a trick with the queen.

   b)  Lead the suit back, trapping declarer's queen. The defenders can take all of the tricks in the suit.

## Exercise Five — Unblocking

In each of the following examples, your partner leads the indicated card, and declarer plays dummy's ace. Which card must you play to allow your side to take four tricks in the suit if you have the only entry outside of this suit?

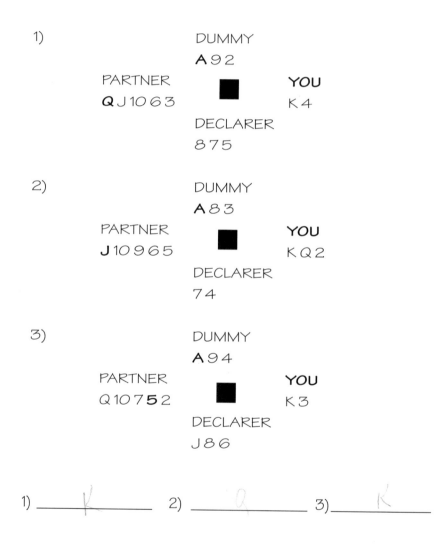

1)
DUMMY
A 9 2

PARTNER
Q J 10 6 3

YOU
K 4

DECLARER
8 7 5

2)
DUMMY
A 8 3

PARTNER
J 10 9 6 5

YOU
K Q 2

DECLARER
7 4

3)
DUMMY
A 9 4

PARTNER
Q 10 7 5 2

YOU
K 3

DECLARER
J 8 6

1) _____K_____     2) _____Q_____     3)_____K_____

**Exercise Five** — Unblocking

    1) King         2) King or Queen        3) King

In all examples, you want to have a low card left to lead back to partner's length in the suit. You want to unblock the suit.

## Exercise Six — Putting It All Together

Your partner leads the indicated card, and the 3 is played from dummy. Which card do you play in each of the following situations?

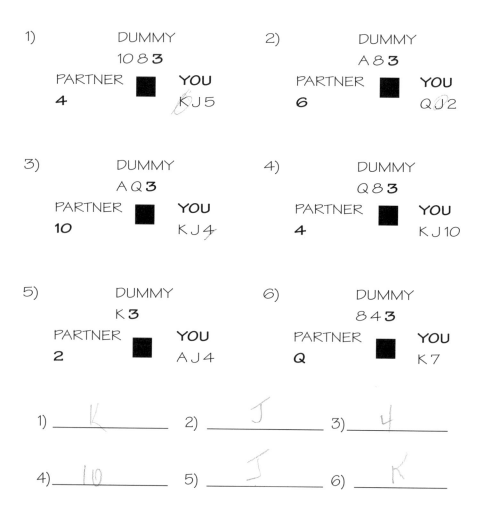

1)
DUMMY
10 8 3
PARTNER    ■    YOU
4        KJ5

2)
DUMMY
A 8 3
PARTNER    ■    YOU
6        QJ2

3)
DUMMY
A Q 3
PARTNER    ■    YOU
10       KJ4

4)
DUMMY
Q 8 3
PARTNER    ■    YOU
4        KJ10

5)
DUMMY
K 3
PARTNER    ■    YOU
2        AJ4

6)
DUMMY
8 4 3
PARTNER    ■    YOU
Q        K7

1) ___K___    2) ___J___    3) ___4___

4) ___10___    5) ___J___    6) ___K___

**Exercise Six** — Putting It All Together

1) King        2) Jack        3) 4

4) 10        5) Jack        6) King

## Exercise Seven — Review of Responses to 1NT Opening Bids

Your partner opens the bidding 1NT. What do you respond with each of the following hands?

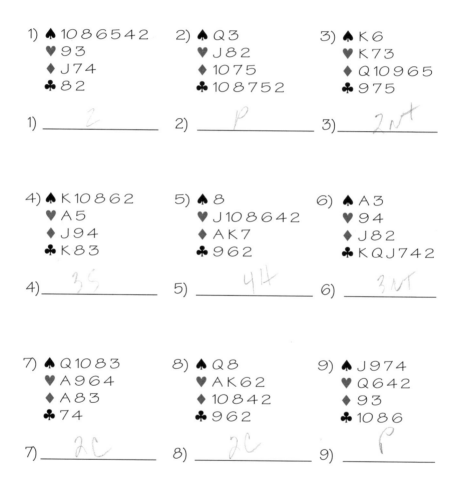

1) ♠ 10 8 6 5 4 2
♥ 9 3
♦ J 7 4
♣ 8 2

2) ♠ Q 3
♥ J 8 2
♦ 10 7 5
♣ 10 8 7 5 2

3) ♠ K 6
♥ K 7 3
♦ Q 10 9 6 5
♣ 9 7 5

1) _____2_____   2) _____P_____   3)_____2 NT_____

4) ♠ K 10 8 6 2
♥ A 5
♦ J 9 4
♣ K 8 3

5) ♠ 8
♥ J 10 8 6 4 2
♦ A K 7
♣ 9 6 2

6) ♠ A 3
♥ 9 4
♦ J 8 2
♣ K Q J 7 4 2

4)_____3 S_____   5) _____4 H_____   6) _____3 NT_____

7) ♠ Q 10 8 3
♥ A 9 6 4
♦ A 8 3
♣ 7 4

8) ♠ Q 8
♥ A K 6 2
♦ 10 8 4 2
♣ 9 6 2

9) ♠ J 9 7 4
♥ Q 6 4 2
♦ 9 3
♣ 10 8 6

7)_____2 C_____   8) _____2 C_____   9) _____P_____

**Exercise Seven —** Review of Responses to 1NT Opening
Bids

1) 2♠          2) Pass          3) 2NT

4) 3♠          5) 4♥          6) 3NT

7) 2♣          8) 2♣          9) Pass

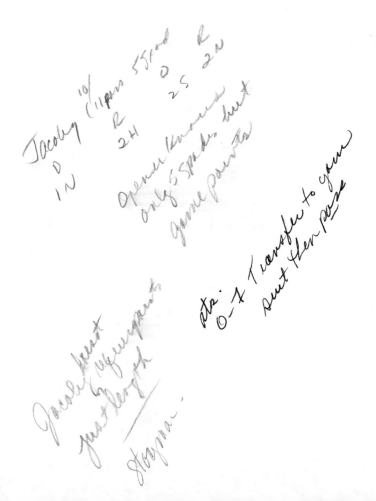

## Exercise Eight — Developing Tricks in Notrump Contracts

What is the maximum number of tricks you can get from each of the following suit combinations if the missing cards are favorably located? How would you plan to play the suit?

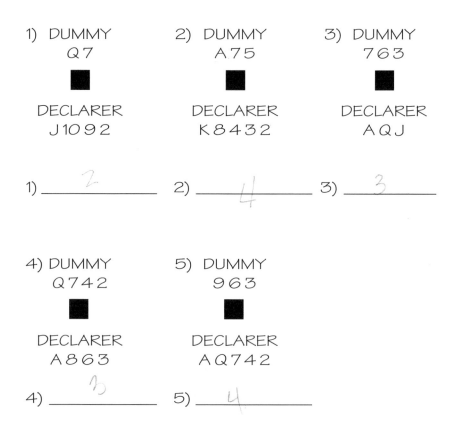

1) DUMMY
Q 7

DECLARER
J 10 9 2

2) DUMMY
A 7 5

DECLARER
K 8 4 3 2

3) DUMMY
7 6 3

DECLARER
A Q J

1) _____ 2 _____   2) _____ 4 _____   3) _____ 3 _____

4) DUMMY
Q 7 4 2

DECLARER
A 8 6 3

5) DUMMY
9 6 3

DECLARER
A Q 7 4 2

4) _____ 3 _____   5) _____ 4 _____

**Exercise Eight** — Developing Tricks in Notrump Contracts

1) Two. Play the suit twice, driving out the ace and the king to promote two winners. Play the queen, high card from the short side, first.

2) Four. Play the suit five times, giving one trick to the opponents so that you can collect four tricks.

3) Three. Take a repeated finesse against the opponent on your right.

4) Three. Lead toward dummy's queen and get an extra trick through length assuming the suit is divided 3–2.

5) Four. Take the finesse against the queen and hope the suit is divided 3–2 so that you also get extra tricks through length.

## Exercise Nine — Third Hand High
### (E-Z Deal Cards: #3, Hand 1 — Dealer, North)

Turn up the cards from the first pre-dealt deal. Put each hand dummy-style at the edge of the table in front of each player.

**The Bidding**

What would North open the bidding? East and West pass throughout. With two four-card suits that can be bid at the one level, which suit does South bid? Is there still room for North to bid a suit at the one level? What does North rebid? How many points does South have? At what level does the partnership belong? Is there a Golden Fit? What does South rebid?

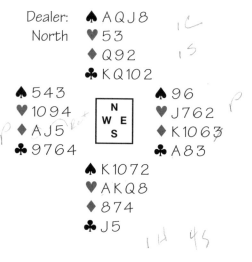

Dealer:    ♠ A Q J 8
North      ♥ 5 3
           ♦ Q 9 2
           ♣ K Q 10 2

♠ 5 4 3              ♠ 9 6
♥ 10 9 4             ♥ J 7 6 2
♦ A J 5             ♦ K 10 6 3
♣ 9 7 6 4           ♣ A 8 3

           ♠ K 10 7 2
           ♥ A K Q 8
           ♦ 8 7 4
           ♣ J 5

How does the auction proceed from there? Who is the declarer?

**The Defense**

Which player makes the opening lead? Which suit would be led? Why? Which card would be led? Which card would West play on the first trick? What would West do next?

**The Play**

Review the steps in declarer's PLAN. How does declarer plan to make the contract?

## Exercise Nine — Third Hand High

### The Bidding

- North opens the bidding 1♣.
- South responds 1♥.
- Yes. North rebids 1♠.
- South has 13 high-card points plus 1 dummy point in support of spades and knows there are enough points for game. The partnership has a Golden Fit in spades. South rebids 4♠.
- The final contract is 4♠ and North is the declarer.

### The Defense

- East leads the ♦3, fourth best from the unbid suit.
- West plays the ♦A, third hand high, and returns the ♦J, top of the remaining doubleton.

### The Play

- Declarer can afford three losers in 4♠ and has one too many. Declarer plans to discard one of the diamond losers on dummy's extra heart winner. After an opening diamond lead and a diamond return, however, the defenders get three diamond tricks before declarer has a chance to discard a loser.

## Exercise Ten — Trapping High Cards

## (E-Z Deal Cards: #3, Hand 2 — Dealer, East)

Turn up the cards from the second pre-dealt deal. Put each hand dummy-style at the edge of the table in front of each player.

### The Bidding

What would East open the bidding? What would South do? Can West bid a suit at the one level? What would West respond? North passes. With a minimum balanced hand, what does East rebid? How does the auction proceed from there? What is the contract? Who is the declarer?

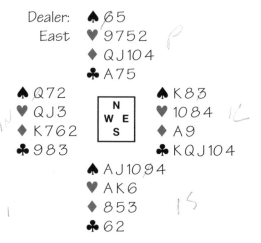

Dealer: ♠ 65
East ♥ 9752
♦ QJ104
♣ A75

♠ Q72
♥ QJ3
♦ K762
♣ 983

♠ K83
♥ 1084
♦ A9
♣ KQJ104

♠ AJ1094
♥ AK6
♦ 853
♣ 62

### The Defense

Which player makes the opening lead? Which suit would be led? Why? Which card would be led? Which card will South play if a small card is played from dummy?

### The Play

Review the steps in declarer's PLAN. How does declarer plan to make the contract?

## Exercise Ten — Trapping High Cards

### The Bidding

- East opens the bidding 1♣.
- South overcalls 1♠.
- With a minimum balanced hand, West bids 1NT.
- All players pass.
- The final contract is 1NT and West is the declarer.

### The Defense

- North leads the ♠6, top of partner's doubleton.
- South will play the ♠9, as high a card as necessary, while still keeping dummy's ♠K trapped.

### The Play

- Declarer needs seven tricks and has only three sure tricks. Four more tricks can be developed in clubs after the opponents' ♣A is driven out. Declarer will need to keep the ♦A in dummy as an entry to the clubs in case the opponents hold up their ♣A.

## Exercise Eleven — Third Hand not so High
### (E-Z Deal Cards: #3, Hand 3 — Dealer, South)

Turn up the cards from the third pre-dealt deal. Put each hand dummy-style at the edge of the table in front of each player.

### The Bidding

What is South's opening bid? West passes. What is North's response? How does the bidding proceed from there? What is the contract? Who is the declarer?

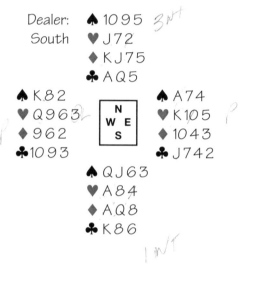

Dealer:  ♠ 10 9 5  *3NT*
South    ♥ J 7 2
         ♦ K J 7 5
         ♣ A Q 5

♠ K 8 2              ♠ A 7 4
♥ Q 9 6 3            ♥ K 10 5
♦ 9 6 2             ♦ 10 4 3
♣ 10 9 3            ♣ J 7 4 2

         ♠ Q J 6 3
         ♥ A 8 4
         ♦ A Q 8
         ♣ K 8 6

         *1NT*

### The Defense

Which player makes the opening lead? What would the opening lead be? Why? If a small card is played from dummy on the first trick, which card should East play? Why?

### The Play

Review the steps in declarer's PLAN. How does declarer plan to make the contract?

## Exercise Eleven — Third Hand not so High

### The Bidding

- South opens the bidding 1NT.
- North responds 3NT.
- All players pass. The final contract is 3NT and South is the delcarer.

### The Defense

- West leads the ♥3, fourth highest from the longest suit.
- East should play the ♥10 to keep dummy's ♥J trapped by the ♥K.

### The Play

- Declarer needs nine tricks and starts with eight sure tricks. The additional trick required can be developed in the spade suit through promotion by driving out the opponents' ♠A and ♠K.

## Exercise Twelve — Unblocking

### (E-Z Deal Cards: #3, Hand 4 — Dealer, West)

Turn up the cards from the fourth pre-dealt deal. Put each hand dummy-style at the edge of the table in front of each player.

### The Bidding

West and North pass. How does East describe this hand? South passes. What does West respond? How does the auction proceed from there? What is the contract? Who is the declarer?

Dealer:   ♠ 10 6 5 2
West      ♥ A 6
          ♦ 7 3 2
          ♣ J 7 5 4

♠ 9 7 3                      ♠ A K Q
♥ 10 4 2        N            ♥ 8 7 3
♦ K 8 4      W     E         ♦ A Q J 9
♣ 10 8 6 2      S            ♣ A K Q

          ♠ J 8 4
          ♥ K Q J 9 5
          ♦ 10 6 5
          ♣ 9 3

### The Defense

Which player makes the opening lead? What would the opening lead be? Which card must North contribute to the first trick? Why?

### The Play

Review the steps in declarer's PLAN. How does declarer plan to make the contract?

## Exercise Twelve — Unblocking

### The Bidding
- East describes this hand by bidding 3NT.
- All players pass and East is the declarer in 3NT.

### The Defense
- South leads the ♥K, top of a three-card sequence.
- North must contribute the ♥A and return a low heart to get back into South's hand. Otherwise, the suit is blocked.

### The Play
- Declarer needs nine tricks and has nine after gaining the lead. Meanwhile, the defenders may have taken enough tricks to defeat the contract.

# CHAPTER 4
## *Second-Hand Play*

If the first card led to a trick is from your right, you are referred to as second hand, since you are contributing the second card to the trick. The situation here is different from playing as third hand. Partner is in the enviable position of being the fourth hand, last to play to the trick. Declarer will have to play a card from both sides of the table before partner has to play. Your role as second hand is to ensure that your side doesn't unnecessarily spend any of its high cards in trying to win the trick.

As with third-hand play, you want to keep declarer's high cards trapped whenever possible. The basic idea is expressed in the saying *aces are meant to take kings*. In addition to winning the trick, an ace is most powerful when capturing an opponent's king at the same time. If the ace captures only small cards from the opponents, its power is lessened. Similarly, you would ideally like to use your kings to capture the opponents' queens, your queens to capture their jacks, and so forth. Of course the actual situation during a deal is seldom so ideal, but the principle is useful to keep in mind. Let's see how it can be put to use when playing second hand to a trick.

## SECOND HAND LOW

One common piece of advice given for second hand play is *second hand low*. This indicates that you should play a low card to the trick when you have nothing else to guide you. Let's see why this is often a good idea.

### Conserving High Cards

Consider the following situation. Declarer leads a small card toward the dummy, and you can see only the following cards in the suit:

DUMMY
Q 7 3
YOU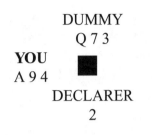
A 9 4
DECLARER
2

Should you play your ace to make sure of winning the trick? If you can see that taking your ace will clearly defeat the contract, it's best to take it and get on with the next board. Otherwise, follow the guideline and play second hand low, contributing the 4

to the trick. If you play the ace, declarer will play the 3 from dummy. Your ace will have captured only two of declarer's low cards, and declarer will still hold all of the high cards.

First, let's suppose declarer has the king and the complete layout looks something like this:

DUMMY
Q 7 3
YOU 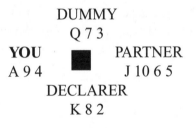 PARTNER
A 9 4     J 10 6 5
DECLARER
K 8 2

If you rise with the ace, declarer ends up with two tricks, one with the queen and one with the king. If you play second hand low, declarer can win the first trick with dummy's queen but now the king remains trapped by your ace and partner's jack and 10. Declarer is held to one trick in the suit. Your ace is meant to take declarer's king, not the 2.

Suppose we give partner the king instead of declarer. Playing the ace right away could still cost your side a trick:

DUMMY
Q 7 3
YOU 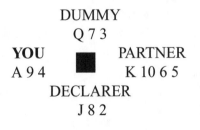 PARTNER
A 9 4     K 10 6 5
DECLARER
J 8 2

If you rise with the ace, declarer will have the queen and the jack left to drive out partner's king and create one trick in the suit. On the other hand, if you play second hand low, partner can capture dummy's queen with the king and your ace remains to stop declarer

from getting a trick with the jack. Declarer doesn't get a trick in the suit. How low is low? When declarer leads the 2 toward dummy, you may be tempted to play the 9, rather than the 4, to encourage declarer to play dummy's queen. There's no need to do this. Declarer is surely not planning to play dummy's 7 to try to win the trick. If you waste the 9, it might cost your side a trick later. To illustrate this, play the 9 in the previous layout, declarer plays the queen, and partner wins the king. The remaining cards now look like this:

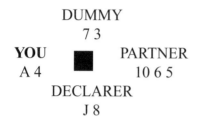

DUMMY
7 3
YOU
A 4
PARTNER
10 6 5
DECLARER
J 8

If partner leads the 10, declarer can cover with the jack to drive out your ace and promote the 8 into a trick since you no longer have the 9. If partner plays a low card, declarer can finesse the 8, again driving out your ace and establishing a trick in the suit. Just as aces were meant to take

kings, 9's were meant to take 8's. Don't waste any of your cards when you don't have to. Let's see the importance of second hand low in a complete deal:

DUMMY
Contract: 6NT
Lead: ♦ 10
♠ A K J
♥ K 7 5
♦ Q 6 3
♣ A J 10 8

YOU
♠ 9 4 2
♥ A J 3
♦ 10 9 8 7
♣ 7 4 3

PARTNER
♠ 10 7 6 3
♥ 9 8 6 2
♦ 5 4 2
♣ 9 6

DECLARER
♠ Q 8 5
♥ Q 10 4
♦ A K J
♣ K Q 5 2

You start off well against the 6NT slam by leading the ♦ 10. If you had led the ♥A, declarer would immediately have 12 tricks. By leading a diamond, you don't give declarer any help. Holding three spade tricks, three diamond tricks, and four club tricks, declarer will have to get two tricks from the heart suit. Your work isn't finished, however. When declarer leads a low heart toward dummy's ♥K, you must again refrain from taking your ♥A and play second hand low. Now your ♥A and ♥J have declarer's ♥Q trapped and there is no way for declarer to establish a 12th trick. Notice once again how you can't afford to play "semi-low" by playing your ♥J on the first trick. Declarer could then win dummy's ♥K and use the remaining ♥Q and ♥10 to drive out your ♥A.

## Making Declarer Guess

Another reason for playing second hand low is to give declarer a chance to make a mistake. Players often have difficulty defending correctly in this type of situation:

DUMMY
A Q 10
**YOU**
K J 5 3
DECLARER
4

When declarer leads a low card toward dummy, you may feel compelled to play the jack or king since these cards are going to be trapped anyway. You don't know what's going on in declarer's mind, however, so play second hand low and leave it up to declarer to decide what to do. Declarer may have a singleton and may be planning to play the ace rather than take a finesse. Declarer may decide to finesse the queen rather than the 10. Now your king and jack will prevent declarer from getting a third trick in the suit.

Playing low can be even more important when declarer has a complete guess. Consider the following layout:

DUMMY
K J
YOU  PARTNER
A 10 8 6 2            Q 9 5 4
DECLARER
7 3

When declarer leads a low card toward dummy, you might feel that it doesn't matter whether or not you play your ace since declarer is always entitled to a trick in the suit with dummy's king. Declarer, however, can't see your cards. If you play second hand low, declarer may think that the actual layout is something like this:

DUMMY
K J
YOU  PARTNER
Q 10 8 6 2           A 9 5 4
DECLARER
7 3

In this layout, declarer should play dummy's jack, taking a finesse against your queen. Since declarer doesn't know which is the actual layout, play low as second hand and let declarer do the guesswork.

In situations like this, where declarer has to guess whether you or your partner holds the ace, it pays to have thought about the guideline ahead of time so that you can play second hand low in tempo. If you hesitate, pondering whether or not to take your ace, declarer won't have much of a guess left by the time you decide to play low.

Here is a similar situation where it's important to play second hand low. Second-hand play can apply whether you are on dummy's left or right. This time you are next to play when a small card is led from dummy:

DUMMY
8 6 4 3
PARTNER 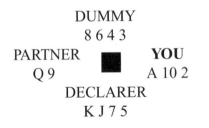 YOU
Q 9                   A 10 2
DECLARER
K J 7 5

If you play low, declarer may play the jack and partner will win the queen. Declarer will lead toward the king later, and you'll get a second trick for your side with the ace. Even if declarer guesses to play the king the first time, your partner is still entitled to a trick with the queen, and you get a trick with the ace. In either case, your side gets two tricks in the suit. Look what might happen if you play the ace when a low card is led from dummy. Declarer plays low and the remaining cards look like this:

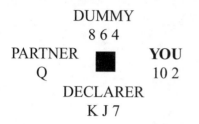

DUMMY
8 6 4

PARTNER
Q

YOU
10 2

DECLARER
K J 7

Declarer may choose to play the king on the next round of the suit, dropping your partner's queen. All of a sudden, your two tricks in the suit have been compressed into one.

## Creating Entry Problems for Declarer

By playing second hand low, you can often create entry problems for declarer.

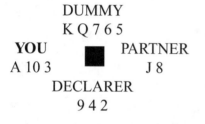

DUMMY
K Q 7 6 5

YOU
A 10 3

PARTNER
J 8

DECLARER
9 4 2

When a low card is led toward dummy, declarer will have no problem establishing the suit if you take the first trick with the ace. Play second hand low and give declarer a more difficult time. Declarer can win the first trick with dummy's queen (or king), but if the remaining high card is played from dummy, you take the trick with the ace and your 10 is established as a winner. Instead, declarer must now travel across the table to lead toward dummy's remaining high card, giving you only one trick with the ace. Declarer may not always have an easy entry back to the other side.

For example, here is a deal where declarer has no chance if you play second hand low:

|  | DUMMY |  |
|---|---|---|
| Contract: 3NT | ♠ 8 4 3 |  |
| Lead: ♣Q | ♥ 7 4 2 |  |
|  | ♦ 9 6 3 2 |  |
|  | ♣ A 8 4 |  |

| PARTNER |  | YOU |
|---|---|---|
| ♠ J 9 2 | N | ♠ Q 10 6 5 |
| ♥ Q 6 3 | W E | ♥ J 10 9 5 |
| ♦ 10 8 | S | ♦ A J 7 |
| ♣ Q J 10 9 3 |  | ♣ 6 2 |

|  | DECLARER |  |
|---|---|---|
|  | ♠ A K 7 |  |
|  | ♥ A K 8 |  |
|  | ♦ K Q 5 4 |  |
|  | ♣ K 7 5 |  |

Declarer starts with six sure tricks, and three remaining tricks must come from the diamond suit. Declarer would like to lead toward the king and queen twice but has only one entry to the dummy. Still, that will be sufficient if, when a low diamond is led from dummy, you play your ace. By playing low, you prevent declarer from taking three diamond tricks. Declarer doesn't have another entry to dummy and will have to go down one.

## SECOND HAND NOT SO LOW

Second hand low is useful advice when you have nothing else to guide you but, as with all guidelines, there are some situations where it doesn't apply.

### Splitting Honors

While you want to avoid wasting any of your high cards, you also want to prevent declarer from winning a trick cheaply. Consider this layout, with declarer leading low from dummy:

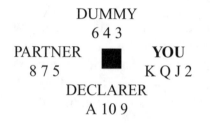

|  | DUMMY |  | If you play the 2 when declarer leads |
|---|---|---|---|
|  | 6 4 3 |  | a low card from the dummy, it's pos- |
| PARTNER |  | YOU | sible that declarer will play the 9 or |
| 8 7 5 |  | K Q J 2 | 10 and win a trick to which the of- |
|  | DECLARER |  | fense is not entitled. To prevent this, |
|  | A 10 9 |  | play one of your high cards when the |

suit is led. This is referred to as splitting your honors. You need play only as high a card as necessary to prevent declarer from winning the trick too cheaply. In the above example, you would play the jack. Declarer is then restricted to one trick in the suit.

Whether or not you need to split your honors depends on the actual layout of the suit and what declarer intends to do. Since you rarely know where all the missing cards are and you can't read declarer's mind, you have to exercise your judgment in most cases. Here is a common situation, with declarer leading a small card toward dummy:

|  | DUMMY |  | Should you split your honors? If you |
|---|---|---|---|
|  | A 10 4 2 |  | don't have much else to go on, it's a |
| YOU |  |  | good idea to split your honors to pro- |
| Q J 6 |  |  | mote one trick in the suit. The com- |
|  | DECLARER |  | plete layout may be something like |
|  | 3 |  | this: |

```
          DUMMY
          A 10 4 2
PARTNER      ■     YOU
Q J 6        ■     9 5
         DECLARER
          K 8 7 3
```

If you play the 6, declarer might decide to insert dummy's 10, which will win the trick since partner doesn't have a higher card. When declarer plays the ace and king, your queen and jack will fall and declarer will end up losing no tricks in the suit.

By splitting your honors and playing the jack on the first trick, declarer is forced to play dummy's ace in order to win the trick. Now, your queen will take a trick when declarer continues playing the suit.

In the above layout, it wouldn't have made much difference if your partner held the king rather than declarer. Partner can let your jack win the trick. There are times, however, when you have additional information which guides you to a different decision. Suppose the bidding indicates that declarer has a five-card suit. This might be the complete layout:

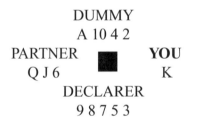

```
          DUMMY
          A 10 4 2
PARTNER      ■     YOU
Q J 6        ■     K
         DECLARER
          9 8 7 5 3
```

If you split your honors, playing the jack, and declarer plays dummy's ace, partner's king will fall on the same trick. Instead of losing two tricks in the suit, declarer ends up losing only one. How could you know that this was the situation? You can't see declarer's cards, but perhaps this is declarer's trump suit. If so, declarer is quite likely to hold at least five cards. If declarer holds five cards in the suit, it's unlikely that declarer is planning to play dummy's 10 even if you do play a small card. For example, suppose this is the actual layout:

DUMMY
A 10 4 2

PARTNER 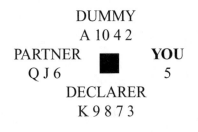 YOU
Q J 6        5

DECLARER
K 9 8 7 3

With nine cards in the combined hands, declarer is probably planning to play dummy's ace and later the king. Declarer hopes the missing cards are divided 2–2 so that it isn't necessary to lose any tricks in the suit. In this case, it's fairly safe not to split your honors, safeguarding against the situation where partner has the singleton king. As you can see, this situation can sometimes become a cat-and-mouse game between declarer and the defenders.

Another time not to split your honors is when there is nothing to gain and you will end up helping declarer.

DUMMY
A K 10

YOU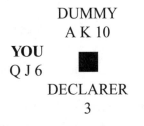
Q J 6

DECLARER
3

When declarer leads a low card toward dummy, you may be tempted to split your honors and play the jack. If there is an entry back to declarer's hand, this won't help your side. After winning the trick with dummy's king and coming back to the hand, declarer can lead another low card toward the ace and 10 in dummy. Whether or not you play the queen, declarer will win all three tricks. There's no reason to panic when you can see that declarer will be able to win the trick with dummy's 10 if you play a low card. Remember that declarer can't see what you hold in the suit. Declarer may be intending to win the first trick with dummy's ace or king and now your queen and jack will prevent three tricks from being taken in the suit.

## The Setting Trick

Another time to avoid automatically playing second hand low is when you can see that by winning the trick you'll be able to defeat the contract. Here is an example in a complete deal:

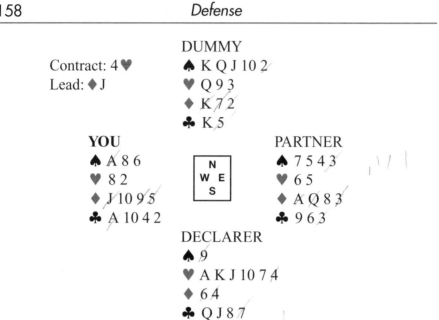

Contract: 4♥
Lead: ♦ J

DUMMY
♠ K Q J 10 2
♥ Q 9 3
♦ K 7 2
♣ K 5

YOU
♠ A 8 6
♥ 8 2
♦ J 10 9 5
♣ A 10 4 2

PARTNER
♠ 7 5 4 3
♥ 6 5
♦ A Q 8 3
♣ 9 6 3

DECLARER
♠ 9
♥ A K J 10 7 4
♦ 6 4
♣ Q J 8 7

You lead the ♦ J, declarer plays dummy's ♦ K, and your partner wins the first trick with the ♦ A. Partner then plays the ♦ Q, which wins the trick and follows with a third round of diamonds, which declarer trumps. Declarer immediately leads a low spade toward dummy. Now is not the time to automatically play low. To defeat the contract, you need to take four tricks. Your side already has two diamond tricks and you also have the ♣ A. By winning this trick with the ♠ A, you can see that you have enough tricks to defeat the contract. If you play low and let declarer win the trick with one of dummy's high spades, you may not get another chance. On this hand, declarer has a singleton spade and will end up losing just three tricks. After winning the ♠ A, don't get careless. You must immediately take the ♣ A as well. Otherwise, declarer will be able to discard all of the club losers on dummy's spades.

On this deal, it's easy to see that taking the ♠ A leads to declarer's defeat. It wouldn't have been as straightforward for you if your partner held the ♠ A rather than you. But, since none of the usual reasons for playing second hand low apply, you shouldn't let declarer slip the single-ton spade by. You won't be saving a trick by playing low — declarer has enough high spades to drive out your ♠A and win all of the remaining spade tricks. Declarer doesn't have to guess which spade to play from dummy, and declarer is unlikely to have any problems with entries to either hand with hearts as the trump suit. As a result, there's no good reason to play second hand low even if you don't hold the ♣A.

Situations where it may be dangerous to play second hand low are quite common in suit contracts. Consider this layout of a side suit in a suit contract where declarer is leading a low card from a doubleton in the dummy:

DUMMY

7 4

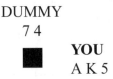  **YOU**

A K 5

If you play low, the trick may be won with the queen if declarer has that card. You would get only one trick in the suit if dummy has some trumps left. It's best to make sure of two tricks in the suit by winning the first trick with your king. You don't want to "go to bed" with your king or your ace, especially if winning those tricks will help your side defeat the contract.

Here's an example which combines the idea of splitting your honors and taking the setting trick:

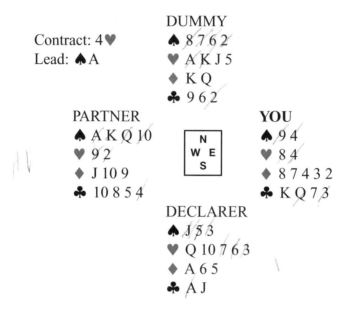

Contract: 4♥
Lead: ♠A

DUMMY
♠ 8 7 6 2
♥ A K J 5
♦ K Q
♣ 9 6 2

PARTNER
♠ A K Q 10
♥ 9 2
♦ J 10 9
♣ 10 8 5 4

YOU
♠ 9 4
♥ 8 4
♦ 8 7 4 3 2
♣ K Q 7 3

DECLARER
♠ J 5 3
♥ Q 10 7 6 3
♦ A 6 5
♣ A J

Partner starts off by taking the ♠A, the ♠K, and the ♠Q and then leading the ♠10, which declarer trumps. Declarer then draws trumps by playing the ♥A and the ♥K and leads a low club from dummy. Here's your first chance to avoid playing second hand low. Even though you can't see declarer's hand, split your club honors and play the ♣Q, promoting your ♣K into a winner. If you play low, declarer will be able to win the trick with the ♣J and could end up making the contract. By playing the ♣Q, you force declarer to play the ♣A to win the trick. If declarer now plays a low diamond over to dummy's ♦Q and leads the remaining low club, you have a second chance to avoid playing second hand low. This time win the trick with the ♣K since it represents the setting trick. If you play low, declarer will win with the ♣J and make the contract.

# COVERING HONORS

Another bridge maxim that requires discretion in its application is *cover an honor with an honor.* This implies that if declarer leads a honor, you cover it with (play) a higher honor if you have one. The saying *second hand low* usually applies when a small card, rather than an honor, is led. To see why you would usually play a higher card in second hand when a high card is led, we need to look at the reasoning behind this advice.

## Promoting Tricks

The theory behind covering an honor with an honor can be seen clearly in this example where declarer leads the queen from the dummy:

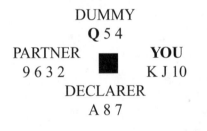

DUMMY
Q 5 4
PARTNER        YOU
9 6 3 2        K J 10
DECLARER
A 8 7

If you were to play low (the 10 or the jack), declarer could play low and win the trick with dummy's queen. Declarer's ace would then make two tricks in the suit. Instead, cover dummy's queen with your king to make declarer play the ace in order to win the trick. Now your jack and 10 are promoted into the highest cards in the suit, and declarer ends up with one trick. By covering the queen with the king, you made declarer use two high cards to capture one of yours. This in turn promoted your lower cards in the suit into winners. This is the idea behind covering an honor with an honor. You want to promote tricks for your side.

Although it's easy to see in the above layout how the jack and the 10 will be promoted by covering dummy's queen, the picture may not be so clear if you don't hold these cards. Suppose these are the only cards you see when the queen is led from dummy:

DUMMY
Q 5 4

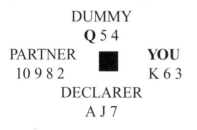 YOU
K 6 3

Should you cover with your king or play second hand low? It doesn't look as if there is anything to promote in your hand by covering with the king. However, there may be something in partner's hand. With nothing else to go on, cover with the king. The complete layout might look something like this:

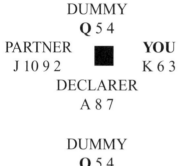

DUMMY
Q 5 4
PARTNER          YOU
J 10 9 2         K 6 3
DECLARER
A 8 7

By covering the queen with the king, you promote partner's jack and 10 into tricks for your side. Of course, declarer may have both the jack and the 10:

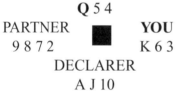

DUMMY
Q 5 4
PARTNER          YOU
9 8 7 2          K 6 3
DECLARER
A J 10

If this is the case, you haven't lost anything by covering with the king. Declarer is always entitled to three tricks. If you don't cover the queen, it will win the trick and declarer can repeat the finesse by leading a low card from dummy to trap your king.

Partner doesn't need both the jack and the 10 to make covering the queen worthwhile. Suppose this is the layout:

DUMMY
Q 5 4
PARTNER          YOU
10 9 8 2         K 6 3
DECLARER
A J 7

If you don't cover the queen with the king, dummy's queen will win the trick. Declarer can then lead a low card from dummy and your king is trapped. Declarer wins three tricks in the suit. If you cover with the king, however, declarer can win with the ace and take a trick with the jack. Now partner's 10 is promoted into the highest card in the suit, and declarer gets only two tricks rather than three.

Covering with the king could be important even if partner holds the ace. Suppose this is the complete layout:

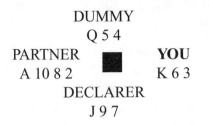

DUMMY
Q 5 4

PARTNER
A 10 8 2

YOU
K 6 3

DECLARER
J 9 7

If you play low when dummy's queen is led, partner can win the trick with the ace. Declarer can get a trick later with the jack, whether or not you play your king, by leading a low card from the dummy. By covering the queen with the king, you prevent declarer from getting any tricks in the suit. Your king wins the trick and declarer's jack remains trapped by partner's ace and 10.

Here's a complete deal to illustrate the importance of covering an honor in order to promote winners for your side:

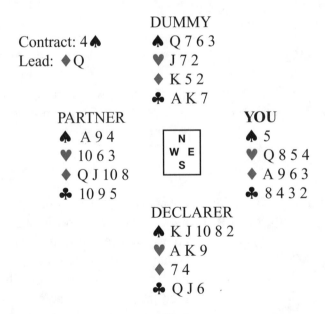

Contract: 4 ♠
Lead: ♦ Q

DUMMY
♠ Q 7 6 3
♥ J 7 2
♦ K 5 2
♣ A K 7

PARTNER
♠ A 9 4
♥ 10 6 3
♦ Q J 10 8
♣ 10 9 5

YOU
♠ 5
♥ Q 8 5 4
♦ A 9 6 3
♣ 8 4 3 2

DECLARER
♠ K J 10 8 2
♥ A K 9
♦ 7 4
♣ Q J 6

Partner leads the ♦Q, and your side takes the first two diamond tricks. When a third round of diamonds is led, declarer ruffs and starts to draw trumps. Partner wins the ♠A, and leads a club which declarer wins.

Declarer draws partner's remaining trumps, takes the club tricks, and then leads the ♥J from the dummy. Here's your chance to shine by covering with the ♥Q. Declarer can win the ♥K and the ♥A, but your partner's ♥10 is promoted into the setting trick.

The opportunity to cover an honor with an honor arises in a variety of circumstances. It's usually right to cover if you can see that your honor will be trapped anyway the next time the suit is led. For example, suppose these are the cards you see in a side suit when declarer leads the 10 toward the dummy:

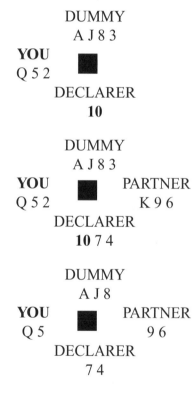

| | DUMMY | | This is your chance to cover and |
| | A J 8 3 | | make declarer use both the 10 and the |
| **YOU** | | | ace to capture your queen. If you play |
| Q 5 2 | | | low, the complete layout might look |
| | DECLARER | | like this: |
| | **10** | | |

| | DUMMY | | If you play a low card, declarer will |
| | A J 8 3 | | play a low card from dummy, and |
| **YOU** | | **PARTNER** | your partner will win the first trick |
| Q 5 2 | | K 9 6 | with the king. The remaining cards |
| | DECLARER | | will now look like this: |
| | **10** 7 4 | | |

| | DUMMY | | Your queen is now trapped by dummy's |
| | A J 8 | | ace and jack. When declarer next leads |
| **YOU** | | **PARTNER** | a low card toward the dummy, there's |
| Q 5 | | 9 6 | no way you can prevent declarer from |
| | DECLARER | | taking the rest of the tricks. If you cover |
| | 7 4 | | the 10 with the queen originally, how- |

ever, the remaining cards would look like this when declarer wins the trick with dummy's ace:

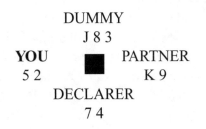

DUMMY
J 8 3
YOU     PARTNER
5 2       K 9
DECLARER
7 4

Now, it's declarer's jack that is trapped by your partner's king and 9. Declarer will have to lose two tricks in the suit.

## When not to Cover

Since the idea of covering an honor with an honor is to promote tricks for your side, you don't cover when there is nothing to promote. For example, suppose the queen is led from dummy in this situation:

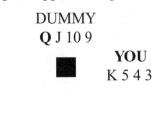

DUMMY
Q J 10 9
     YOU
     K 5 4 3

Since you can see the jack, the 10, and the 9 in the dummy, there's nothing to promote for your side by covering the queen with the king. In fact, it may cost you a trick:

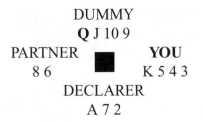

DUMMY
Q J 10 9
PARTNER     YOU
8 6       K 5 4 3
DECLARER
A 7 2

If you cover the queen, declarer will win the ace and end up with four tricks in the suit. By refusing to cover each time the suit is led from dummy, declarer will get only three tricks in the suit.

The situation isn't so clear when there are two touching high cards in the dummy:

DUMMY
Q J 4

YOU
K 7 3

Should you cover the queen with the king? You can see that the jack is in the dummy, but partner may have the 10. In such situations, the guideline is to cover the last high card led when you have nothing else to go on. One reason for this can be seen when partner holds the ace:

DUMMY
Q J 4
PARTNER        YOU
A 10 9 5      K 7 3
DECLARER
8 6 2

By letting partner win the first trick with the ace, your king remains to trap dummy's jack. Declarer gets no tricks in the suit. If you were to win the first trick with the king, declarer could later lead toward dummy's remaining jack and would get one trick whether or not partner chose to play the ace.

A more subtle reason for not covering occurs when partner has only the 10, as in this layout:

DUMMY
Q J 4
PARTNER        YOU
10 6 5       K 7 3
DECLARER
A 9 8 2

If you cover the queen with the king, declarer wins the trick with the ace and the remaining cards look like this:

DUMMY
J 4
PARTNER        YOU
10 6        7 3
DECLARER
9 8 2

Declarer can lead the 9 and partner's 10 is trapped. Whether or not partner plays the 10, declarer can take all of the tricks in the suit. If you don't cover the first honor led from dummy, the remaining cards will look like this:

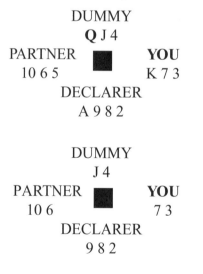

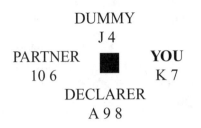

DUMMY
J 4

PARTNER          YOU
10 6                   K 7

DECLARER
A 9 8

Declarer can no longer avoid losing a trick in the suit. If dummy's jack is played, you cover the last high card led from dummy and promote partner's 10 into a trick. If declarer plays dummy's 4, you play second hand low, and whichever card declarer plays, your side gets a trick. It's difficult to foresee complicated combinations such as this, but using the guideline of covering the last high card led will provide the help you need.

There are other times when you need to be careful about covering an honor with an honor, and it may be impossible to know exactly what to do without being able to see declarer's cards. This is especially true when it comes to declarer's trump suit. For example, suppose declarer leads the jack of trumps toward the dummy in this situation:

DUMMY
A 7 3

YOU
Q 6 2

DECLARER
J

It might be right to cover with the queen if partner has some high cards in the suit. But, since this is declarer's trump suit, that's unlikely to be the case. It's more likely that the layout is something like this:

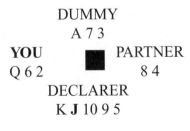

DUMMY
A 7 3

YOU                    PARTNER
Q 6 2                   8 4

DECLARER
K J 10 9 5

Why is declarer leading the jack? Declarer doesn't want to lose a trick to the missing queen and is hoping that you will unthinkingly cover an honor with an honor to help out. If you play a small card, declarer, assuming that your partner has the queen, will probably win the trick with dummy's ace and play a card from dummy, intending to finesse the 10 if your partner plays a small card. Of course, if you think too long before playing a small card, declarer will no longer have to guess what to do.

Covering the jack would also be disastrous if this were the layout:

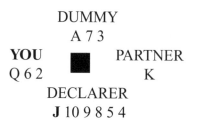

When declarer plays dummy's ace on your queen, it will be a pleasant surprise to find that there are no losers in the suit!

Here is a similar situation where declarer leads the queen of trumps from the dummy:

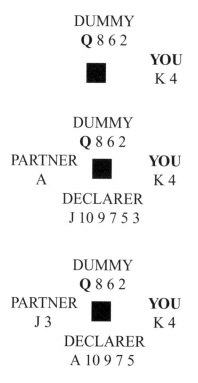

You would be disappointed if you covered the queen with the king and this was the complete layout:

Then again, it would be unfortunate if you didn't cover and the layout turned out to look like this:

Sometimes it may seem as though the game is too difficult! Is it second hand low or cover an honor with an honor? Which guideline applies? The underlying theme is that you want to cover an honor with an honor if it will promote one or more tricks for your side.

This challenge arises because you can't look into partner's hand to see if there is something to promote. Sometimes, you have to guess and sometimes, you will be lucky. Let's finish off with some straightforward examples where you have nothing else to guide you and must play after a card is led from dummy or declarer's hand:

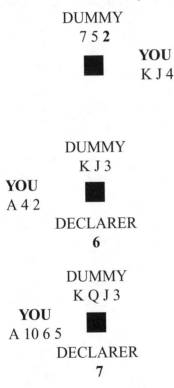

DUMMY
7 5 **2**

**YOU**
K J **4**

When a low card is led from dummy, conserve your high cards and play second hand low, the **4**. There's no need to help declarer out by playing either the king or the jack.

DUMMY
K J 3

**YOU**
A 4 **2**

DECLARER
**6**

When a low card is played toward the dummy and declarer can't be sure which card to finesse, play the **2**, second hand low, and keep declarer guessing.

DUMMY
K Q J 3

**YOU**
A 10 6 **5**

DECLARER
**7**

When a low card is led toward dummy, play low, the **5**, when declarer could be faced with entry problems. If you play the ace, declarer has three tricks, the king, the queen, and the jack. If you play low, declarer may not have enough entries to come back and repeat the finesse. If a high card is led from dummy, you can win the ace and restrict declarer to two tricks in the suit.

DUMMY
A 9 3

YOU
Q J 5

When a low card is led from dummy, split your honors and play the **jack**. This will prevent declarer from winning a cheap trick when holding both the king and the 10.

DUMMY
J 5 2

YOU
K 4 3

If the jack is led from dummy, cover it with the **king**, covering an honor with an honor. If a low card is led from dummy, play second hand low, the **3**.

DUMMY
Q J 10 9 8

YOU
K 4 3

With nothing to promote in either your hand or partner's, play the **3**, second hand low when the queen is led from the dummy.

# BIDDING REVIEW

The opening bidder tries to describe the hand so that partner, the responder, can determine the level and the denomination in which the partnership belongs. The opening bid starts the description, but responder often needs more information before deciding on the best contract. Opener's second bid, the rebid, is used to further describe the strength and distribution of opener's hand. Opener's choice of rebid will also be influenced by the bidding message given by responder's bid. Responder may have made a signoff, an invitational, or a forcing bid. Opener must listen and act accordingly.

## Opener's Rebid after Opening the Bidding 1NT

By bidding 1NT, opener has given responder a good description of both the strength and distribution of the hand. Responder is often able to make a signoff bid in partscore (2♦, 2♥, or 2♠) or in game (3NT, 4♥, or 4♠). Responder has made the final decision for the partnership, and opener must pass.

If more information about opener's strength is needed, responder makes an invitational bid. For example, responder can invite game by raising to 2NT or invite slam by raising to 4NT. Opener has shown 16 to 18 points and rejects the invitation by passing when holding the minimum range, 16 points, and accepts by bidding game, or slam, with a maximum, 17 to 18 points (17 points is borderline and opener could pass).

If more information is needed about opener's distribution, responder makes a forcing bid. For example, responder can ask opener about a four-card major suit by bidding 2♣ (Stayman) or about three-card support for a major suit by bidding 3♥ or 3♠. Opener can't pass a forcing response and has to make a further descriptive bid. If responder bids 2♣, opener bids a four-card major whenever possible, otherwise opener bids 2♦. If responder bids 3♥ or 3♠, opener raises to 4♥ or 4♠ respectively with three-card or longer support. Otherwise opener rebids 3NT.

## Opener's Rebid after Opening the Bidding 2NT

The situation is similar after opening the bidding 2NT. If responder makes a signoff bid by bidding game or slam (3NT, 4♥, 4♠, 6NT, etc.), opener passes. If responder invites opener to slam by bidding beyond game (4NT, 5♥, etc.), opener accepts with the top of the range, otherwise passes. If responder makes a forcing bid such as 3♣ (Stayman) or 3♥ or 3♠ (asking for three-card support), opener makes a descriptive rebid.

## Opener's Rebid after Opening the Bidding One of a Suit

An opening suit bid at the one level covers a much wider range of both strength and distribution than an opening notrump bid. Responder isn't in a position to make a signoff bid (except by passing) and makes either an invitational or forcing response. In choosing a rebid, opener classifies the strength of the hand as minimum (13 to 16 points), medium (17 or 18 points), or maximum (19 to 21 points) and bids accordingly. As a general guideline, the more strength opener has, the more (higher) opener bids.

For example, responder's raise of opener's suit to the two level is an invitational bid showing support and 6 to 10 points. With a minimum, opener passes. With a medium strength hand, opener raises to the three level. With a maximum, opener bids game.

Similarly, a response of 1NT is invitational, showing 6 to 10 points without support for opener's suit and with no other suit that can be bid at the one level. With balanced distribution, opener passes with a minimum or raises to 3NT with a maximum (opener would open 1NT with a medium strength balanced hand). With an unbalanced hand, opener can bid a second suit (jump shifting with a maximum hand) or rebid the original suit (at the two level with a minimum hand, at the three level with a medium hand, and at game level with a maximum hand).

A new suit by responder is forcing and opener can't pass, even with a minimum hand. Opener makes the most descriptive rebid. With support for responder's suit, opener raises to the next level with a minimum hand, jumps a level with a medium hand, and jumps two levels with a maximum hand. With an unbalanced hand, opener can bid a second suit (jump shifting with a maximum hand) or rebid the original suit (at the cheapest level with a minimum hand, jumping a level with a medium hand, and jumping two levels with a maximum hand). With a balanced hand, opener rebids notrump at the cheapest level with a minimum hand and jumps a level with a maximum hand.

## Opener's Rebid after Opening the Bidding Two of a Suit

An opening strong two-bid is forcing to the game level, so opener continues to describe the hand with the rebid. The partnership is committed to playing at least at the game level but there may be enough combined strength to play at the slam level. Since some of the bidding room has already been used up by opening at the two level, there's no need for opener to jump again to show strength. Opener must keep in mind that a bid of 2NT by responder is artificial and shows a weak hand (0 to 5 points).

## Opener's Rebid after Opening the Bidding Three of a Suit

Responder will usually pass when opener makes a preemptive bid at the three level or higher. If responder signs off in game, then opener must pass. If responder bids a new suit below the game level, however, that is still forcing and opener must make a suitably descriptive rebid.

# PLAY OF THE HAND REVIEW

## Leading toward High Cards

The basic principle of the finesse is to lead toward the high card which you are hoping will win a trick:

DUMMY

K 3

DECLARER

4 2

By leading toward the king, you get a trick whenever the opponent on your left holds the ace, whether the card is played or not. With touching high cards, you may have a repeating finesse:

DUMMY

K Q 3

DECLARER

6 5 4

If you lead toward dummy and win the first trick with the queen (or king), you may be able to cross back to your hand with an entry in another suit to lead toward dummy's remaining honor. If the ace is on your left, you end up with two tricks. Notice how your opponent can make it more difficult for you by playing second hand low on your first lead toward dummy when that opponent actually holds the ace.

When the high cards aren't touching, the general guideline is to lead toward the lower card first:

DUMMY

K J 3

DECLARER

6 5 4

With no other considerations, you would play the jack if your left-hand opponent plays a low card when you lead toward dummy. That will give you two tricks if both the ace and the queen are on your left since you can later lead toward the king. If the jack loses to the queen, you still have a chance for one trick by leading toward the king later. The following situation, however, is a little different:

DUMMY

K J

DECLARER

4 3

When you lead a low card toward dummy, you have to guess whether to play the jack or the king unless both the ace and the queen are on your left. If the queen is on your left and the ace on your right, you must finesse the jack to get one trick. If the ace is on your left and the queen is on your right, you must play dummy's king on the first trick, otherwise you won't get a trick. Notice how your left-hand opponent makes things difficult by playing second hand low. How are you to know what to do? You might be able to deduce from the bidding which opponent is more likely to have the ace. An opponent who opened the bidding or overcalled is more likely to hold a missing ace than an opponent who passed throughout the auction.

Here's another situation where you have to guess what to do:

DUMMY

K 7 6 2

DECLARER

Q 5 4 3

It isn't possible to win by leading toward both high cards since one of the opponents must have the ace. The best way to play this suit is to lead toward the high card that you think will win the trick. If this works, play a low card from both hands when you lead the suit a second time. Your hope is that the ace is now singleton. For example, if you think that the ace is on your left, lead toward dummy's king, playing for this layout:

DUMMY

K 7 6 2

PARTNER          YOU

A 10            J 9 8

DECLARER

Q 5 4 3

When you lead toward dummy, West will play the 10, and you'll win the trick with dummy's king. Since you now know West has the ace, it doesn't do any good to lead toward the queen. Instead, play a small card from both hands and you'll end up with three tricks. If East has the ace, you need to lead from dummy toward your queen originally. Of course, there is no guarantee that either opponent started with exactly a doubleton ace, but with a good guess and a little luck, who knows?

## Leading High Cards

Since a defender will frequently cover an honor with an honor, you lead a high card only when you can afford to have it covered:

DUMMY
A Q 4 2

DECLARER
J 10 9 3

You can afford to lead the jack (or 10 or 9) to try to trap the king on your left. You don't mind if the jack is covered by the king since all of your remaining cards will be promoted into winners. On the other hand, if your holding isn't as strong:

DUMMY
A Q 4 2

DECLARER
J 6 5 3

You can't afford to lead the jack, since if it's covered, the opponents' 10 will be promoted into a winner. Instead, you must lead a low card toward dummy and hope for this position:

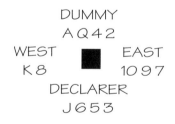

DUMMY
A Q 4 2
WEST                    EAST
K 8                     10 9 7
DECLARER
J 6 5 3

You lead a low card to dummy's queen and then take the ace. After West's king falls, your carefully preserved jack prevents East from winning a trick with the 10. There are many variations of this theme, but the general idea is to consider whether or not you can afford to have the opponents cover an honor with an honor before you lead a high card. If you can't afford to cover, you may want to look for other options.

# SUMMARY

When a low card is led from declarer's hand or from the dummy and you are the second person to play to the trick, a useful guideline is *second hand low*. Your partner will play last to the trick, and you don't want to waste your high cards capturing only low cards from declarer. Ideally, you would like to use your aces to capture declarer's kings, your kings to capture declarer's queens, and so forth.

There are exceptions:

- You don't want to play a low card if it will allow declarer to win a trick too cheaply. With a strong holding in the suit, you may need to **split your honors**.
- You don't want to play second hand low if you could defeat the contract by playing high.

If declarer leads a high card, you should generally **cover an honor with an honor** if you have a higher card. You should do this, however, only if it's likely to promote a trick for your side. If declarer leads from touching high cards, you should generally wait to **cover the last high card led**.

**Exercise One** — When Declarer Leads a Low Card

In each of the following layouts, declarer leads the 2 toward dummy. How many tricks can declarer take if you play low (a)? How many tricks can declarer take if you play high (b)?

1)                      DUMMY
                        Q 7 5

     **YOU**                              PARTNER
     K 8 4                                A 10 9 3

                        DECLARER
                        J 6 2

2)                      DUMMY
                        A Q J

     **YOU**                              PARTNER
     K 8 4                                10 9 7 6 5 3

                        DECLARER
                        2

3)                      DUMMY
                        A 10 9

     **YOU**                              PARTNER
     K 8 4                                J 7 5 3

                        DECLARER
                        Q 6 2

1) a) _____ L . 0 _____   2) a) _____ L 2 _____   3) a) _____ L - 2 _____

   b) _____ 1 _____       b) _____ 7 _____        b) _____ H  B _____

**Exercise One** — When Declarer Leads a Low Card

1) a) Play low and declarer takes no tricks because your king keeps declarer's jack trapped and partner's ace keeps the queen trapped.

   b) Play high and declarer gets one trick with either the queen or the jack.

2) a) Play low and declarer gets two tricks, since declarer can't repeat the finesse to trap your king.

   b) Play high and declarer takes three tricks.

3) a) Play low and declarer takes two tricks.

   b) Play high and declarer can take all three tricks, since declarer's ace takes your king and partner's jack is trapped by declarer's queen.

## Exercise Two — When Dummy Leads a Low Card

In each of the following layouts, declarer leads the 2 from dummy. Which card must you play to ensure that your side gets all of the tricks to which it's entitled? How do you expect declarer to play the suit?

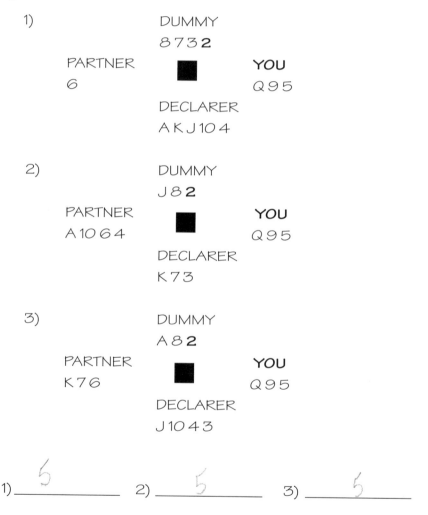

1)
DUMMY
8 7 3 **2**

PARTNER
6

YOU
Q 9 5

DECLARER
A K J 10 4

2)
DUMMY
J 8 **2**

PARTNER
A 10 6 4

YOU
Q 9 5

DECLARER
K 7 3

3)
DUMMY
A 8 **2**

PARTNER
K 7 6

YOU
Q 9 5

DECLARER
J 10 4 3

1) _____5_____     2) _____5_____     3) _____5_____

**Exercise Two** — When Dummy Leads a Low Card

1)  Play low (the 5) hoping declarer will play the ace and the king (eight ever, nine never), and your queen will be a winner.

2)  Play low (the 5) and partner's ace traps declarer's king, and your queen traps dummy's jack.

3)  Play low (the 5) and partner gets a trick with the king, and you'll get a trick with your queen later, since it lies behind the ace in the dummy.

## Exercise Three — Splitting Honors

In each of the following layouts, declarer leads the 2 toward dummy. Which card must you play to ensure that your side gets all of the tricks to which it's entitled?

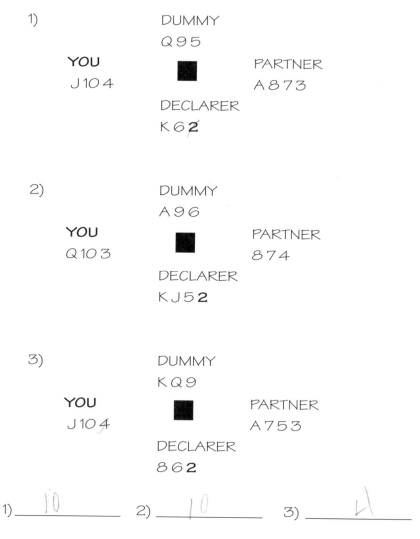

1)                  DUMMY
                    Q95
       **YOU**                        PARTNER
       J 10 4                         A 8 7 3
                    DECLARER
                    K 6 2

2)                  DUMMY
                    A 9 6
       **YOU**                        PARTNER
       Q 10 3                         8 7 4
                    DECLARER
                    K J 5 2

3)                  DUMMY
                    K Q 9
       **YOU**                        PARTNER
       J 10 4                         A 7 5 3
                    DECLARER
                    8 6 2

1)____10____    2)____10____    3)____J____

**Exercise Three —** Splitting Honors

1) Play the 10 (or jack) , splitting your honors.

2) Play the 10, making sure declarer doesn't win a trick with dummy's 9.

3) Play the 4, hoping declarer plays the king or the queen, which will be declarer's only winner in the suit.

## Exercise Four — Covering Honors

In each of the following layouts, how many tricks does declarer get if you cover with an honor when the jack is led from dummy (a)? How many tricks does declarer get if you don't cover (b)?

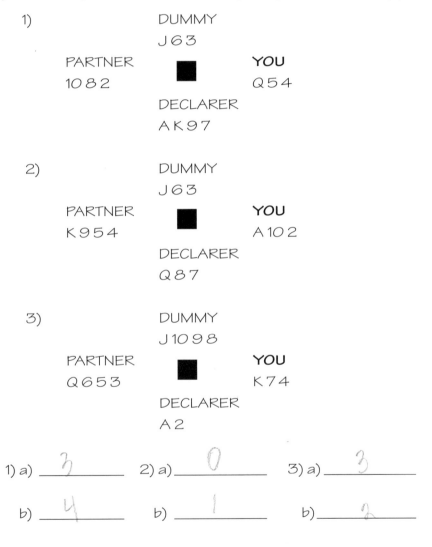

1)                          DUMMY
                            J 6 3
          PARTNER                        YOU
          10 8 2                         Q 5 4
                            DECLARER
                            A K 9 7

2)                          DUMMY
                            J 6 3
          PARTNER                        YOU
          K 9 5 4                        A 10 2
                            DECLARER
                            Q 8 7

3)                          DUMMY
                            J 10 9 8
          PARTNER                        YOU
          Q 6 5 3                        K 7 4
                            DECLARER
                            A 2

1) a) _____2_____    2) a) _____0_____    3) a) _____3_____

   b) _____4_____       b) _____1_____       b) _____2_____

## Exercise Four — Covering Honors

1)  a)  Declarer gets three tricks.

    b)  Declarer gets four tricks.

2)  a)  Declarer gets no tricks.

    b)  Declarer gets one trick.

3)  a)  Declarer gets three tricks.

    b)  Declarer's gets only two tricks. In the last example, you don't cover because you have nothing to promote.

## Exercise Five — Covering Second Honors

In each of the following layouts, should you play your high card when the jack is led from dummy?

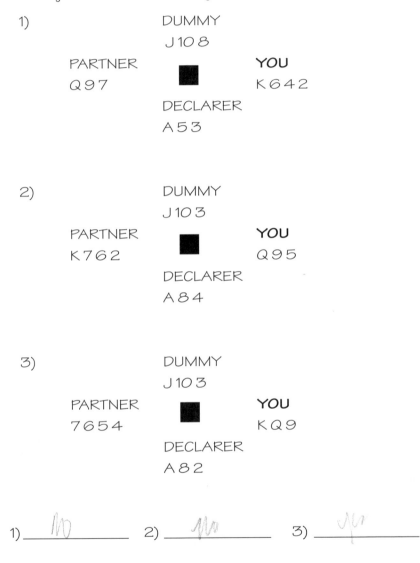

1) DUMMY
J 10 8

PARTNER          YOU
Q 9 7            K 6 4 2

DECLARER
A 5 3


2) DUMMY
J 10 3

PARTNER          YOU
K 7 6 2          Q 9 5

DECLARER
A 8 4


3) DUMMY
J 10 3

PARTNER          YOU
7 6 5 4          K Q 9

DECLARER
A 8 2


1) _____ 2) _____ 3) _____

**Exercise Five** — Covering Second Honors

    1) No        2) No        3) Yes

## Exercise Six — Putting It All Together

Which card do you play in each of the following situations when declarer leads the indicated card toward dummy?

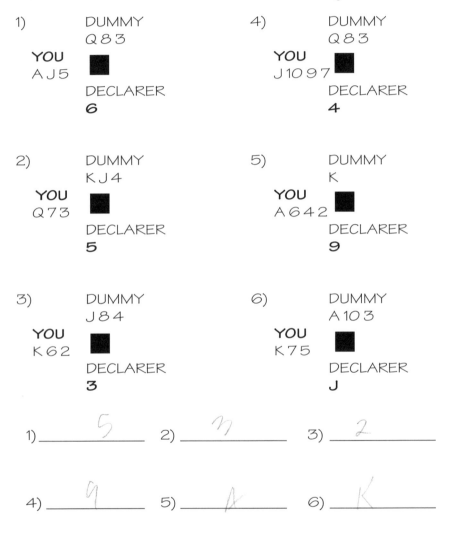

1)　　DUMMY
　　　Q 8 3
　YOU　　■
　A J 5
　　　DECLARER
　　　6

2)　　DUMMY
　　　K J 4
　YOU　　■
　Q 7 3
　　　DECLARER
　　　5

3)　　DUMMY
　　　J 8 4
　YOU　　■
　K 6 2
　　　DECLARER
　　　3

4)　　DUMMY
　　　Q 8 3
　YOU　　■
　J 10 9 7
　　　DECLARER
　　　4

5)　　DUMMY
　　　K
　YOU　　■
　A 6 4 2
　　　DECLARER
　　　9

6)　　DUMMY
　　　A 10 3
　YOU　　■
　K 7 5
　　　DECLARER
　　　J

1) _____5_____  2) _____7_____  3) _____2_____

4) _____9_____  5) _____X_____  6) _____K_____

**Exercise Six —** Putting It All Together

1) 5          2) 3          3) 2

4) 9          5) Ace          6) King

## Exercise Seven — Review of Rebids by Opener

You open the bidding 1♥ and your partner responds 1♠. What do you rebid with each of the following hands?

1) ♠ 10 8 4 2
♥ A K J 7 3
♦ K 9
♣ J 10

1) _____ 3̶5̶

2) ♠ Q 4
♥ K J 10 7 3
♦ A 10 4
♣ Q J 6

2) _____ 1 N

3) ♠ 7
♥ Q J 9 7 5 3
♦ J 4 2
♣ A K J

3) _____ 2♦

4) ♠ 7 4
♥ A Q 6 4 2
♦ K J 6 3 2
♣ A

4) _____ 2♦

5) ♠ K Q 6 3
♥ A Q J 7 2
♦ 4
♣ K 9 4

5) _____ 3♠

6) ♠ Q 2
♥ A K J 8 4 3 2
♦ A 4
♣ 9 5

6) _____ 3♥

7) ♠ K 10
♥ A J 10 8 2
♦ K Q 9
♣ A Q 2

7) _____ 2NT

8) ♠ A 4
♥ K Q 10 7 3
♦ K 5
♣ A K J 2

8) _____ 3♣

9) ♠ A J 8 4
♥ A K Q 7 5
♦ 8
♣ Q J 2

9) _____ 4♠

Romeo
3NT

**Exercise Seven** — *Review of Rebids by Opener*

1) 2♠          2) 1NT          3) 2♥

4) 2♦          5) 3♠          6) 3♥

7) 2NT          8) 3♣          9) 4♠

## Exercise Eight — Review of Finesses

What is the maximum number of tricks you can get from each of the following suit combinations if the missing high cards are favorably located? How would you plan to play the suit?

|  | 1) | 2) | 3) | 4) | 5) |
|---|---|---|---|---|---|
| DUMMY: | Q J 7 | 7 5 4 | Q J 10 | Q 7 4 | Q 7 5 |
| DECLARER: | 6 4 2 | A J 10 | A 7 5 | A J 6 | K 8 6 |

1) _____1_____

2) _____2 - find_____

3) _____3_____

4) _____3_____

5) _____2_____

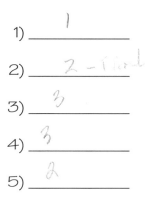

**Exercise Eight** — Review of Finesses

1) One. Lead twice toward the dummy, hoping either the ace or the king are on the left.

2) Two. Lead toward your hand, planning to finesse the 10 if a low card appears. If the first finesse loses, repeat the finesse, hoping either the king or the queen is on the right.

3) Three. Lead a high card from the dummy, since you can afford to have it covered, and hope the king is on your right.

4) Three. Lead low from the dummy, finessing the jack, and then play the ace hoping that your left-hand opponent started with a singleton or doubleton king.

5) Two. Lead toward one of the honors and then play a low card from both hands, hoping one defender started with a doubleton ace.

## Exercise Nine — *Second Hand Low*

### (E-Z Deal Cards: #4, Hand 1 — Dealer, North)

Turn up the cards from the first pre-dealt deal. Put each hand dummy-style at the edge of the table in front of each player.

### The Bidding

With a balanced hand, why can't North open the bidding 1NT? What bid would North make to open the bidding? East and West pass throughout. Does South have a suit that can be bid at the one level? What does South respond? How does North show support for South's suit and the strength of the hand? How does the auction proceed from there? Who is the declarer?

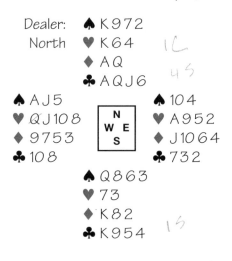

Dealer: ♠ K 9 7 2
North ♥ K 6 4
♦ A Q
♣ A Q J 6

♠ A J 5            ♠ 10 4
♥ Q J 10 8    ♥ A 9 5 2
♦ 9 7 5 3      ♦ J 10 6 4
♣ 10 8           ♣ 7 3 2

♠ Q 8 6 3
♥ 7 3
♦ K 8 2
♣ K 9 5 4

### The Defense

Which player makes the opening lead? What would the opening lead be? If declarer plays trump by leading a small spade toward dummy, which card does West play? Why?

### The Play

Review the steps in declarer's PLAN. How can declarer avoid losing two trump tricks?

## Exercise Nine — Second Hand Low

### The Bidding

- North has too many points (19) to open 1NT and so bids 1♣.

- Yes. South responds 1♠.

- North rebids 4♠, showing the strength of the hand and support for partner.

- The final contract is 4♠ and South is the declarer.

### The Defense

- West leads the ♥Q, top of touching honors.

- If declarer plays trumps by leading a low spade toward dummy, West should play second hand low, the ♠5, to keep declarer's ♠Q trapped.

### The Play

- Declarer can afford only three losers and potentially has four losers. Declarer has to try to avoid more than one loser in the trump suit. Declarer hopes that one opponent has a doubleton ♠A. The plan is to lead toward one of the spade honors and, if this wins, to play a small card from both hands, hoping that an opponent has to play the ♠A.

## Exercise Ten — Giving Declarer a Guess

### (E-Z Deal Cards: #4, Hand 2 — Dealer, East)

Turn up the cards from the second pre-dealt deal. Put each hand dummy-style at the edge of the table in front of each player.

### The Bidding

What would East open the bidding? North and South pass throughout. What does West respond? How does East show support for West's suit and the strength of the hand? Does West have enough information to place the contract? What does West rebid? What is the contract? Who is the declarer?

Dealer:  ♠ A 9 5 4
East     ♥ 9 2
         ♦ J 10 9 8 2
         ♣ 10 3

♠ 8 3              ♠ K J
♥ A K 8 6 4        ♥ Q J 7 5
♦ 6 4              ♦ K 7 3
♣ A Q 8 4          ♣ K J 9 5

         ♠ Q 10 7 6 2
         ♥ 10 3
         ♦ A Q 5
         ♣ 7 6 2

### The Defense

Which player makes the opening lead? What is the opening lead? What will South do if a small card is played from dummy? What must North be prepared to do when West leads a spade toward dummy?

### The Play

Review the steps in declarer's PLAN. How can declarer avoid a spade loser?

## Exercise Ten — Giving Declarer a Guess

### The Bidding

- East opens the bidding 1♣.
- West responds 1♥.
- East rebids 2♥.
- West knows that the contract belongs in game and rebids 4♥.
- The final contract is 4♥ and West is the declarer.

### The Defense

- North leads the ♦J, top of a sequence.
- South will play the ♦5 if a low card is played from the dummy.
- When West leads a spade toward the dummy, North must be prepared to play second hand low so that declarer has to guess whether to play dummy's ♠J or ♠K.

### The Play

- Declarer can afford three losers and has one too many. With the ♦A in the South hand, there's no way to avoid two diamond losers after the opening lead. Declarer can plan to eliminate one of the spade losers, however, by leading a low spade toward dummy's ♠K and ♠J. Declarer has to guess whether to finesse the ♠J, playing North for the ♠Q, or to finesse the ♠K, playing North for the ♠A.

## Exercise Eleven — Covering an Honor

### (E-Z Deal Cards: #4, Hand 3 — Dealer, South)

Turn up the cards from the third pre-dealt deal. Put each hand dummy-style at the edge of the table in front of each player.

### The Bidding

South and West pass. What is North's opening bid? After East passes, what does South respond? What is the contract? Who is the declarer?

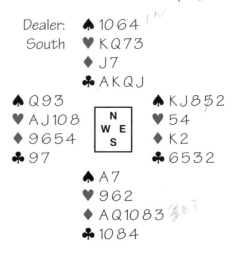

```
Dealer:      ♠ 10 6 4
South        ♥ K Q 7 3
             ♦ J 7
             ♣ A K Q J
♠ Q 9 3              ♠ K J 8 5 2
♥ A J 10 8    N      ♥ 5 4
♦ 9 6 5 4   W   E    ♦ K 2
♣ 9 7         S      ♣ 6 5 3 2
             ♠ A 7
             ♥ 9 6 2
             ♦ A Q 10 8 3
             ♣ 10 8 4
```

### The Defense

Which player makes the opening lead? What would the opening lead be? Why? If a small card is played from dummy on the first trick, which card should West play? Why? If declarer leads a small diamond toward dummy, which card should East play? Which card should East play if declarer leads a diamond honor toward dummy?

### The Play

Review the steps in declarer's PLAN. How does declarer plan to make the contract?

## Exercise Eleven — Covering an Honor

### The Bidding

- North opens the bidding 1NT.

- South responds 3NT.

- The final contract is 3NT and North is the declarer.

### The Defense

- East leads the ♠5, fourth highest from the longest and strongest suit. West should play third hand high, the ♠Q, if a low card is played from dummy.

- If declarer leads a small diamond toward dummy, East should play the ♦2, second hand low.

- If declarer leads a diamond honor, East should cover with the ♦K, covering an honor with an honor.

### The Play

- Declarer needs nine tricks and starts with six. The three extra tricks can come from diamonds. Declarer can't afford to lose a diamond trick to the opponents, however, if the missing spades are divided 5-3. Declarer can hold up the ♠A only one round and must plan to finesse for the ♦K, hoping to develop enough tricks in the suit before having to give the lead to the opponents.

# Exercise Twelve — Waiting to Cover
## (E-Z Deal Cards: #4, Hand 4 — Dealer, West)

Turn up the cards from the fourth pre-dealt deal. Put each hand dummy-style at the edge of the table in front of each player.

## The Bidding

West and North pass. Why doesn't East open 1 NT? What bid does East make to open the bidding? South passes. Does West have a suit that can be bid at the one level? What does West respond? North passes. How does East finish describing this strong balanced hand? South passes. What does West rebid? What's the contract? Who is the declarer?

Dealer: **♠** K J 5
West    **♥** 10 8 3 2
        **♦** K 8 6 2
        **♣** Q 10

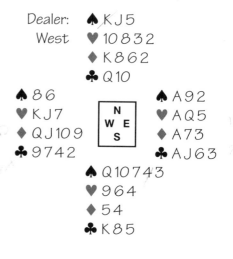

**♠** 8 6          **♠** A 9 2
**♥** K J 7        **♥** A Q 5
**♦** Q J 10 9     **♦** A 7 3
**♣** 9 7 4 2      **♣** A J 6 3

**♠** Q 10 7 4 3
**♥** 9 6 4
**♦** 5 4
**♣** K 8 5

## The Defense

Which player makes the opening lead? What would the opening lead be? Which card must North contribute to the first trick? Why? Should North cover if a diamond is led from dummy? Why not?

## The Play

Review the steps in declarer's PLAN. How does declarer plan to make the contract?

## Exercise Twelve — Waiting to Cover

### The Bidding

- East has too many points (19) to open 1NT and starts with 1♣.
- Yes. West responds 1♦.
- East shows a strong hand by rebidding 2NT.
- West rebids 3NT.
- The final contract is 3NT and East is the declarer.

### TheDefense

- South leads the ♠4, fourth-highest card.
- North should play third hand high and contribute the ♠K.
- If a diamond is led from the dummy, North shouldn't cover since there's nothing to promote for the defense.

### The Play

- Declarer needs nine tricks and has six. The best chance to develop extra tricks is in the diamond suit. By leading a high diamond from dummy and taking the finesse, declarer can hope to develop extra tricks if North has the ♦K. If North had fewer than four diamonds, declarer could end up with four tricks in the diamond suit, enough to make the contract.

# CHAPTER 5

## *Defensive Signals*

The defenders work as a team trying to defeat declarer's contract. They get tricks in the same fashion as declarer, developing tricks through promotion, length, and finesses, as well as by using the trump suit to ruff their opponent's winners. Unlike declarer, who can also see the dummy's hand, the defenders can't look into each other's hands to see their strengths and weaknesses. This is a disadvantage which they want to overcome as quickly as possible, and *defensive signals* are a way of helping them do this. By playing specific cards in certain situations, each defender can paint a picture of the hand to give partner the information needed to make an appropriate decision.

You have already seen some of the signals the defenders can give each other. By leading the top of touching honors, for example, information is passed from one defender to the other. If partner leads a queen against a notrump contract, you can assume partner also has the jack, and likely the 10 as well, but not the king. If you can't see the king in dummy or in your hand, you know declarer holds it. Notice that the specific card played by partner gives you information not only about partner's hand but also, by inference, about declarer's holding in the suit. This happens often enough to help you defeat the contract.

What type of information do the defenders want to give each other through their signals? The information that is of most value to partner normally falls into one of these categories:

- **Attitude.** An *attitude signal* tells partner whether or not you like a particular suit. "Like" here means you have positive values or distribution in that particular suit. If it's known that you like a suit, partner can lead or continue to lead that suit at the first opportunity. Conversely, if it's known that you don't like a particular suit, partner can lead a different suit when the opportunity arises. The attitude signal may also be used to help partner in discarding.

- **Count.** A *count signal* tells partner how many cards you have in a suit. Since partner can see how many cards there are in partner's hand and in the dummy, it's possible to determine how many cards declarer has. This can help partner decide how many tricks your side can take in the suit, when to take a trick, or which cards to hold when it's necessary to discard.

• **Suit Preference.** A *suit preference* signal tells partner which of two suits you prefer. Again, such information will be helpful in letting partner know which suit to lead when the opportunity arises or which cards to hold when it's necessary to discard.

Let's take a look at how the various types of signals work and how to put them into practice.

## ATTITUDE SIGNALS

You can give a signal only when you have a choice of cards to play. If partner has led a suit and you're trying to win the trick by playing third hand high, you may be forced to play your only high card and won't be able to give partner a signal. On the other hand, if a card played by partner or declarer is already winning the trick, you may have a choice of cards to play to the trick which won't affect whether the current trick is won or lost. In such cases, the specific card you choose may be used to give a signal to partner. For example, consider the following situation where partner leads the 3 against a notrump contract:

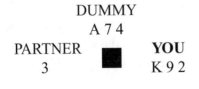

DUMMY
A 7 4
PARTNER          YOU
3                K 9 2

If a low card is played from dummy, you have no choice — you must play the king, third hand high, in order to win the trick for your side. On the other hand, if the ace is played from dummy, you can't win the trick and are in a position to choose which of your cards to play. You don't want to play the king, since that card is now established as a winner, but you have a choice between the 9 and the 2. Neither card is likely to have any significance as far as winning tricks is concerned, so the one you choose can be used to give partner a signal.

## High Cards Encourage, Low Cards Discourage

What message do you want to give partner? One of the most important pieces of information you can give to partner is your attitude toward the suit. You give an *attitude signal* by playing *a high card to encourage and a low card to discourage.* In the above example, you like the suit that partner has led since you hold the king. You can give an encouraging signal by playing the highest card you can afford, the 9, rather than the 2. Suppose we change your holding in the suit:

DUMMY
A 7 4
PARTNER  YOU
3  9 6 2

If the ace is played from dummy, you have a choice of three cards to play. With no high cards in the suit, you can make a discouraging signal by playing the lowest card you can afford, the 2. Giving a discouraging signal doesn't stop partner from playing the suit again if partner wants to. It merely suggests that you have no particular interest in the suit and, by inference, would prefer another suit.

Both partners must cooperate if the message is to be successfully communicated. One partner must be giving the appropriate signal and the other partner must be watching for it. If your partner doesn't bother to look to see if you played the 9 or the 2, the message won't be delivered. On the other hand, if you carelessly play the 2 when you want to encourage, or the 9 when you want to discourage, partner will get the wrong message. Likewise, when the roles are reversed and your partner is giving the signal, you must be watching the cards as they are played to see whether partner likes or dislikes the suit.

Let's take a look at two deals to see how important it can be to give an appropriate encouraging or discouraging signal. We will give your partner and the dummy the identical cards in both hands. Your hand and declarer's hand will be changed slightly to show how an attitude signal can help defeat the contract in both cases. Your partner starts by leading the ♠Q against a contract of 4♥. Here is the first deal:

```
                         DUMMY
    Contract: 4♥         ♠ A 7 5
    Lead: ♠Q             ♥ J 9 4 2
                         ♦ K Q 10
                         ♣ K 8 3
        PARTNER                      YOU
        ♠ Q J 10 6      ┌─────┐      ♠ K 9 2
        ♥ 8             │  N  │      ♥ Q 10 7
        ♦ A 7 6 5 3     │W   E│      ♦ 9 8 2
        ♣ 10 9 7        │  S  │      ♣ J 5 4 2
                        └─────┘
                         DECLARER
                         ♠ 8 4 3
                         ♥ A K 6 5 3
                         ♦ J 4
                         ♣ A Q 6
```

Declarer wins the first trick with dummy's ♠A and starts to draw trumps by playing the ♥A and the ♥K. When the trumps divide 3–1, declarer has a heart loser to go along with the two spade losers and the diamond loser. It's not all over yet, since declarer may be able to discard one of the spade losers on an extra diamond winner in dummy once the ♦A is driven out. So declarer leads the ♦J and your partner wins the ♦A.

What does partner do now? There's no problem if you helped out by giving an attitude signal on the first trick by playing the ♠9. Since you encouraged by playing a high card, partner can play another spade. You'll win a trick with your ♠K and partner will get a trick with the ♠J. Together with the ♦A and the ♥Q, that's enough to defeat the contract. If partner led any suit other than a spade after winning the ♦A, declarer could win and discard one of the spade losers on dummy's extra diamond winner. Declarer would end up making the contract, losing only one spade trick, one heart trick, and one diamond trick.

It looks easy enough for partner to continue leading spades after winning the ♦ A. It may appear as though it doesn't matter whether you play the 9 or the 2 on the first trick. But let's exchange a couple of cards in your hand and declarer's hand while leaving partner's hand and dummy's hand the same:

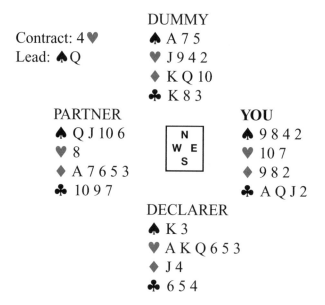

DUMMY

Contract: 4 ♥          ♠ A 7 5
Lead: ♠ Q              ♥ J 9 4 2
                      ♦ K Q 10
                      ♣ K 8 3

PARTNER                              YOU
♠ Q J 10 6                           ♠ 9 8 4 2
♥ 8                                  ♥ 10 7
♦ A 7 6 5 3                          ♦ 9 8 2
♣ 10 9 7                             ♣ A Q J 2

DECLARER
♠ K 3
♥ A K Q 6 5 3
♦ J 4
♣ 6 5 4

From partner's point of view, everything looks the same. On defense against a 4 ♥ contract, partner leads the ♠ Q. Declarer wins the first trick with dummy's ♠ A and plays the ♥ A and the ♥ K to draw trumps. Next declarer leads the ♦ J and partner wins the trick with the ♦ A. Look what happens if partner leads another spade! Declarer wins the trick with the carefully concealed ♠ K and proceeds to discard one of the club losers on dummy's extra diamond winner. Declarer makes the contract, losing just one diamond trick and two club tricks.

Of course, you don't let partner fall into this trap. When the first trick is won with dummy's ♠ A, you give a discouraging signal by playing the ♠ 2. When partner later wins a trick with the ♦ A, your message has already let it be known that you don't like spades. Since partner doesn't have any trumps and declarer has diamond winners in the dummy, the only hope for the defense is that you have some strength in the club suit. Instead of leading another spade, partner leads the ♣10 and dummy's ♣K is trapped. Your side takes three club tricks to go along with the ♦A, and you defeat the contract.

It's important to see that partner has no way of knowing whether or not it's correct to lead another spade without your help. Only your attitude signal can give partner the necessary information. If you were to automatically play your lowest card, the ♠2, in both cases, partner would have to guess what to do later. Naturally partner would go wrong about half the time. Once you and your partner start using attitude signals, you get a chance to defeat declarer in both situations.

## When to Signal

Once you and your partner start signaling, you can't suddenly stop. In situations similar to those in the previous deals, partner will be expecting to see an attitude signal when on lead. This means that you will have to decide whether you want to encourage or discourage when partner expects an attitude signal. Consider the following layout where partner leads the queen against a notrump contract and the ace is played from dummy:

DUMMY
A 5
PARTNER          YOU
Q                10 7 2

Since partner led the top card of a sequence, declarer must have the king. Should you give a discouraging signal to partner by playing the 2, to say that you don't have the king?

You must always consider the entire hand before deciding whether or not to encourage. If there appears to be a better suit that partner could switch to in order to defeat the contract, you should make a discouraging signal. If you can't see anything better, you may want to encourage partner to lead the suit again. With the above holding, you probably want to encourage partner since you hold the 10. Partner must have led the top of a broken sequence, such as Q–J–9–6–4, and, if you discourage by playing the 2, partner won't want to lead the suit again, fearing that declarer has both the king and the 10. Since you have the missing 10, you can give an encouraging signal by playing the highest card you can afford, the 7. This tells partner it's safe to continue leading the suit.

Here is a deal where you want to discourage partner from leading a suit again, even though you could win the next trick in the suit:

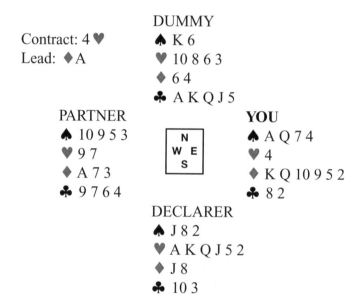

Contract: 4 ♥
Lead: ♦ A

DUMMY
♠ K 6
♥ 10 8 6 3
♦ 6 4
♣ A K Q J 5

PARTNER
♠ 10 9 5 3
♥ 9 7
♦ A 7 3
♣ 9 7 6 4

YOU
♠ A Q 7 4
♥ 4
♦ K Q 10 9 5 2
♣ 8 2

DECLARER
♠ J 8 2
♥ A K Q J 5 2
♦ J 8
♣ 10 3

The opponents declare 4 ♥ after you have opened the bidding 1 ♦. Your partner dutifully leads your suit, and selects the ♦ A since partner doesn't want to lead away from an ace against a suit contract. It may appear that you want to encourage partner to lead the suit again since you can win the next trick. Looking at the dummy, however, you see that this would allow declarer to make the contract. After winning the second diamond trick, what next? If you lead a spade, declarer will get a trick with dummy's ♠ K. If you don't lead a spade, declarer will discard the spade losers on dummy's club winners after drawing trumps. You are no longer in a position to defeat the contract.

Instead, you must play the ♦ 2, a discouraging signal, to say that you don't want partner to lead another diamond. Looking at all of those club winners in dummy, partner probably will figure out that you must want a spade lead to trap dummy's ♠K. If partner does lead a spade, you'll get two spade tricks and you can then take your second diamond trick to defeat the contract. Of course, when you give a discouraging signal in diamonds, you still may not get a spade lead, but at least you have given partner a chance to find the winning defense.

## How High Is High?

When giving a discouraging signal, you play the lowest card you hold in the suit, and when giving an encouraging signal, you play as high a card as you can afford. Ideally, a card lower than a 6 would usually be interpreted by partner as a discouraging card, whereas a card higher than a 6 would be seen as an encouraging card. Unfortunately, you may not always have the ideal card with which to give a clear-cut signal. Suppose this is the layout:

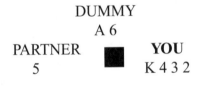

|  | DUMMY |  |
|---|---|---|
|  | A 6 |  |
| PARTNER |  | YOU |
| 5 |  | K 4 3 2 |

Partner leads the 5 and declarer wins the trick with dummy's ace. Holding the king, you'd like to encourage but the highest card you can afford is the 4. You'll have to play the 4 and hope partner is able to interpret that this is the highest card you could afford. Partner should notice that both the 2 and the 3 are missing, and this will indicate that you are making an encouraging signal.

You may also get a chance to clarify the situation later in the play. For example, if you are discarding on another suit, you can throw the 2. Since the first card you played was the 4, partner will know that you meant that as an encouraging signal. The concept of playing a high card followed by a low card to encourage was first developed by Joseph Elwell and is called an echo. When you play a high card to encourage, you are starting an echo. You may or may not get an opportunity to complete the high-low echo later in the play.

This idea can be carried over when you are trying to discourage partner. Suppose you are faced with this situation:

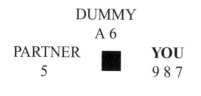

| | DUMMY | | If dummy's ace is played when part- |
| | A 6 | | ner leads the 5, the lowest card you |
| PARTNER | | YOU | have is the 7. Partner may be able to |
| 5 | | 9 8 7 | interpret this as a discouraging card |

when the remaining smaller cards are visible, but if you get an opportunity later, you can clarify the situation by playing or discarding the 8 (or 9). Since you played low–high rather than high-low, partner will know you are giving a discouraging signal in the suit.

## Getting a Ruff

You usually give an encouraging signal when you have strength in the suit partner has led. In a trump contract, however, you may want to encourage partner to lead a suit in which you have shortness because you can ruff declarer's winners. Let's look at an example in a complete deal:

|  | DUMMY |
| Contract: 4♠ | ♠ Q 10 8 7 4 |
| Lead: ♥A | ♥ Q 8 3 |
| | ♦ K 8 5 |
| | ♣ A K |

| PARTNER | | YOU |
| ♠ 9 | | ♠ 5 2 |
| ♥ A K 9 6 2 | N W E S | ♥ 10 4 |
| ♦ 10 9 2 | | ♦ A 7 6 4 |
| ♣ 10 8 4 3 | | ♣ J 9 7 5 2 |

DECLARER
♠ A K J 6 3
♥ J 7 5
♦ Q J 3
♣ Q 6

Partner leads the ♥A against 4♠. Although you don't have any high cards in hearts, you want to encourage partner to continue leading the suit since you can ruff on the third round. Play the ♥10, an encouraging card. When partner continues by leading the ♥K, you'll complete your echo by playing the ♥4. Partner should realize that the reason you are encouraging a heart lead is that you started with two of them. When partner leads the suit again, you can ruff and take your ♦A to defeat the contract. Good cooperation by the defenders.

To see the importance of encouraging in this situation, let's exchange a couple of cards in your hand with those in declarer's hand:

DUMMY

Contract: 4♠ ♠ Q 10 8 7 4
Lead: ♥A ♥ Q 8 3
♦ K 8 5
♣ A K

PARTNER YOU
♠ 9 ♠ 5 2
♥ A K 9 6 2 ♥ 10 5 4
♦ 10 9 2 ♦ A Q 7 4 3
♣ 10 8 4 3 ♣ J 9 5

N
W   E
S

DECLARER
♠ A K J 6 3
♥ J 7
♦ J 6
♣ Q 7 6 2

The deal looks the same to partner, but if the ♥A, the ♥K, and another heart are played, declarer will make the contract. Declarer can discard a diamond loser on dummy's ♥Q and ends up losing only two heart tricks and a diamond trick. To prevent this, you must play a discouraging card, the ♥4, when partner leads the ♥A. Even if partner continues by leading the ♥K, perhaps thinking that you started with a singleton ♥4, you can clarify the situation by playing the ♥5 (or ♥10).

Since you played low-high rather than high-low, partner will realize that you're not encouraging a continuation of the suit. Looking at the club winners in dummy, partner will probably lead a diamond through dummy's king, allowing you to take two diamond tricks and defeat the contract. Once again, the only way partner can distinguish between this situation and the previous one is by watching the attitude signal that you give.

## Attitude Discards

While you usually give attitude signals in the suit that is currently being played, you can also give attitude signals for other suits when you are discarding. Consider the following deal:

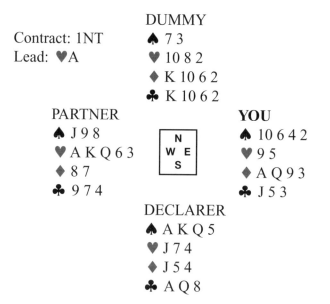

```
                         DUMMY
   Contract: 1NT         ♠ 7 3
   Lead: ♥A              ♥ 10 8 2
                         ♦ K 10 6 2
                         ♣ K 10 6 2
   PARTNER                              YOU
   ♠ J 9 8              ┌─────────┐     ♠ 10 6 4 2
   ♥ A K Q 6 3         │   N     │     ♥ 9 5
   ♦ 8 7               │ W   E   │     ♦ A Q 9 3
   ♣ 9 7 4             │   S     │     ♣ J 5 3
                        └─────────┘
                         DECLARER
                         ♠ A K Q 5
                         ♥ J 7 4
                         ♦ J 5 4
                         ♣ A Q 8
```

On partner's heart lead you make a discouraging signal of the ♥5 since you don't have any help in the suit. This doesn't deter partner from continuing to take five tricks in the suit. On the third heart trick, you must decide what to discard. Stop and think about the message you want to send partner. When partner has finished taking all of the heart tricks, you want a diamond lead, since dummy's king is trapped by your ♦ A and ♦ Q, giving you two tricks in the suit. How can you get this message across to partner? Using encouraging and discouraging signals gives you a number of ways to accomplish what you want, since you'll be making three discards. You could start by discarding the ♦ 9, an encouraging card in diamonds. You could follow by discarding the ♦ 3, completing the high-low echo, to confirm your interest in diamonds. Finally, you could discard a low card in one of the other suits to discourage partner from leading that suit. Alternatively, you could start by discarding the ♠ 2 to tell partner you're not interested in spades. Your next discard could be the ♣ 3 to say you're not interested in clubs. On your last discard, you could play the ♦ 9 to encourage partner to lead that suit. Whatever you choose, you should be able to get the message across to partner and defeat the contract.

## Putting It All Together

Here are some examples of giving attitude signals when partner makes the opening lead against a notrump contract:

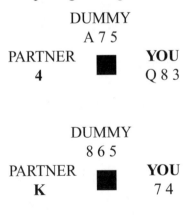

Partner leads the 4 and the ace is played from dummy. Play the **8**, an encouraging signal. Holding the queen, you tell partner you would like the suit led again.

When partner leads the king and the 5 is played from dummy, play the **4**, a discouraging card. You want to tell partner you have no help cards in the suit. If you were defending a suit contract, you might play an encouraging card from your doubleton, hoping that partner would be able to give you a ruff in the suit before trumps are drawn.

DUMMY
A 3
PARTNER                 YOU
K                                    J 5 2

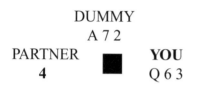

When partner leads the king and the ace is played from dummy, it looks as though partner is leading from a holding headed by the king, the queen, and the 10. Therefore, the jack is an important card and you want to encourage by playing the **5**, the highest card you can afford.

DUMMY
A 7 2
PARTNER                 YOU
4                                    Q 6 3

If dummy plays the 2 on partner's lead of the 4, play the **queen**, third hand high. This isn't a situation in which you can signal since you don't have a choice about the card to play.

# COUNT SIGNALS

Not all situations require an attitude signal. Partner may already know whether or not you like a particular suit. When you don't need to give an attitude signal, you may be able to tell partner how many cards you hold in the suit. This can be a vital piece of information for partner. Once one member of the partnership knows how many cards the other holds in a suit, it's possible to determine how many cards declarer holds, since that player can also see how many cards there are in hand and in the dummy. You may be able to take things further than that. Once you know how many cards declarer has in one suit, you may be able to figure out how many cards declarer has in other suits. This will be very helpful as you defend.

## High-low

How do you tell partner how many cards you have in a suit? You give a *count signal* by playing *high-low to show an even numbers of cards* and *low-high to show an odd number of cards*. Notice that a count signal doesn't tell partner exactly how many cards you hold in the suit. If you play high–low, you are showing an even number of cards, which could be two, four, six, or eight. Usually, partner will be able to determine exactly how many you  have from other clues such as the bidding or the other cards in the suit that can be seen. Similarly, if you play low-high, you are showing an odd number of cards. Again, partner can usually tell whether you are more likely to hold three cards rather than five or seven.

It's also important to recognize whether the situation calls for an attitude signal or a count signal. After all, a high card followed by a low card is used as an encouraging signal when showing attitude and to show an even number of cards when giving a count signal. Partner will need to know which type of signal applies. A useful guideline is that attitude signals are given priority, and you *give a count signal only when attitude clearly doesn't apply*. A typical situation arises when declarer is playing a long suit. There is usually no reason to show your attitude toward that suit since declarer is playing it anyway. Instead, it may be more important to tell partner how many cards you hold. This is very useful when partner is considering making a defensive *holdup play.* Let's look at an example in a complete deal:

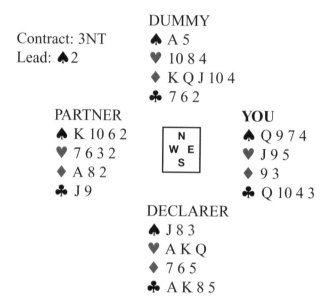

Contract: 3NT
Lead: ♠2

DUMMY
♠ A 5
♥ 10 8 4
♦ K Q J 10 4
♣ 7 6 2

PARTNER
♠ K 10 6 2
♥ 7 6 3 2
♦ A 8 2
♣ J 9

YOU
♠ Q 9 7 4
♥ J 9 5
♦ 9 3
♣ Q 10 4 3

DECLARER
♠ J 8 3
♥ A K Q
♦ 7 6 5
♣ A K 8 5

Partner leads the ♠2 against 3NT and declarer plays dummy's ♠5. You play the ♠Q, third hand high, which wins the trick, and lead back a spade, returning partner's suit. Declarer is forced to win this trick with dummy's ♠A. Needing nine tricks, declarer has one sure spade trick, three heart tricks, and two club tricks. The remaining tricks that declarer needs can come from the diamond suit, once the ♦A is driven out. There is a problem, however. There is no outside entry to dummy's diamond winners once they are established, because dummy's ♠A has already been played. Declarer will have to hope that the defenders win the first or second round of diamonds with the ♦A, leaving a small diamond in declarer's hand as an entry to dummy's winners.

Of course, the defenders want to counter declarer's plan by holding up with the ♦A until declarer doesn't have any left, leaving the remaining diamond winners stranded in the dummy. When declarer leads a high diamond from dummy, partner doesn't need to win the first trick. But should partner win the second trick or the third trick? Partner needs to know how many diamonds declarer has in order to be able to tell when declarer has run out. Here is where you can help by giving a count signal. Obviously, it isn't necessary to show attitude toward the diamond suit since that's the suit declarer is trying to establish. Instead, the specific order in which you play your cards can be used to give a count signal. With two cards in the suit, you want to show an even number by playing high-low. When the first diamond is led from dummy, play the ♦9, starting the "high" part of the signal. When the next diamond is led from dummy, you play the ♦3, completing the "low" part of the signal.

How does partner know that you have two cards in the suit rather than four or six? There are only 13 cards in the suit and partner can see five in dummy and three in hand. Even before the suit is played, partner knows you can't have six, since that would add up to more than 13 cards in the suit. In fact, if declarer has opened the bidding 1NT, showing a balanced hand, partner can also figure out ahead of time that you can't have four cards in the suit. That would mean that declarer started with a singleton and wouldn't have a balanced hand. This will be confirmed anyway when declarer plays a diamond on the second round of the suit. So when you play high-low in diamonds, partner has enough clues to determine that you must be showing exactly two cards in the suit. With five cards in dummy and three in hand, declarer is left with exactly three cards in the suit.

This tells partner to hold up the ♦A until the third round of the suit. At that point, declarer won't have any diamonds left and dummy's winners will be stranded. After winning the ♦A, partner can take two remaining spade winners and lead a heart or a club. Declarer is left with only eight tricks, a spade trick, three heart tricks, the first two diamond tricks, and two club tricks. With careful play, the defense prevails.

Defeating the contract isn't easy. Partner must realize the importance of holding up the ♦ A. Partner must watch your count signal and use the information to figure out exactly when to win the ♦ A. You must cooperate by realizing the need to give a count signal in the diamond suit and then by playing your diamonds in the correct order.

Was the count signal really necessary? Couldn't partner hold up with the ♦ A as long as possible just to be sure that declarer didn't have any diamonds left? That would have worked on this hand. Let's change the hand slightly leaving partner's cards and the dummy's cards looking exactly the same:

DUMMY

Contract: 3NT      ♠ A 5
Lead: ♠2         ♥ 10 8 4
              ♦ K Q J 10 4
              ♣ 7 6 2

PARTNER                    YOU
♠ K 10 6 2            ♠ Q 9 7 4
♥ 7 6 3 2     N        ♥ 9 5
♦ A 8 2     W   E     ♦ 9 5 3
♣ J 9        S        ♣ Q 10 4 3

           DECLARER
           ♠ J 8 3
           ♥ A K Q J
           ♦ 7 6
           ♣ A K 8 5

The bidding and contract are the same, partner makes the same opening lead, and the play to the first couple of tricks goes the same way. Now, suppose partner waits until the third round of diamonds to win the ♦ A, takes the established spade winners, and leads a heart or a club. This time, declarer makes the contract! Declarer has one spade trick, four heart tricks, the two diamond tricks, and two club tricks. The extra heart winner in hand gives declarer enough tricks once partner ducks the first two rounds of diamonds. To defeat the contract, partner has to win the second round of diamonds with the ♦A, restricting declarer to only one diamond trick while still stranding the remaining diamond winners in dummy.

How does partner know to win the second diamond trick rather than the third? Partner has to rely on your count signal. With an odd number of cards, start by playing a low diamond, the ♦3, when the first diamond is led from dummy. On the second round, follow with the ♦5 (or ♦9), a higher diamond. By playing low-high, you show partner an odd number of diamonds. Since it can't be one or five, partner can figure out that you have exactly three diamonds. That leaves declarer with exactly two diamonds. By winning the second round of diamonds with the ♦A, partner prevents declarer from getting any more tricks than declarer is entitled to in the suit. Again, the contract is defeated through careful defense. Partner has to trust you to give the right information, and you have to cooperate by making the appropriate signal.

## Count when Discarding

You can also give count signals when discarding. Of course, both you and partner must realize that the situation calls for count rather than attitude. One of the important reasons for giving a count signal is to help partner know which cards to hold on to while discarding. At least one of the defenders must hold on to enough cards in a suit to prevent declarer's little cards from becoming established through length. Here is a dramatic example:

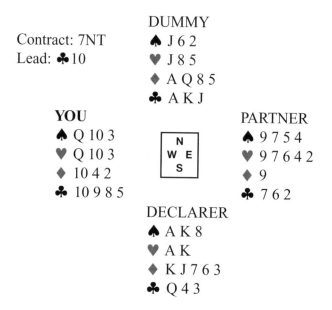

Contract: 7NT
Lead: ♣10

DUMMY
♠ J 6 2
♥ J 8 5
♦ A Q 8 5
♣ A K J

YOU
♠ Q 10 3
♥ Q 10 3
♦ 10 4 2
♣ 10 9 8 5

PARTNER
♠ 9 7 5 4
♥ 9 7 6 4 2
♦ 9
♣ 7 6 2

DECLARER
♠ A K 8
♥ A K
♦ K J 7 6 3
♣ Q 4 3

This time you will be cast in the role of the defender receiving the signals rather than sending them. The opponents reach a grand slam contract of 7NT and you make the safe lead of the ♣10, top of a sequence. You hope that one of your queens will later take a trick to defeat the contract. Things won't be easy, however, as declarer quickly takes the first 12 tricks. There are two spade tricks, two heart tricks, five diamond tricks, and three club tricks. When it comes to the last trick, declarer has only one card left. Which card are you holding on to, the ♠Q or the ♥Q?

Looking at declarer's hand, it's easy to see that you have to hold on to the ♠Q rather than the ♥Q, since declarer's last card will be the ♠8. Unfortunately, at the table, you can't see into declarer's hand. When it comes to making that crucial discard on the 12th trick, will you be able to tell whether declarer's last card is a spade or a heart? You can be sure only if your partner is careful to provide you with the information you need, and you watch the cards that partner plays. Even without holding any high cards, partner plays a key role in the defense. Since declarer has all of the missing high cards, partner doesn't need to give an attitude signal for any suit. Instead, this is a situation for count signals. Partner must realize that you will need to know what to hold on to at the end of the hand in order to defeat the contract.

Partner can start on the first trick, when declarer wins with one of dummy's high clubs. Partner plays the ♣2, starting to play low-high, to show an odd number. The auction and subsequent play will help you confirm that partner started with exactly three clubs. This tells you that declarer also has exactly three clubs. When it comes time to find a discard, you can throw away one of your clubs without giving anything away. When declarer starts to take the diamond tricks, partner's first card will be the ♦9. This may look like the start of a high-low to show an even number, but when the next discard is made on the next diamond trick, you'll know that partner started with only one diamond and that declarer has five. The crucial information will come from partner's discards on the diamonds as declarer takes the diamond winners. Partner must throw a high spade and then a low spade to show an even number of spades and a low heart and then a high heart to show an odd number of hearts.

Now it's up to you to put all of the information together. With partner showing an even number of spades, you can determine from the auction that partner has four rather than two (giving declarer a five-card suit) or six (giving declarer a singleton), leaving declarer with exactly three. When partner shows an odd number of hearts, you can determine that partner has five rather than three (giving declarer a four-card suit) or seven (giving declarer a void). This leaves declarer with exactly two hearts. When

it comes down to the critical decision, you can confidently discard the
♥Q and hold on to the ♠Q, knowing that declarer started with three
spades and only two hearts.

## Practice Makes Perfect

Defending in this manner may seem like hard work, but it gets easier
with practice. You'll soon find that the necessary information can be
gathered very quickly and is very helpful on most hands. Experienced
defenders probably would have exchanged all of the necessary information by the time the first three tricks had been played on the above deal
and could defend in comfort after that point.

For example, suppose declarer wins the first club trick and then starts
off by taking two diamond tricks. East plays the ♣2 on the first trick, the
♦9 on the second trick, and discards the ♥2 on the third trick. Assuming that declarer has a balanced hand, West will know that declarer has
three clubs from partner's play of the ♣2 to the first trick and five diamonds since partner showed out on the second trick. That leaves only
five cards unaccounted for. East's discard of the ♥2, showing an odd
number of hearts, marks declarer with an even number, probably two,
leaving room for exactly three spades. West can conclude that declarer
has a 3–2–5–3 distribution and can defend accordingly. Any subsequent
signals by East will merely help confirm West's picture of the deal. No
wonder experts always seem to know which cards to hang on to at the
end!

Here are some examples to see how quickly you can get information
from your partner's count signals. Declarer has opened the bidding 1NT
and has been left to play there. After winning the first trick in hand,
declarer is trying to establish a long suit in dummy to which there are no
outside entries, and you must decide how long to hold up your winner.
Assuming that partner is trying to give you a count signal, let's look at
how many rounds you plan to hold up in each of the following situations:

DUMMY
K Q J 10 7

PARTNER 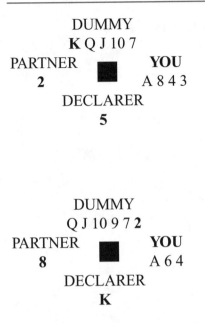 YOU
2 A 8 4 3

DECLARER
5

Declarer leads the 5, partner plays the 2, and the king is played from dummy. Partner's 2, a low card, shows an odd number. Partner can't have three, since that would give declarer a singleton. Therefore partner must have only one card. That leaves declarer with three cards and you plan to win your ace on the **third round** of the suit.

DUMMY
Q J 10 9 7 2

PARTNER YOU
8 A 6 4

DECLARER
K

Declarer leads the king, partner plays the 8, and the 2 is played from dummy. Partner's 8, a high card, looks like the start of a high-low, showing an even number. If partner has two cards in the suit, declarer has two cards, and you plan to win the **second round** of the suit. Of course partner will show out on the next round if partner started with a singleton 8, in which case you'll know that declarer has three cards. Then you'll have to wait until the third round before playing your ace.

DUMMY
K Q 10 5 4

PARTNER 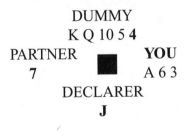 YOU
7 A 6 3

DECLARER
J

Declarer leads the jack, partner plays the 7, and the 4 is played from dummy. Since you can't see the 2, it's not clear whether partner is trying to show an even number or an odd number. If partner started with the 7–2, the play of the 7 is the start of a high-low to show a doubleton. If partner started with 9-8-7, the 7 is the start of a low-high, to show three cards. You'll have to **wait** until you see partner's next card before deciding what to do. If partner has a doubleton, you'll win the ace on the third round. If partner has three, declarer has only two, and you'll win the ace on the second round of the suit.

# SUIT-PREFERENCE SIGNALS

When the card you choose to play is clearly not needed for either an attitude signal or a count signal, you may be able to give partner a *suit-preference signal*.

## High-Low Again

A suit preference signal is used when partner will need to know which of two suits to lead at the next opportunity. *A high card shows preference for the higher-ranking suit* and *a low card shows preference for the lower-ranking suit.* This can be illustrated more clearly with the aid of a complete hand:

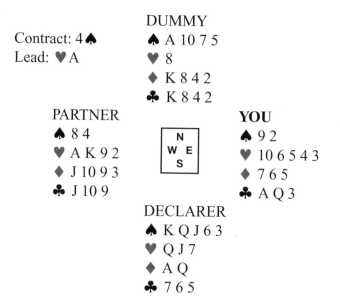

Contract: 4♠
Lead: ♥ A

DUMMY
♠ A 10 7 5
♥ 8
♦ K 8 4 2
♣ K 8 4 2

PARTNER
♠ 8 4
♥ A K 9 2
♦ J 10 9 3
♣ J 10 9

YOU
♠ 9 2
♥ 10 6 5 4 3
♦ 7 6 5
♣ A Q 3

DECLARER
♠ K Q J 6 3
♥ Q J 7
♦ A Q
♣ 7 6 5

Against declarer's 4♠ contract, your partner leads the ♥A. The singleton heart accompanied by all of those trumps in dummy indicates there is little future in that suit. There's not much need for you to tell partner your attitude toward hearts. Whether you like the suit or not, your side is unlikely to get more than one trick in the suit since declarer can ruff heart losers in the dummy. Likewise, there's not much point in using your signaling opportunity to tell partner how many cards you have in the suit. Instead, the key piece of information partner needs to know is what to lead next.

Since attitude and count signals don't apply, this is an ideal situation to employ a suit-preference signal. Partner is no longer interested in the heart suit and spades is declarer's trump suit. What partner is interested in knowing is which of the remaining two suits, diamonds and clubs, you prefer. Holding the ♣A and the ♣Q, you prefer that partner lead a club, the lower-ranking of the two suits. Therefore, you play the ♥3, a low card, as suit preference for the lower-ranking suit. Provided partner is in step with you, partner will lead the ♣J and your side will quickly take three club tricks to defeat the contract. Without the use of a suit preference signal, partner might have guessed to lead a diamond rather than a club. Declarer would win the trick and, after drawing trumps, discard a club loser on the extra diamond winner in dummy to make the contract.

If you held the ♦A and the ♦Q instead of the ♣A and the ♣Q, you'd play the ♥10, telling partner you prefer the higher-ranking suit, diamonds. What if you have no preference, perhaps having high cards in both suits or neither? Play a medium-sized heart, such as the ♥5 or the ♥6, to indicate no particular preference. Partner would then decide what to do next based on partner's own holdings in the suits and the knowledge that you had no preference.

## Finding an Entry

The suit-preference signal is much less common than attitude and count signals since the conditions have to be exactly right. Both partners must be aware that the situation doesn't call for either an attitude signal or a count signal and there must be a choice between only two suits. This is sometimes the circumstance when you need to find an entry to your partner's hand. Take a look at the following layout:

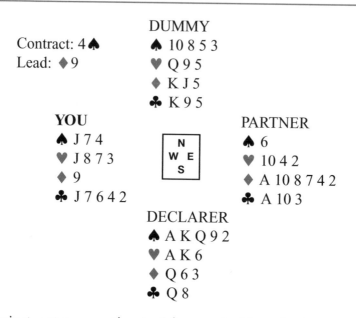

DUMMY
Contract: 4♠          ♠ 10 8 5 3
Lead: ♦9              ♥ Q 9 5
                     ♦ K J 5
                     ♣ K 9 5

YOU                                    PARTNER
♠ J 7 4                                ♠ 6
♥ J 8 7 3         N                    ♥ 10 4 2
♦ 9            W     E                  ♦ A 10 8 7 4 2
♣ J 7 6 4 2        S                   ♣ A 10 3

                  DECLARER
                  ♠ A K Q 9 2
                  ♥ A K 6
                  ♦ Q 6 3
                  ♣ Q 8

Against a strong auction to 4♠, you decide to lead your singleton diamond in the hope that partner can lead the suit again for you to ruff. You are justly rewarded when partner wins the first trick with the ♦A and leads one back for you to ruff. What now? You'd like to find an entry back to partner's hand so partner can lead another diamond for you to ruff, but is it best to lead a heart or a club?

If you and your partner are aware that this is a suit-preference situation, there should be no problem. Partner should return the lowest diamond, the ♦2, to tell you that clubs, the lower-ranking suit, is preferred. You lead a club to partner's ace and partner leads another diamond for you to ruff to defeat the contract. If partner had held the ♥A instead of the ♣A, partner would have returned the ♦10, asking for the higher-ranking suit, hearts. Notice how partner must anticipate your problem before leading back a diamond for you to ruff. Partner must also recognize that there will be only two logical suits for you to choose from, hearts and clubs. If partner didn't have a preference, a medium-sized diamond would be returned and the decision on what to lead next would be left up to you.

# BIDDING REVIEW

Responder's role is that of captain, steering the partnership to the appropriate contract. As opener describes the hand, responder uses the information to determine the level at which the partnership belongs — partscore, game, or slam — and the denomination in which the partnership should play. By the time opener has rebid, responder is usually in a position to place the contract.

## Rebids by Responder when Opener Shows a Minimum Hand

If opener's rebid describes a minimum hand of 13 to 16 points, responder adds the strength of the hand to that promised by opener and bids accordingly. With 6 to 10, responder wants to stop in the best partscore and makes a signoff bid. With 11 or 12 points, responder wants to invite opener to game and makes an invitational bid. Opener can reject the invitation with 13 or 14 points and accept with the top of the minimum range, 15 or 16 points. With 13 to 16 points, responder makes sure the partnership gets to game by signing off in game or by making a forcing bid. With 17 or 18 points, responder invites opener to slam. With 19 or more, responder makes sure the partnership gets to slam.

Responder can use the following guidelines when choosing a rebid to make sure that opener receives the right type of message:

| RANGE | OPTIONS | MESSAGE |
|---|---|---|
| 6 to 10 | • Pass. | Signoff |
| | • 1NT. | Signoff |
| | • Two-level bid of a suit already bid by the partnership. | Signoff |
| 11 or 12 | • 2NT. | Invitational to game |
| | • Three-level bid of a suit already bid by the partnership. | Invitational to game |
| 13 to 16 | • Game (3NT, 4♥, 4♠). | Signoff |
| | • Bid of a new suit at the three level. | Forcing |
| 17 or 18 | • Bid one level beyond game (4NT, 5♥, 5♠). | Invitational to slam |
| 19 or more | • Slam. | Signoff |
| | • Bid of a new suit at the three level. | Forcing |

*Take Note*

## Rebids by Responder when Opener Shows a Medium Hand

If opener's rebid describes a medium hand of 17 or 18 points, responder wants to stop in partscore only when holding about 6 to 8 points; otherwise responder wants to be in game or higher. The following guidelines can be used to select a rebid:

| RANGE | OPTIONS | MESSAGE |
|---|---|---|
| 6 to 8 | • Pass. | Signoff |
| | • Cheapest bid of a suit already bid by the partnership. | Signoff |
| 9 to 14 | • Game (3NT, 4♥, 4♠). | Signoff |
| | • Bid of a new suit . | Forcing |
| 15 or 16 | • Bid one level beyond game (4NT, 5♥, 5♠). | Invitational to slam |
| 17 or more | • Slam. | Signoff |
| | • Bid of a new suit. | Forcing |

## Rebids by Responder when Opener Shows a Maximum Hand

If opener's rebid describes a maximum hand of 19 to 21 points, the partnership is forced to at least the game level, so any bid by responder below the game level is still forcing.

Responder can use the following guidelines:

| RANGE | OPTIONS | MESSAGE |
|---|---|---|
| 6 to 12 | • Pass, if already in game | Signoff |
| | • Game (3NT, 4 ♥, 4 ♠) | Signoff |
| | • Any bid other than game | Forcing |
| 13 or 14 | • Bid one level beyond game (4NT, 5 ♥, 5 ♠) | Invitational to slam |
| 15 or more | • Slam | Signoff |
| | • Any bid other than game | Forcing |

# PLAY OF THE HAND REVIEW

The techniques for developing tricks in notrump are all available to declarer when trying to eliminate extra losers in a suit contract. In addition, declarer has the possibility of ruffing losers or discarding them.

## Ruffing Losers

Consider the following side suit that you hold in a trump contract:

DUMMY
6

DECLARER
9 4 2

You have three losers in the suit, but since dummy has fewer cards in the suit than you do, there's an opportunity to ruff losers in the dummy. To be able to ruff your losers in dummy, you must first give up a trick to the opponents so that dummy is void in the suit. You must be careful to keep enough trumps in dummy to ruff your losers. In the above layout, you need two trumps in dummy to ruff two of your losers. Don't forget that the opponents may lead trumps when they get the lead, so often you have to delay drawing trumps when you're planning to ruff losers in the dummy. One other thing to watch out for is the entries to your hand. After ruffing one of your losers in dummy, you need an entry back to your hand to ruff the second loser.

## Discarding Losers

Consider the following side suit in a trump contract:

DUMMY
K Q 3

DECLARER
A 6

With only two cards in your hand, and holding both the ace and the king, you have no losers in this suit. In fact, holding the queen as well, you have an extra winner in the dummy. This provides the opportunity to discard one of your losers in another suit after taking tricks with the ace and the king. Here the extra winner is already established. In some cases, you'll have to work to create extra winners in the dummy on which you can discard your losers.

When planning to discard losers on extra winners, you must consider whether or not you can afford to draw trumps first. Whenever possible, you should draw trumps before discarding your losers to avoid the risk of having one of your winners ruffed by an opponent. If you may have to give up the lead while drawing trumps, however, you must first decide whether or not you have too many quick losers. Quick losers are the tricks the opponents can take as soon as they get the lead. If you have too many quick losers, you'll have to discard some of them before giving up the lead.

# SUMMARY

Since the defenders can't see each other's hands, they must try to communicate information about their strength and distribution through the use of defensive signals. They have the opportunity to make a signal whenever they have a choice of cards to play to a trick. The types of signals the defenders can use, in order of priority, are:

**Attitude Signals** — When you want to tell partner whether or not you like a particular suit, *a high card is an encouraging signal, a low card is a discouraging signal.*

**Count Signals** — When you want to tell partner how many cards you hold in a suit, *a high card followed by a low card shows an even number of cards, a low card followed by a high card shows an odd number of cards.*

**Suit-Preference Signals** — When partner will have a choice of leading one of two suits, *a high card shows preference for the higher-ranking suit, a low card shows preference for the lower-ranking suit.*

Both partners will need to be aware of which type of signal the situation calls for. While one partner is doing the signaling, the other partner must be watching the cards played by partner in order to receive the signal.

## Exercise One — *Giving an Attitude Signal*

In each of the following layouts, you're defending against a notrump contract. Your partner leads the king, and the 3 is played from dummy. Decide whether you want to encourage or discourage. Which card do you play?

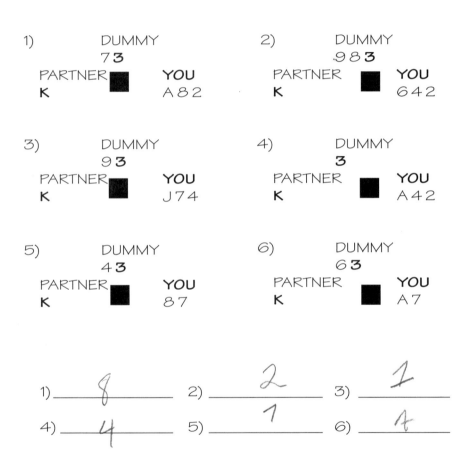

1)  DUMMY
    7 3
PARTNER ■  YOU
K          A 8 2

2)  DUMMY
    .9 8 3
PARTNER ■  YOU
K          6 4 2

3)  DUMMY
    9 3
PARTNER ■  YOU
K          J 7 4

4)  DUMMY
    3
PARTNER ■  YOU
K          A 4 2

5)  DUMMY
    4 3
PARTNER ■  YOU
K          8 7

6)  DUMMY
    6 3
PARTNER ■  YOU
K          A 7

1) _____ *8* _____   2) _____ *2* _____   3) _____ *1* _____
4) _____ *4* _____   5) _____ *1* _____   6) _____ *7* _____

**Exercise One** — Giving an Attitude Signal

1) Encourage with the 8.

2) Discourage with the 2.

3) Encourage with the 7.

4) Encourage with the 4.

5) Discourage with the 7.

6) Unblock with the ace.

**Exercise Two** — When Partner Signals

You're defending a notrump contract with the following hand and lead the ♦Q:

DUMMY

♠ J 3 2
♥ K 7 4
♦ A 2
♣ K Q 9 7 4

YOU

♠ K 5 4
♥ 8 6 3
♦ Q J 10 5
♣ 8 5 3

What can you deduce about partner's hand under each of the following circumstances:

1) Declarer wins the first trick in dummy, and partner plays the ♦3.

2) Declarer wins the first trick in dummy, and partner plays the ♦8.

3) After winning the first trick, declarer starts taking the club tricks and partner discards the ♠6 on the third round.

4) After winning the first trick, declarer starts taking the club tricks and partner discards the ♥9 on the third round.

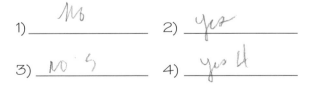

1) _____ Mb _____  2) _____ yes _____

3) _____ NO 5 _____  4) _____ yes u _____

## Exercise Two — When Partner Signals

1) Partner dislikes diamonds.    2) Partner likes diamonds.

3) Partner dislikes spades.    4) Partner likes hearts.

## Exercise Three — Giving a Count Signal

You're defending a contract of 6NT holding the following hand:

♠ 9 7 6 5 2
♥ 8 7 5 3
♦ 10 6 4
♣ J

Declarer starts taking tricks in the club suit, and you have to discard after the first round. With no information to give partner other than the number of cards you have in each suit, which two cards would you discard to give partner one of the following signals:

1) The number of cards you hold in the spade suit.

2) The number of cards you hold in the heart suit.

3) The number of cards you hold in the diamond suit.

1) _____2 - 5_____ 2) _____8 - 3_____ 3) _____4 - 6_____

---

**Answers to Exercise**

## Exercise Three — Giving a Count Signal

1) ♠2 then ♠5 (low-high).

2) ♥8 then ♥3 (high-low).

3) ♦4 then ♦6 (low-high).

## Exercise Four — Interpreting a Count Signal

After an opening bid of 1NT on your right, you lead the ♠4 against a contract of 3NT. This is the dummy:

DUMMY
♠ A
♥ 9 7 4
♦ K Q J 10 9
♣ J 7 6 3

YOU
♠ Q 8 5 4 2
♥ 8 6
♦ A 8 3
♣ 8 4 2

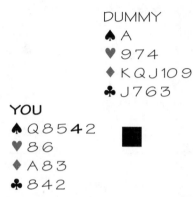

Declarer wins the first trick with dummy's ♠A and starts leading dummy's diamonds to drive out your ♦A. On which round should you take your ♦A if:

1)  Partner plays the ♦7 and then the ♦4.

2)  Partner plays the ♦2 and then the ♦6

3)  Partner plays the ♦5 and then discards the ♥2.

1)_____  2) _____  3) _____

---

## Answers to Exercise

## Exercise Four — Interpreting a Count Signal

1) Third round     2) Second round     3) Doesn't matter

## Exercise Five — *Giving Suit Preference*

Partner leads what looks like a singleton club against declarer's contract of 4♥. After winning your ♣A, which club do you lead back for partner to ruff from each of the following hands?

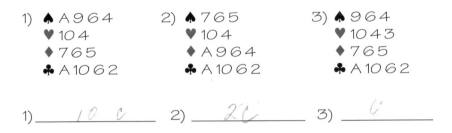

1) ♠ A 9 6 4
   ♥ 10 4
   ♦ 7 6 5
   ♣ A 10 6 2

2) ♠ 7 6 5
   ♥ 10 4
   ♦ A 9 6 4
   ♣ A 10 6 2

3) ♠ 9 6 4
   ♥ 10 4 3
   ♦ 7 6 5
   ♣ A 10 6 2

1) _____ *10 C* _____   2) _____ *2C* _____   3) _____ *6* _____

## Exercise Six — *Putting It All Together*

You hold the following hand:

♠ K 9 2
♥ 8 4 2
♦ K 7 6 3
♣ 9 5 4

During the play, you get an opportunity to give partner a signal.

1) Which card would you play to tell partner that you would like to have a spade led?

2) Which card would you play to tell partner that you don't like clubs?

3) Which card would you play to start to give a count signal in hearts?

4) Which card would you play to start to give a count signal in diamonds?

5) Which club could you play to tell partner that you prefer spades to hearts?

1) _____  2) _____  3) _____  4) _____ 5) _____

**Exercise Five** — Giving Suit Preference

1) 10, showing preference for spades.

2) 2, showing preference for diamonds.

3) 6, showing no preference for either suit.

**Exercise Six** — Putting It All Together

1) ♠9    2) ♣4    3) ♥2

4) ♦7    5) ♣9

## Exercise Seven — *Review of Rebids by Responder*

Your partner opens the bidding 1♦, you respond 1♠, and partner rebids 1NT. What do you rebid with each of the following hands?

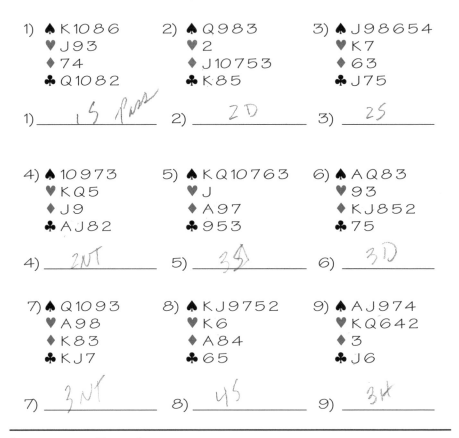

1) ♠ K 10 8 6
♥ J 9 3
♦ 7 4
♣ Q 10 8 2

1)_____ 1 5 *Pass*

2) ♠ Q 9 8 3
♥ 2
♦ J 10 7 5 3
♣ K 8 5

2)_____ 2 D

3) ♠ J 9 8 6 5 4
♥ K 7
♦ 6 3
♣ J 7 5

3)_____ 2 S

4) ♠ 10 9 7 3
♥ K Q 5
♦ J 9
♣ A J 8 2

4)_____ 2NT

5) ♠ K Q 10 7 6 3
♥ J
♦ A 9 7
♣ 9 5 3

5)_____ 3 S

6) ♠ A Q 8 3
♥ 9 3
♦ K J 8 5 2
♣ 7 5

6)_____ 3 D

7) ♠ Q 10 9 3
♥ A 9 8
♦ K 8 3
♣ K J 7

7)_____ 3 NT

8) ♠ K J 9 7 5 2
♥ K 6
♦ A 8 4
♣ 6 5

8)_____ 4 S

9) ♠ A J 9 7 4
♥ K Q 6 4 2
♦ 3
♣ J 6

9)_____ 3 H

---

### Answers to Exercise

## Exercise Seven — *Review of Rebids by Responder*

1) Pass

2) 2♦

3) 2♠

4) 2NT

5) 3♠

6) 3♦

7) 3NT

8) 4♠

9) 3♥

**Exercise Eight** — Developing Tricks in a Suit Contract

How would you plan to make your contract of 4♠ on the following hand after the opening lead of the ♣Q? Can you draw trumps immediately?

DUMMY
♠ Q J 9 3
♥ A K 8 3
♦ 6
♣ 9 5 4 2

Lead: ♣Q

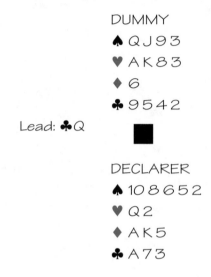

DECLARER
♠ 10 8 6 5 2
♥ Q 2
♦ A K 5
♣ A 7 3

**Answers to Exercise**

**Exercise Eight** — Developing Tricks in a Suit Contract

Declarer can afford three losers in 4♠. There are two spade losers, a diamond loser, and two club losers. The diamond loser can be ruffed in dummy, and one of the club losers can be discarded on the extra heart winner in dummy. Drawing trumps will have to be delayed until a club loser is discarded, because once the defenders get the lead, they can take four quick tricks.

# Exercise Nine — *Giving Attitude*

## (E-Z Deal Cards: #5, Hand 1 — Dealer, North)

Turn up the cards from the first pre-dealt deal. Put each hand dummy-style at the edge of the table in front of each player.

## The Bidding

What would North open the bidding? East and West pass throughout. What would South respond? How does North show both the strength of the hand and support for responder's suit? Does South know the level at which the partnership belongs? Does South know the denomination in which the partnership belongs? What does South rebid? How does the auction proceed from there? Who is the declarer?

Dealer:　♠ 10 8 7 3
North　♥ A K 6
　　　　♦ Q J 10 2
　　　　♣ K 9

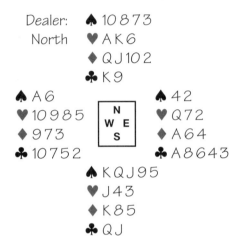

♠ A 6　　　　　　　♠ 4 2
♥ 10 9 8 5　　　　♥ Q 7 2
♦ 9 7 3　　　　　　♦ A 6 4
♣ 10 7 5 2　　　　♣ A 8 6 4 3

♠ K Q J 9 5
♥ J 4 3
♦ K 8 5
♣ Q J

## The Defense

Which player makes the opening lead? What would the opening lead be? Which card would East play on the first trick if dummy wins the trick? Why?

## The Play

Review the steps in declarer's PLAN. How does declarer plan to make the contract?

## Exercise Nine — Giving Attitude

### The Bidding

- North would open the bidding 1♦.
- South would respond 1♠.
- North rebids 2♠ and South rebids 4♠.
- All players pass. South is the declarer in 4♠.

### The Defense

- West leads the ♥10, the top of a sequence.
- East encourages with the ♥7. The defenders have to work to get the ♥Q to go along with their three aces to defeat the contract.

### The Play

- Declarer has one loser in each suit. He'll try to discard the heart loser on dummy's extra diamond winner after driving out the ♦A. Declarer will have to draw trumps first, otherwise the opponents will be able to ruff the extra diamond winner once it's established.

## Exercise Ten — Getting a Ruff
### (E-Z Deal Cards: #5, Hand 2 — Dealer, East)

Turn up the cards from the second pre-dealt deal. Put each hand dummy-style at the edge of the table in front of each player.

### The Bidding

East and South pass. What would West open the bidding? North passes. Which suit does East bid at the one level? Why? South passes? Counting dummy points, does West have a minimum, medium, or maximum hand in support of partner's suit? What does West rebid? North passes. What does East know about West's hand? What does East rebid? What is the contract? Who is the declarer?

Dealer:   ♠ 10 5
East    ♥ A 10 4 2
     ♦ 10 5
     ♣ K J 10 9 2

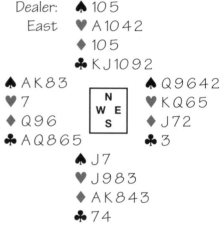

♠ A K 8 3        ♠ Q 9 6 4 2
♥ 7            ♥ K Q 6 5
♦ Q 9 6        ♦ J 7 2
♣ A Q 8 6 5     ♣ 3

     ♠ J 7
     ♥ J 9 8 3
     ♦ A K 8 4 3
     ♣ 7 4

### The Defense

Which player makes the opening lead? What would the opening lead be? Which card would North play? Why? What will South lead next?

### The Play

Review the steps in declarer's PLAN. How does declarer plan to make the contract?

## Exercise Ten — Getting a Ruff

### The Bidding

- West opens the bidding 1♣.
- East responds 1♠.
- West has a medium hand in support of spades and rebids 3♠.
- East knows West has spade support and 17 or 18 points.
- East bids 4♠ and the others pass. East is the declarer in 4♠.

### The Defense

- South leads the ♦A, the top of touching high cards.
- North encourages with the ♦10.
- South will play the ♦K and another diamond, based on partner's encouraging signal.

### The Play

- Declarer plans to ruff heart losers in dummy after driving out the ♥A.

## Exercise Eleven – *Giving Count*

### (E-Z Deal Cards: #5, Hand 3 — Dealer, South)

Turn up the cards from the third pre-dealt deal. Put each hand dummy-style at the edge of the table in front of each player.

### The Bidding

South passes. What is West's opening bid? North passes. What does East respond? South passes. Does West accept East's invitation? How does the bidding proceed from there? What is the contract? Who is the declarer?

Dealer: ♠ K Q J 9
South   ♥ 9 3
     ♦ A 7 6
     ♣ J 10 6 5

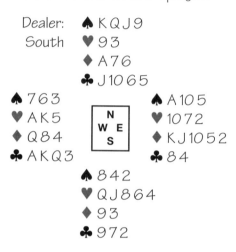

♠ 7 6 3           ♠ A 10 5
♥ A K 5           ♥ 10 7 2
♦ Q 8 4           ♦ K J 10 5 2
♣ A K Q 3        ♣ 8 4

     ♠ 8 4 2
     ♥ Q J 8 6 4
     ♦ 9 3
     ♣ 9 7 2

### The Defense

Which player makes the opening lead? What would the opening lead be? Which card does South play on the first trick? Why? When declarer leads diamonds, what card should South play? Why? Should North win the first diamond trick? If not, which round should North win? Why?

### The Play

Review the steps in declarer's PLAN. How does declarer plan to make the contract?

## Exercise Eleven – Giving Count

### The Bidding

- West opens the bidding 1NT.
- East raises to 2NT.
- West accepts the invitation and bids 3NT.
- West is the declarer in 3NT.

### The Defense

- North leads the ♠K, top of touching honors.
- South plays the ♠2 to tell partner there is no help in spades.
- When declarer leads diamonds, South plays the ♦9 to give count, showing an even number of diamonds.
- No. North holds up until the third round. With the ♠A already played, declarer doesn't have an entry to dummy and dummy's good diamonds are stranded.

### The Play

- Declarer has six sure tricks and needs three more.
- Declarer needs to promote diamond winners by driving out the ♦A. The defenders, however, can make it difficult by stranding East's winners.

# Exercise Twelve — Giving Suit Preference

## (E-Z Deal Cards: #5, Hand 4 — Dealer, West)

Turn up the cards from the fourth pre-dealt deal. Put each hand dummy-style at the edge of the table in front of each player.

### The Bidding

West passes. What is North's opening bid? East passes. How does South show the support for partner's suit and the strength of the hand? West passes. What does North know about the combined strength of the hands? What does North rebid? What is the contract? Who is the declarer?

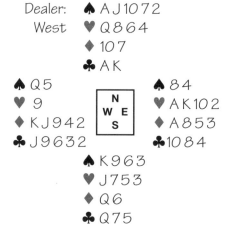

Dealer: ♠ A J 10 7 2
West ♥ Q 8 6 4
♦ 10 7
♣ A K

♠ Q 5　　　　♠ 8 4
♥ 9　　　　　♥ A K 10 2
♦ K J 9 4 2　♦ A 8 5 3
♣ J 9 6 3 2　♣ 10 8 4

♠ K 9 6 3
♥ J 7 5 3
♦ Q 6
♣ Q 7 5

### The Defense

Which player makes the opening lead? What would the opening lead be? Which card does East play to the second trick? Which card does East play to the third trick? Why? Which suit does West lead to the fourth trick? Why?

### The Play

Review the steps in declarer's PLAN. How does declarer plan to make the contract?

## Exercise Twelve — Giving Suit Preference

### The Bidding

- North opens the bidding 1♠.

- South bids 2♠.

- Everyone passes and North is the declarer in 2♠.

### The Defense

- East leads the ♥A, top of touching honors.

- After West's encouraging ♥9, East plays the ♥K.

- West shows out and East plays the k10, showing a suit-preference signal for diamonds, rather than clubs.

- West leads diamonds after ruffing the heart.

### The Play

- Declarer plans to draw trumps by playing the ♠A and the ♠K, hoping the ♠Q will drop. Declarer hopes that the hearts will be divided 3–2 and the defenders won't get a ruff.

# CHAPTER 6
## *Developing Defensive Tricks*

The defenders get tricks the same way as declarer — they take their sure tricks, promote winners, establish long suits, take finesses, and trump declarer's winners. They can't see each other's hands, however, and sometimes it's more difficult for them to get the tricks to which they are entitled. They need to recognize the various possibilities, often using partner's signals to guide them. In this chapter, we look at the techniques the defenders use to get the tricks coming to them, starting with the straightforward one, taking their established winners.

## TAKING SURE TRICKS

When a suit is divided evenly between the defenders' hands, usually there's no problem taking sure tricks, those that are already established as winners. The suit itself provides the necessary entries back and forth between the two hands. When the suit is unevenly divided, winners may get stranded if the defenders aren't careful.

### Unblocking

When faced with the problem of taking sure tricks in a suit that is unevenly divided, declarer follows the guideline of *playing the high card from the short side first*. This is straightforward for declarer, who can see all of the cards in dummy's hand and declarer's own hand but requires some imagination from the defenders' perspective. Consider this suit layout where partner leads the king against a notrump contract:

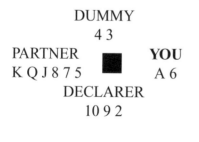

DUMMY
4 3
PARTNER       YOU
K Q J 8 7 5     A 6
DECLARER
10 9 2

Through no fault of your own, the defense has a problem that declarer doesn't face. If declarer were playing this suit, declarer would start by leading a low card to the ace, winning the first trick in the short side, and then leading the 6 back over to the remaining winners. Unfortunately, your partner couldn't see your hand when making the opening lead. Not knowing where the ace was, partner made the normal lead of the top of three touching honors.

It's up to you to recover by overtaking partner's king with the ace and leading the 6 back to partner's established winners. In the chapter on third-hand play, we saw that this is called *unblocking* the suit. The general idea is that when partner is playing a long suit and taking tricks, you want to end up with a low card, not a winner, as the last card in that suit. Once you are able to visualize the problem, it's not so difficult to come up with the solution.

## Signaling

In the above layout, you could afford to overtake partner's king with your ace since your side had all of the high cards in the suit. The defenders won't always be able to afford to play two of their high cards on the same trick. Sometimes, however, it won't be necessary. Consider this layout where, once again, partner leads the king against a notrump contract:

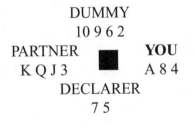

DUMMY
10 9 6 2
PARTNER          YOU
K Q J 3          A 8 4
DECLARER
7 5

If you overtake partner's king with your ace and lead the suit back, partner will play the queen and then the jack. At that point, dummy's 10 becomes established as a trick. You get only three of the four tricks to which you are entitled. You have two lower cards to go along with your ace, so you don't need to unblock on the first trick by playing the ace on partner's king. Now that you know about attitude signals, make an encouraging signal on partner's king by playing the 8, the highest card you can afford.

Now, it's up to partner to cooperate in taking the tricks to which you are entitled. When partner's king wins the trick, it will be tempting to continue by leading the queen or the jack. This would make it impossible for your side to take the first four tricks. Instead, seeing your encouraging 8, partner must next lead a low card, the 3, over to your ace. Since you are the shorter side, partner wants you to play your high card first. You lead back the 4 and your side quickly has the first four tricks.

## Blocked Suits

It won't always be possible to unblock your sure tricks as in the earlier examples. Suppose we change the previous layout slightly:

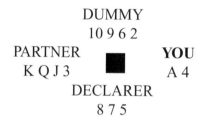

DUMMY
10 9 6 2
PARTNER     YOU
K Q J 3     A 4
DECLARER
8 7 5

As declarer, you would have no trouble taking four tricks in this suit. When partner, with no x-ray vision available, leads the king against a notrump contract, the suit becomes hopelessly blocked. If you play the ace on partner's king, declarer will eventually get a trick with dummy's 10. If you play the 4, partner can lead a low card to your ace, but you have no low cards left to lead back to partner's queen and jack.

After partner's lead of the king, usually the best you can do is to play the 4, to avoid giving declarer a trick in the suit. Although this is a low card and may look like a discouraging signal to partner, you can hope partner recognizes the situation when declarer doesn't win the trick with the ace. If partner now plays the 3 over to your ace, you'll have to try to find an entry to partner's hand in another suit.

Sometimes you can recover from situations similar to this when defending against a suit contract. Consider the following deal:

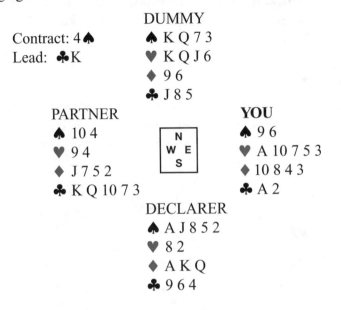

Contract: 4♠
Lead: ♣K

DUMMY
♠ K Q 7 3
♥ K Q J 6
♦ 9 6
♣ J 8 5

PARTNER
♠ 10 4
♥ 9 4
♦ J 7 5 2
♣ K Q 10 7 3

YOU
♠ 9 6
♥ A 10 7 5 3
♦ 10 8 4 3
♣ A 2

DECLARER
♠ A J 8 5 2
♥ 8 2
♦ A K Q
♣ 9 6 4

Partner leads the ♣K against 4♠, and you are faced with a problem. It looks as though your side is entitled to three tricks in clubs as well as the ♥A, enough to defeat the contract. If you play the ♣2 on the first trick, however, the suit is blocked. Even if partner leads a low club over to your ♣A, there's no way to get back to partner's hand. Declarer will eventually be able to discard a club loser and make the contract. If you overtake partner's ♣K with your ♣A, dummy's ♣J could become a winner on the third trick.

Since you're defending a suit contract, however, there's a potential solution to your problem. Partner can lead another club and you can ruff dummy's ♣J. Instead of taking three club tricks, you end up taking two club tricks and a trump trick! Partner will have to recognize why you decided to overtake the ♣K with your ♣A rather than give an encouraging signal. Only partnership cooperation can help you untangle the four sure tricks you started with.

# PROMOTING TRICKS

When the defenders are trying to promote tricks by driving out declarer's high cards, they must be aware of the problem of entries between the two hands.

## More Signaling

Declarer follows the guideline of playing the high card from the short side when promoting tricks. As a defender, you may have to be careful to apply the same principle. In this example, it's on the second round that the suit may become blocked:

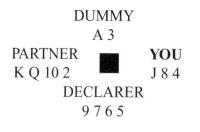

DUMMY
A 3
PARTNER        YOU
K Q 10 2        J 8 4
DECLARER
9 7 6 5

Partner leads the king, top of a broken sequence, against declarer's notrump contract, and the ace is played from dummy. Holding the jack, you give an encouraging signal by playing the 8. If you get the lead next, lead the jack, high card from the short side, and then the 4 over to partner's winners. If partner gets the lead before you do, things will be more difficult but the same principle applies. Based on the encouraging signal, partner must lead the 2 over to your jack. You then lead the 4 back to partner's winners.

Here is a similar situation. This time, you are the defender making the opening lead against a notrump contract. We won't give you the benefit of seeing either partner's or declarer's hand right away.

```
                        DUMMY
Contract: 3NT        ♠ A 9 4
Lead: ♦ 6            ♥ K 8 3
                     ♦ 7 4
                     ♣ Q J 10 6 2
                              YOU
              ┌─────┐      ♠ 8 6 2
              │  N  │      ♥ 7 6 4
              │ W E │      ♦ K 9 8 6 3
              │  S  │      ♣ K 5
              └─────┘
```

You lead the ♦ 6, the ♦ 4 is played from dummy, partner plays the ♦ J, and declarer wins with the ♦ A. Declarer plays a low spade over to dummy's ♠ A and then leads dummy's ♣ Q, taking a finesse. After winning the ♣ K, what do you lead next?

Since the ♦ A has been driven out, your ♦ K is established as a winner. It looks as though partner has the ♦ Q, since declarer won the first trick with the ♦ A. Holding both the ♦ Q and the ♦ J, partner would have played the ♦ J, since third hand plays the lower of touching cards when there is a choice. As you have the length, you want the next trick to be won from the short side. Lead the ♦ 3, expecting partner to have the ♦ Q and hoping partner has another diamond to lead back to your established diamonds.

The complete deal might look like this:

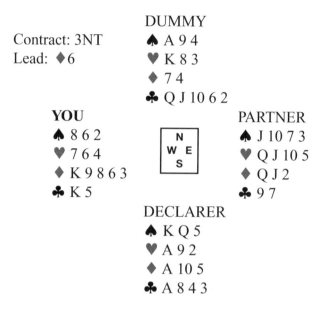

DUMMY
Contract: 3NT       ♠ A 9 4
Lead: ♦ 6           ♥ K 8 3
                    ♦ 7 4
                    ♣ Q J 10 6 2

YOU                                    PARTNER
♠ 8 6 2                                ♠ J 10 7 3
♥ 7 6 4                                ♥ Q J 10 5
♦ K 9 8 6 3                            ♦ Q J 2
♣ K 5                                  ♣ 9 7

DECLARER
♠ K Q 5
♥ A 9 2
♦ A 10 5
♣ A 8 4 3

The play of the diamond suit is the key to the defense. When you get the lead with the ♣K, if you play your ♦K and a diamond to partner's ♦Q, the suit blocks. Your side gets two diamond tricks but partner doesn't have a small card left to get to your winners. It's the play to the second diamond trick that is important. You must lead a low diamond.

## More Unblocking

There are times when you need to unblock on the first trick. For example, consider this layout:

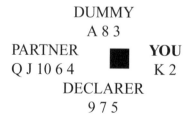

DUMMY
A 8 3
PARTNER          YOU
Q J 10 6 4       K 2
DECLARER
9 7 5

If it were possible to see your hand, partner would lead a small card to your king, planning to play the high card from the short side first. Partner's normal opening lead, however, is the queen. Whether or not declarer plays dummy's ace on the first trick, you must unblock by playing the king. The underlying theme in unblocking is that when partner has the length, you *want to be left with a low card* rather than a high card as your last card in the suit. This idea can be helpful in more complicated situations such as this:

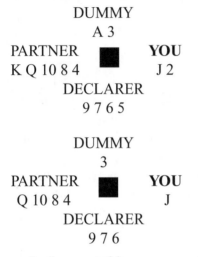

Partner leads the king, top of a broken sequence, against a notrump contract and declarer plays dummy's ace. If you play the 2, the remaining cards will look like this:

If partner next gets the lead for your side, a low card can be played to your jack, but you won't have a low card to return to partner's winners. If you get the lead first and lead the jack, partner can overtake with the queen and play the 10, but declarer's 9 becomes a winner.

Is there anything you can do? Knowing that you generally want to have a low card rather than a high card left when trying to establish partner's long suit, play the jack on the first trick, leaving this layout:

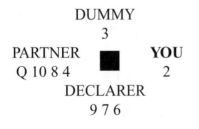

If partner next gets the lead, you're no better off. Declarer's 9 will be established as a trick if the winners in partner's hand are played. The difference arises if you get the next opportunity to lead the suit. When you lead the 2, declarer's 9 is trapped. Whichever card declarer plays, your partner can take all four tricks.

Positions such as this may be difficult to foresee when you are defending. Nonetheless, they become easier to visualize once you are aware that the defenders, like declarer, must try to play the high card from the short side first when promoting tricks.

# ESTABLISHING LONG SUITS

Against notrump contracts the defenders want to take tricks from their long suits just as declarer does. They are faced with the same problems. They have to be willing to lose the lead while establishing their winners, and they have to be aware of the importance of having an entry to get to their established winners.

## Returning Partner's Suit

When trying to establish a long suit, the defenders try to follow the same principles as declarer. That's why guidelines such as *return your partner's suit* can be useful. The defenders want to adopt a consistent approach to the defense. If one partner is trying to establish a long suit, it doesn't help if partner is working at cross-purposes to try to establish another suit. When making the opening lead against a notrump contract, partner has picked a suit to establish. Help partner out by leading that suit back whenever you get the opportunity, unless you can clearly see a better alternative. Here is a typical example:

```
                          DUMMY
        Contract: 3NT     ♠ 10 6 5
        Lead: ♠3          ♥ A 7 2
                          ♦ J 6
                          ♣ A 10 9 7 5
        PARTNER                        YOU
        ♠ A Q 7 3 2       ┌─────┐      ♠ 8 4
        ♥ 6 4             │  N  │      ♥ K Q J 10 3
        ♦ 10 8 5 2        │W   E│      ♦ 9 7 4 3
        ♣ 8 2             │  S  │      ♣ K 4
                          └─────┘
                          DECLARER
                          ♠ K J 9
                          ♥ 9 8 5
                          ♦ A K Q
                          ♣ Q J 6 3
```

On partner's lead of the ♠3, the ♠5 is played from dummy, you play third hand high, the ♠8, and declarer wins the trick with the ♠9. Then declarer plays the ♣Q, taking a finesse which loses to your ♣K. You may have been a little disappointed to see partner's opening lead since you have such a fine heart suit. If partner had originally led a heart, you could have established four heart tricks, enough for you to defeat the contract when you won the ♣K. It may occur to you to lead a heart now, establishing four heart tricks for the defense, but this would be inconsistent with partner's line of defense. Instead, return the ♠4, partner's suit, hoping the layout is something like that on the actual deal. The spade return is the only way to defeat the contract. If you lead a heart, declarer will win the ♥A and end up with nine tricks.

When returning partner's suit, look at the **remaining** cards you hold in that suit and return the card that you would normally have led: top of a doubleton; top of touching high cards; or low from three or more cards (*e.g., J–4, 9–4–2, 10–9–5, Q–6–3*).

## Ducking

Consider how declarer would play the following suit with no entries to dummy other than the high cards in the suit:

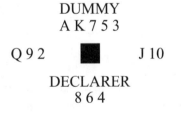

DUMMY
A K 7 5 3

Q 9 2          J 10

DECLARER
8 6 4

If declarer played the ace and the king and then gave up a trick, the remaining two cards in dummy would be established as winners but would be stranded. Instead, declarer must *duck* either the first or second trick, keeping a high card in dummy as an entry. Declarer takes the losses early to retain communication between the two hands.

The defenders must employ similar tactics on the following deal. Declarer is in a contract of 3NT after you have opened the bidding 1♠. Partner dutifully leads your suit, the ♠10, top of a doubleton:

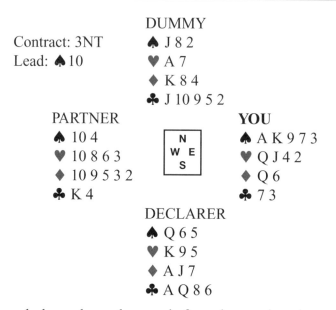

DUMMY
Contract: 3NT    ♠ J 8 2
Lead: ♠ 10       ♥ A 7
                 ♦ K 8 4
                 ♣ J 10 9 5 2

PARTNER                          YOU
♠ 10 4                           ♠ A K 9 7 3
♥ 10 8 6 3                       ♥ Q J 4 2
♦ 10 9 5 3 2                     ♦ Q 6
♣ K 4                            ♣ 7 3

DECLARER
♠ Q 6 5
♥ K 9 5
♦ A J 7
♣ A Q 8 6

When declarer plays a low spade from dummy, here is your chance to shine by playing low. If you win the trick with the ♠K and play the ♠A and another spade, you'll establish two more winners in the spade suit. Unfortunately, they'll be stranded, since it's unlikely you can gain the lead and partner has no spades left to lead. Instead, take your losses early and duck the first spade trick. You're hoping partner will get the lead and have a spade left to lead to your established winners. You can play the ♠9 as an encouraging signal to partner to lead the suit again given the opportunity. Declarer wins the trick with the ♠Q, plays a low heart to dummy's ♥A and tries the club finesse by leading the ♣J from dummy, hoping you have the ♣K. Unluckily for declarer, your partner wins the trick with the ♣K and is now able to lead the ♠4 over to your spade winners. You always had to lose one spade trick. By choosing to lose it early, partner was left with a spade to return to your winners.

The need to let declarer win tricks while establishing your long suit often arises when defending a contract. Consider the following deal. Again you are defending 3NT. This time, partner is on lead and leads fourth highest from the longest suit in the hand, the ♥4:

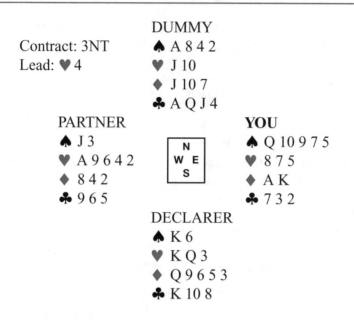

Contract: 3NT
Lead: ♥ 4

DUMMY
♠ A 8 4 2
♥ J 10
♦ J 10 7
♣ A Q J 4

PARTNER
♠ J 3
♥ A 9 6 4 2
♦ 8 4 2
♣ 9 6 5

YOU
♠ Q 10 9 7 5
♥ 8 7 5
♦ A K
♣ 7 3 2

DECLARER
♠ K 6
♥ K Q 3
♦ Q 9 6 5 3
♣ K 10 8

Declarer wins the first trick with dummy's ♥ 10 and, needing to promote tricks in the diamond suit to make the contract, leads dummy's ♦ J, which you win with the ♦ K. You return partner's suit. Declarer plays the ♥ Q, and now it's partner's turn to stop and think. Partner knows declarer has the ♥ K since you would have played that card earlier if you held it. If partner wins the ♥ A and leads another heart, your last heart disappears. Partner's remaining hearts will be established as winners, but there will be no entry to play them. Partner must duck the heart trick, giving declarer a second trick in the suit. When declarer leads another diamond to drive out your ♦ A, you'll still have a small heart to lead back. Partner wins declarer's ♥ K with the ♥ A and can now take the other two established heart winners to defeat the contract.

Notice that both defenders have to be on their toes to defeat the contract. You must continue to return partner's suit, even though declarer wins the first two heart tricks. Partner must recognize the need to duck a heart trick to preserve communication between the defenders' hands. Notice also how both defenders must be careful to hang on to all of their low hearts. If declarer took four club tricks before playing diamonds, neither defender could afford to discard a heart.

## FINESSING

The defenders trap declarer's high cards using the principle of the *finesse* in the same way that declarer traps their high cards. The defenders have to visualize where there is an opportunity to finesse based on the cards they can see and partner's signals.

### Partnership Cooperation

Let's consider how the defenders approach a finesse. You're defending against a suit contract and partner leads the ace:

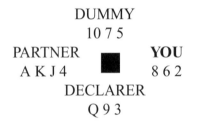

DUMMY
10 7 5
PARTNER     YOU
A K J 4    8 6 2
DECLARER
Q 9 3

If partner continues by leading the king, declarer's queen will become established as a winner. First you must make use of an attitude signal and discourage partner by playing your lowest card, the 2. Partner has to recognize this as a discouraging signal and refrain from continuing to lead the suit. Instead, partner will have to *shift* to another suit, hoping to find an entry to your hand. When you do get the lead, you must cooperate by leading the original suit back, recognizing why partner did not continue leading it.

Notice declarer wouldn't have the same problem deciding how to play such a combination. Looking at both hands, declarer would see the need to lead the suit from your hand in order to trap the missing queen. The defenders have to work a lot harder to bring about the same result.

Let's see how it might look in practice, this time putting you on lead:

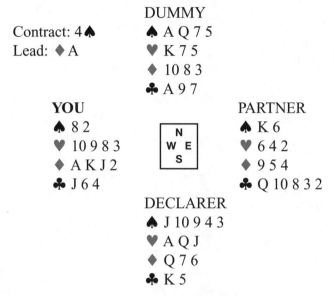

DUMMY
Contract: 4♠
Lead: ♦ A
♠ A Q 7 5
♥ K 7 5
♦ 10 8 3
♣ A 9 7

YOU
♠ 8 2
♥ 10 9 8 3
♦ A K J 2
♣ J 6 4

PARTNER
♠ K 6
♥ 6 4 2
♦ 9 5 4
♣ Q 10 8 3 2

DECLARER
♠ J 10 9 4 3
♥ A Q J
♦ Q 7 6
♣ K 5

Against 4♠, you lead the ♦ A and partner plays the ♦ 4. Since you can see the ♦ 2 in your hand and the ♦ 3 in dummy, you know partner has played the lowest diamond out, a discouraging signal. It looks as if declarer must have the ♦ Q. Since you want diamonds led from partner's side in order to trap declarer's ♦ Q, you must be patient and switch to another suit. Your partner's ♦ 4 is only an attitude signal, not a suit preference signal, so you haven't had a chance to find out which of the other suits partner prefers. It's up to you to decide by looking at the dummy and gathering any useful information from the bidding. On this deal, it turns out that it doesn't make much difference, as long as you don't lead another diamond. Suppose you switch to the ♥ 10. Declarer will win in hand and take the spade finesse, hoping you have the ♠K. Partner will win this trick. Now it's up to partner to recognize why you didn't continue leading diamonds and visualize the type of holding you must have. Diamonds must be led from partner's side, so partner cooperates and leads back a diamond. Your patience is rewarded when you get two more diamond tricks to defeat the contract.

Here is a similar type of situation defending against a notrump contract:

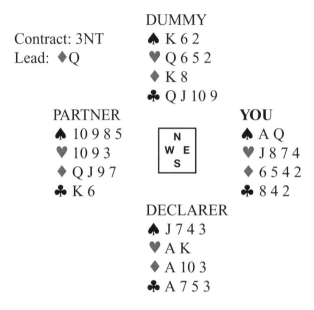

DUMMY
Contract: 3NT     ♠ K 6 2
Lead: ♦Q          ♥ Q 6 5 2
                  ♦ K 8
                  ♣ Q J 10 9

PARTNER                        YOU
♠ 10 9 8 5                     ♠ A Q
♥ 10 9 3                       ♥ J 8 7 4
♦ Q J 9 7                      ♦ 6 5 4 2
♣ K 6                          ♣ 8 4 2

DECLARER
♠ J 7 4 3
♥ A K
♦ A 10 3
♣ A 7 5 3

Partner leads the ♦Q, top of a broken sequence, and declarer wins the first trick with dummy's ♦K, carefully keeping the ♦A and the ♦10 in hand. Since you don't have any help in the diamond suit, play a discouraging card, the ♦2. Next declarer leads dummy's ♣Q and takes a finesse, losing to partner's ♣K. Partner knows declarer holds the ♦A, since you would have won the first trick if you held that card. What partner wants to know is who holds the ♦10? Having led from a suit headed by the ♦Q and the ♦J, partner has to hope you would recognize the importance of the ♦10. If you held it, you would have given an encouraging signal rather than a discouraging signal. Partner, therefore, correctly assumes declarer holds the ♦10 and concludes that it would be unsafe to lead the suit again. Instead, partner must patiently switch to another suit.

On the actual deal, it doesn't matter which suit other than a diamond partner leads next. Let's suppose partner leads a spade, and you win the trick with the ♠Q after declarer plays a low spade from dummy. Things are back in your ballpark. Instead of happily taking your ♠A as well, you must ask yourself why partner didn't continue leading diamonds from a suit headed by the queen and the jack. Once you are able to visualize the potential problem, you can switch back to diamonds from your side, trapping declarer's ♦ 10. Now the defense can establish two diamond tricks to go along with their two spade tricks and their club trick.

## Leading through Strength

Another useful guideline to help the defenders visualize finessing situations is *lead through strength and lead up to weakness.* The logic behind the guideline comes from an examination of the following layout:

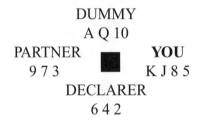

DUMMY
A Q 10
PARTNER ... YOU
9 7 3 ... K J 8 5
DECLARER
6 4 2

For the defenders to get all of the tricks to which they are entitled, partner needs to lead through dummy's strength, trapping dummy's high cards. At the same time, partner would also be leading up to the weakness in declarer's hand. Contrast this with what would happen if you lead the suit. You would be leading through declarer's weakness and up to the strength in the dummy, not an effective way to try for tricks in the suit.

Let's look at a deal:

|                  | DUMMY        |                |
|------------------|--------------|----------------|
| Contract: 2 ♥    | ♠ K 6 3      |                |
| Lead: ♦ A        | ♥ A K J 5    |                |
|                  | ♦ Q J 7 4    |                |
|                  | ♣ 9 5        |                |

| YOU          |         | PARTNER        |
|--------------|---------|----------------|
| ♠ 10 9 7     | N       | ♠ A Q J 8      |
| ♥ 8 4 3      | W   E   | ♥ 9 7          |
| ♦ A K 9 5    | S       | ♦ 10 6 2       |
| ♣ K 8 4      |         | ♣ 10 7 3 2     |

|         | DECLARER     |
|---------|--------------|
|         | ♠ 5 4 2      |
|         | ♥ Q 10 6 2   |
|         | ♦ 8 3        |
|         | ♣ A Q J 6    |

Against 2 ♥, you start off leading the ♦ A and get a discouraging signal of the ♦ 2 from partner. It doesn't do any good to lead another diamond — you would only be helping declarer by establishing dummy's ♦ Q and ♦ J as winners. Which suit should you switch to? Although you have some strength in clubs and not much in spades, you might use the guideline to help you. You want to lead through dummy's strength in spades, up to declarer's assumed weakness in the suit, rather than leading through dummy's weakness in clubs up to declarer's assumed strength. You don't actually know what declarer has in spades and clubs, but you can see your hand and the dummy. With that information, you can try to imagine what declarer and partner might hold. On the actual deal, the defense can defeat the contract if you switch to a spade. Dummy's ♠ K would be trapped and partner can take three spade tricks. Partner can cooperate after winning the spade tricks by leading clubs, through declarer's assumed strength, up to the weakness in dummy. You'll get a trick with the ♣ K to go with the three spade tricks and two diamond tricks, just enough to defeat the contract.

Here is a similar example:

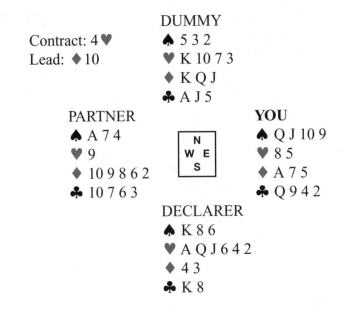

DUMMY

Contract: 4 ♥        ♠ 5 3 2

Lead: ♦ 10        ♥ K 10 7 3

♦ K Q J

♣ A J 5

PARTNER        YOU

♠ A 7 4        ♠ Q J 10 9

♥ 9        ♥ 8 5

♦ 10 9 8 6 2        ♦ A 7 5

♣ 10 7 6 3        ♣ Q 9 4 2

DECLARER

♠ K 8 6

♥ A Q J 6 4 2

♦ 4 3

♣ K 8

Partner leads the top of a diamond sequence against 4 ♥ and you win with the ♦ A. Although your first consideration is to return partner's suit, you can see that dummy has nothing but winners in that suit. Instead, you want to switch to a suit that will help your side take tricks. The spade weakness and club strength in dummy convince you to switch to a spade, through declarer's assumed strength and up to dummy's weakness. You lead back the ♠ Q and declarer's ♠ K is trapped. The defense takes three spade tricks to defeat the contract. Spades have to be led from your side, not partner's, to trap declarer's ♠ K.

# RUFFING

The defenders also take tricks in a suit contract by ruffing declarer's winners when they get the opportunity. This is similar to the way declarer ruffs losers in dummy.

## Giving Partner a Ruff

Take a look at the following deal:

```
                        DUMMY
Contract: 2♠            ♠ 9 7 5 4
Lead: ♥A                ♥ J 7 4
                        ♦ A K 10
                        ♣ 9 6 4
        YOU                             PARTNER
        ♠ 6 3          ┌─────┐          ♠ J 8
        ♥ A K 8 3      │  N  │          ♥ 10 6
        ♦ 9 6 4        │W   E│          ♦ Q 8 7 3 2
        ♣ A 10 8 5     │  S  │          ♣ Q J 3 2
                       └─────┘
                        DECLARER
                        ♠ A K Q 10 2
                        ♥ Q 9 5 2
                        ♦ J 5
                        ♣ K 7
```

We've seen examples in previous lessons of how defenders can get ruffs. It's a combination of recognizing the possibility and making appropriate use of defensive signals. This is another example:

You lead the ♥A against 2♠ and partner cooperates by playing an encouraging ♥10. At this point, you don't know why partner is giving you an encouraging signal. Partner may want to ruff or may hold the ♥Q. In either case, you can continue with the ♥K and another heart.

Which heart do you lead on the third round? Since you don't need to show attitude or count in this situation, the heart you choose to play should be a suit preference signal. Holding the ♣A, you prefer clubs to diamonds and therefore play the ♥3 rather than the ♥8. It turns out that partner can ruff the third round. Now it's up to partner who should interpret your ♥3 as suit preference for clubs. Even if partner isn't sure, the guideline of leading through strength and up to weakness dictates a club return rather than a diamond. Visualizing the situation, partner can lead back the ♣Q to trap declarer's ♣K. It wouldn't do any harm if you held the ♣K and declarer the ♣A instead of the actual layout.

When you win the ♣A, it's time for you to do some thinking. Both you and declarer still have one heart left while there are no hearts in either partner's hand or the dummy. Although dummy can ruff hearts, you should lead another heart anyway, hoping that partner can *overruff* if declarer ruffs the heart in dummy. This proves to be the case. When you lead your remaining ♥8, declarer can ruff with dummy's ♠9, but partner can overruff with the ♠J to win the trick. The defense ends up with two heart tricks, two club tricks, and the two spade tricks from partner's trumps.

## Getting a Ruff

You must always be alert to the possibility of using your trumps to ruff one of declarer's winners. Take a look at the following deal where the defense must be on its toes to defeat the contract:

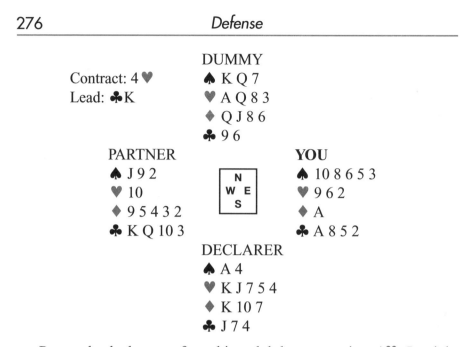

Contract: 4 ♥
Lead: ♣K

DUMMY
♠ K Q 7
♥ A Q 8 3
♦ Q J 8 6
♣ 9 6

PARTNER
♠ J 9 2
♥ 10
♦ 9 5 4 3 2
♣ K Q 10 3

YOU
♠ 10 8 6 5 3
♥ 9 6 2
♦ A
♣ A 8 5 2

DECLARER
♠ A 4
♥ K J 7 5 4
♦ K 10 7
♣ J 7 4

Partner leads the top of touching club honors against 4 ♥. It might seem natural for you to encourage with the ♣8 since you have the ♣A. However, before doing so, you should be deciding on your plan to defeat the contract. It looks as if you have two club tricks and the ♦ A. Where's the fourth defensive trick going to come from? With the singleton ♦ A, there's an opportunity for a defensive ruff, but how can you get partner to cooperate? You might try playing a discouraging ♣2 on the first trick, hoping that partner will switch to a diamond. You can then win the ♦ A, get back to partner's hand by leading a club to the ♣Q and partner can lead another diamond for you to ruff. Partner might figure it all out, but is partner really going to know to lead a diamond rather than a spade if you make a discouraging signal in clubs?

Instead, take matters into your own hands since you can see what needs to be done. Overtake partner's ♣K with your ♣A and play your singleton ♦A. Now lead a club back to partner's ♣Q. Partner, realizing why you have gone to all of this trouble, should cooperate by leading another diamond for you to ruff. Difficult perhaps, but not so hard once you have considered the possibility of ruffing declarer's winners in combination with the knowledge that partner has the ♣Q when leading the ♣K.

# BIDDING REVIEW

When the opponents have opened the bidding, you can compete by making an overcall or a takeout double. When you make an overcall, you're suggesting the suit for your side. When you make a takeout double, you're asking partner to choose the suit.

## Making an Overcall

When the opponents have started the auction, use the following guidelines to decide whether or not to make an overcall:

### Requirements for an Overcall in a Suit

- A five-card or longer suit.
- 13 or more points (less with a good suit if non-vulnerable and at the one level).

### Requirements for a 1NT Overcall

- 16 to 18 points.
- Balanced hand.
- Some strength in the opponent's suit.

## Responding to an Overcall

If partner overcalls 1NT, use the same responses as when partner opens 1NT. If partner overcalls in a suit, use the following guideline:

*With a minimum hand (6 to 10 points):*

- Pass if already at the two level.
- Raise partner's suit to the two level with three-card or longer support.
- Bid a new suit at the one level.
- Bid 1NT with some strength in the opponent's suit and a balanced hand.

*Strong hand - Dbl - then bid suit 2xto*

*With a medium hand (11 or 12 points):*

- Raise partner's suit to the three level with three-card or longer support.
- Bid a new suit (even if it is at the two level).
- Bid 2NT with some strength in the opponent's suit and a balanced hand.

*With a maximum hand (13 or more points):*

- Raise partner's suit to game with three-card or longer support.
- Bid a new suit.
- Bid 3NT with some strength in the opponent's suit and a balanced hand.

## Making a Takeout Double

Another way to compete is by making a takeout double. You can tell whether a double is for takeout or penalty as follows:

- If neither partner has bid anything except pass and the opponents' contract is a partscore, double is for takeout.
- If either partner has bid or the contract is game, the double is for penalty.

## Requirements for a Takeout Double

- 13 or more points (counting dummy points).
- Support for the unbid suits.

*Shortness in opponents suit*

*add in distribution*

## Responding to a Takeout Double

Responder must not pass partner's takeout double unless the right-hand opponent bids. Choose a response using the following guideline:

*With a minimum hand (0 to 10 points):*

- Bid a four-card or longer major suit at the cheapest level.
- Bid a four-card or longer minor suit at the cheapest level.
- Bid 1NT.

*With a medium hand (11 or 12 points):*

- Jump in a four-card or longer major suit
- Jump in a four-card or longer minor suit
- Jump to 2NT

*With a maximum hand (13 or more points):*

- Jump to game in a four-card or longer major suit
- Jump to 3NT

## Rebids by the Takeout Doubler

Having made a takeout double, don't bid again unless partner shows more than a minimum hand or you have more than a minimum hand. Use the following guideline:

*With a minimum hand (13 to 16 points):*

- Pass if partner bids at the cheapest level.
- Pass with 13 or 14 points if partner jumps a level. Bid game with 15 or 16 points if partner jumps.

With a medium hand (17 or 18 points):

- Raise one level if partner bids at the cheapest level.
- Bid game if partner jumps a level.

With a maximum hand (19 t o 21 points):

- Jump raise if partner bids at the cheapest level.
- Bid game if partner jumps a level.

# PLAY OF THE HAND REVIEW

An entry is a way of getting from one hand to the other. As declarer, you must be careful to watch for entries between your hand and the dummy when making your PLAN. You need entries to take finesses, get to your winners, and so on.

## Preserving an Entry

One way to preserve entries is by playing the high card from the short side first when taking sure tricks or promoting winners. For example:

|               |                                                                                          |
| ------------- | ---------------------------------------------------------------------------------------- |
| DUMMY         | It's straightforward to take your four                                                   |
| A K J 2       | sure tricks in this suit if you win the                                                  |
| ■             | first trick with the queen. You then have the 4 left in your hand to lead to             |
| DECLARER      | dummy's winners. If you win the first                                                    |
| Q 4           | trick with a high card in dummy, you create an entry problem. You can't                  |

play another high card from dummy since your queen will have to be played on the same trick. If you lead the 2 over to your queen, dummy's last two winners are stranded unless you have an entry to dummy in another suit. Even if you *do* have an outside entry to dummy, it may be needed for something more important than untangling this suit. Notice how much more difficult it is for the defenders to take their tricks in this suit — they can't see each other's hand.

Don't confuse playing the high card from the short side with this situation:

|               |                                                                                          |
| ------------- | ---------------------------------------------------------------------------------------- |
| DUMMY         | You have only two sure tricks and can                                                    |
| K 7 3         | take them in any order. This type of                                                     |
| ■             | suit can be used for entry purposes. When making your PLAN, look to see                  |
| DECLARER      | how these entries can best be put to                                                     |
| A 8           | use.                                                                                     |

Another way of preserving entries is by taking your losses early and ducking tricks to the opponents when necessary, as in this type of situation:

DUMMY

K 8 6 4 2

DECLARER

A 9 5

If the king is your only entry to dummy, you can't afford to play it too soon if you are trying to establish winners in this suit. Either play the ace and then duck a trick to the opponents or duck the first trick completely. If the missing cards divide 3-2, the suit is established and there is still an entry left to dummy.

## Creating an Entry

You may have to create your own entry when there is none readily available. For example, in this layout, you can create a sure entry to the dummy through promotion:

DUMMY

K Q

DECLARER

7 5

When you lead this suit, the defenders can't prevent you from getting to dummy, whether or not they win the first trick. On the other hand, the entry will not be so sure in this layout:

DUMMY

K 8 3

DECLARER

7 5 2

The best you can do is to lead toward dummy, hoping the ace is on your left — a 50-50 chance. If you held the queen in your hand, you could try leading it first. You hope that one of the opponents will play the ace, making the king a sure entry. If they can see what you are trying to do, however, they may not cooperate.

Another way to create entries is through your long suits. Consider this layout:

DUMMY

7 6 5 2

DECLARER

A K Q 3

If the missing cards are divided 3-2, you have an entry to dummy in this suit. After playing the ace, the king, and the queen to eliminate the opponents' cards, you can play your 3 over to dummy — provided you kept a higher card in the dummy than the 2!

In a suit contract, your trump suit is often the longest suit in the combined hands and may provide a good source of entries between the two hands. When making your PLAN, decide how you want to play the trump suit to make the best use of your entries.

# SUMMARY

The defenders want to develop and take their tricks using the same techniques as declarer. They are hampered by not being able to see their combined holdings in each suit. However, the defenders can overcome much of this disadvantage through the use of signals and by trying to visualize the layout of a suit based on the auction and the way the play has gone.

When taking their winners, the defenders must be careful not to block a suit when it's unevenly divided between the two hands. The hand with the fewer cards needs to have a low card, rather than a high card, as the last card left in the suit. One defender may have to unblock the suit by overtaking partner's high card. At other times, a defender may have to lead a low card to partner's winner(s) in the short hand before taking the winners in the long hand.

The defenders must also try to maintain communication between the two hands when developing tricks. They may have to take their losses early by ducking a trick to keep an entry to the long suit and to avoid stranding their winners.

The defenders must cooperate to take finesses and trap declarer's and dummy's high cards. Each defender must try to visualize the layout of the suit to see the possibility of trapping high cards. A useful guideline is **lead through strength and lead up to weakness.** By leading through the high cards held on your left and up to the low cards held on your right, you give partner a chance to get tricks with high cards when they are favorably placed.

## Exercise One — Taking Sure Tricks

In each of the following layouts, which card would your partner lead against a notrump contract? How would you work with partner to take all of your sure tricks in the suit?

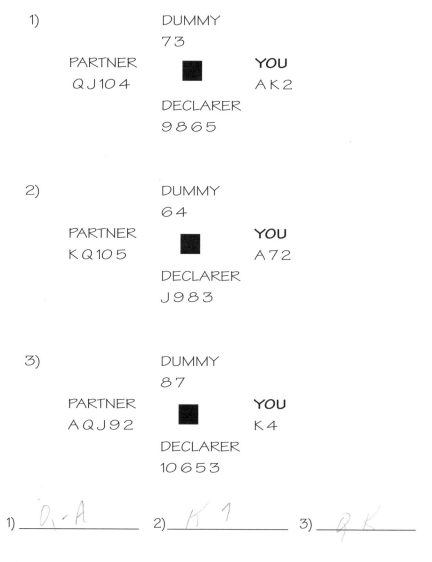

1)
DUMMY
7 3

PARTNER                 YOU
Q J 10 4                 A K 2

DECLARER
9 8 6 5

2)
DUMMY
6 4

PARTNER                 YOU
K Q 10 5                 A 7 2

DECLARER
J 9 8 3

3)
DUMMY
8 7

PARTNER                 YOU
A Q J 9 2                K 4

DECLARER
10 6 5 3

1) _____Q - A_____    2) ___K 7___    3) ___Q K___

**Exercise One** — Taking Sure Tricks

1) Partner would lead the queen and you would overtake with your ace or king. Then you lead your other honor followed by a low card.

2) Partner would lead the king and you would encourage with the 7.

3) Partner would lead the queen and you would overtake with the king and lead back the 4.

## Exercise Two — Promoting Tricks

You're defending a notrump contract and lead the indicated card. Which card will partner play on the first trick (a)? If declarer wins the first trick with the ace, which card in the suit will you lead next when you regain the lead (b)? Why?

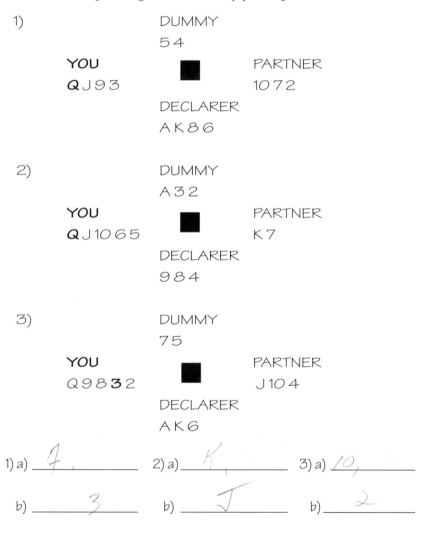

1)

          DUMMY
          5 4
YOU                      PARTNER
Q J 9 3                  10 7 2
          DECLARER
          A K 8 6

2)

          DUMMY
          A 3 2
YOU                      PARTNER
Q J 10 6 5               K 7
          DECLARER
          9 8 4

3)

          DUMMY
          7 5
YOU                      PARTNER
Q 9 8 3 2                J 10 4
          DECLARER
          A K 6

1) a) _____ Q , _____    2) a) _____ K , _____    3) a) _____ 10 , _____

b) _____ 3 _____         b) _____ J _____         b) _____ 2 _____

**Exercise Two** — Promoting Tricks

1) a) The 7 to encourage.

b) You return the 3 so that partner can play the high card and still have a card to lead back to your winners.

2) a) The king.

b) You return one of your high cards, the jack or the 10, and take the rest of the tricks in the suit.

3) a) The lower of equal cards, the 10.

b) You play a low card, the 2, when you next gain the lead.

## Exercise Three — Establishing Long Suits

You're defending a notrump contract and partner leads the indicated card in a suit you've bid. If you don't have any entries in an outside suit, which card do you play on the first trick (a)? Which card do you play the second time the suit is led (b)?

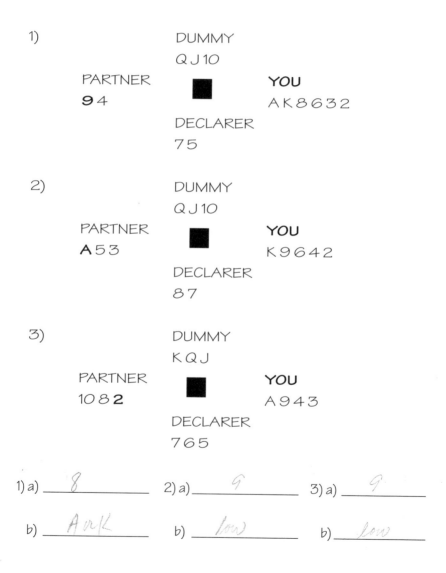

1)

DUMMY
Q J 10

PARTNER
9 4

YOU
A K 8 6 3 2

DECLARER
7 5

2)

DUMMY
Q J 10

PARTNER
A 5 3

YOU
K 9 6 4 2

DECLARER
8 7

3)

DUMMY
K Q J

PARTNER
10 8 2

YOU
A 9 4 3

DECLARER
7 6 5

1) a) _____8_____     2) a) _____9_____     3) a) _____9_____

   b) ___A n K___      b) ___low___      b) ___low___

## Exercise Three — Establishing Long Suits

1) a) The 8, ducking the first trick.

   b) The next time you get the lead, play the high cards and take the rest of the tricks.

2) a) The 9 to encourage.

   b) When partner leads the suit again, duck (play a low card) to preserve the entry to your long suit.

3) a) The 9 to encourage when your partner leads the suit.

   b) Duck the next trick and eventually take the ace and one other trick.

## Exercise Four — The Defensive Finesse

Which card would you lead against a suit contract in each of the following layouts (a)? Which card would partner play to the first trick if a low card is played from dummy (b)? Which defender must lead the suit next if the defenders are to take all of the tricks to which they are entitled (c)?

1)
```
              DUMMY
              A 5 4
YOU                      PARTNER
K Q 10        ■          8 7 6 2
              DECLARER
              J 9 3
```

2)
```
              DUMMY
              7 3 2
YOU                      PARTNER
Q J 9 5       ■          8 6 4
              DECLARER
              A K 10
```

3)
```
              DUMMY
              K 6 5
YOU                      PARTNER
Q J 10 7      ■          A 8 3
              DECLARER
              9 4 2
```

1) a) _____K_____   2) a) _____Q_____   3) a) _____Q_____

   b) _____2_____      b) _____4_____      b) _____8_____

   c) ___partner___    c) ___partner___    c) _____you_____

**Exercise Four** — The Defensive Finesse

1) a) The king.

   b) Partner will discourage with the 2.

   c) When gaining the lead, however, partner should return the suit so that your queen and 10 are in a position to trap the jack.

2) a) The queen, top of a broken sequence.

   b) Partner discourages.

   c) You want partner to return the suit in order to trap declarer's 10.

3) a) The queen.

   b) Partner can encourage with the 8.

   c) You can lead the suit again and dummy's king is trapped.

## Exercise Five — Leading through Strength

In each of the following layouts, who has to lead the suit, you or your partner, in order for the defenders to get all of the tricks to which they are entitled?

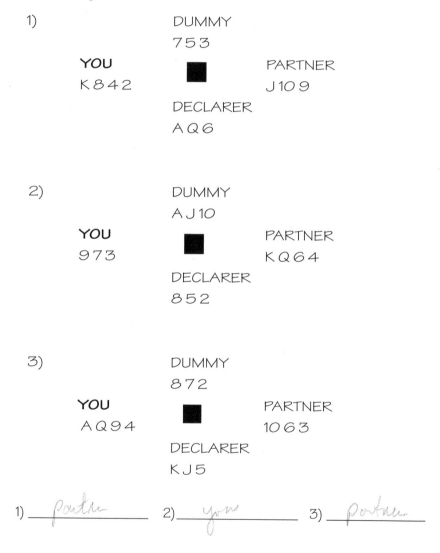

1)

DUMMY
753

YOU
K 8 4 2

PARTNER
J 10 9

DECLARER
A Q 6

2)

DUMMY
A J 10

YOU
9 7 3

PARTNER
K Q 6 4

DECLARER
8 5 2

3)

DUMMY
8 7 2

YOU
A Q 9 4

PARTNER
10 6 3

DECLARER
K J 5

1) _partner_    2) _you_    3) _partner_

**Exercise Five** — Leading through Strength

1) Partner.

2) You.

3) Partner.

## Exercise Six — Trumping Declarer's Winners

On each of the following deals, how will the defenders cooperate to defeat 4♠ after the opening lead of the ♦ 3?

1)

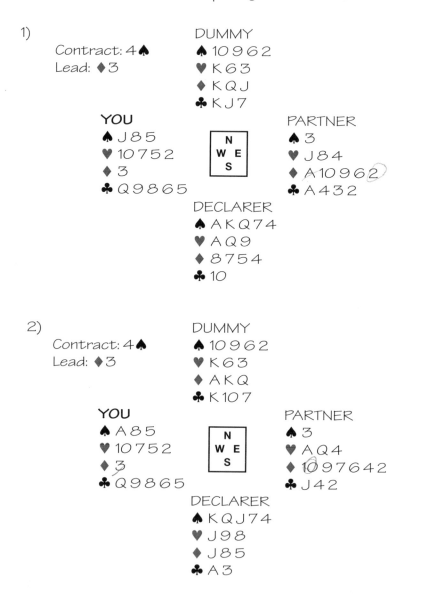

Contract: 4♠
Lead: ♦3

**DUMMY**
♠ 10 9 6 2
♥ K 6 3
♦ K Q J
♣ K J 7

**YOU**
♠ J 8 5
♥ 10 7 5 2
♦ 3
♣ Q 9 8 6 5

N
W   E
S

**PARTNER**
♠ 3
♥ J 8 4
♦ A 10 9 6 2
♣ A 4 3 2

**DECLARER**
♠ A K Q 7 4
♥ A Q 9
♦ 8 7 5 4
♣ 10

2)

Contract: 4♠
Lead: ♦3

**DUMMY**
♠ 10 9 6 2
♥ K 6 3
♦ A K Q
♣ K 10 7

**YOU**
♠ A 8 5
♥ 10 7 5 2
♦ 3
♣ Q 9 8 6 5

N
W   E
S

**PARTNER**
♠ 3
♥ A Q 4
♦ 10 9 7 6 4 2
♣ J 4 2

**DECLARER**
♠ K Q J 7 4
♥ J 9 8
♦ J 8 5
♣ A 3

## Exercise Six — Trumping Declarer's Winners

1) East takes the first trick with the ♦ A and returns the ♦ 2 showing a preference for clubs. After ruffing the diamond, West leads back a club and East gives West a second ruff.

2) East plays the 10, a suit preference signal for hearts. When gaining the lead, West plays a heart. East wins and returns a diamond for West to ruff. West leads a second heart, and East wins and leads another diamond for West to ruff.

## Exercise Seven — Review of Competitive Bidding

The opponent on your right opens the bidding 1♥. What do you call with each of the following hands?

1) ♠ K Q 10 8 6 2    2) ♠ Q 10 8 3    3) ♠ 5 4
    ♥ J 3      *11*     ♥ 2       *13*     ♥ 7       *13*
    ♦ A J 4           ♦ A Q 10 3      ♦ A J 10 6 3
    ♣ 9 2             ♣ K Q 7 5       ♣ A K J 7 5

1) ___*1 S*___     2) ___*D*___     3) ___*2 D*___

4) ♠ J 3          5) ♠ K 7 6 3     6) ♠ 8 3
 *11* ♥ K Q 5     *10* ♥ —         *13* ♥ A Q J 9 3
    ♦ K Q J 9        ♦ A 9 7 5 2      ♦ 8 5 2
    ♣ A J 9 2        ♣ K J 9 3       ♣ A K 5

4) ___*1 NT*___     5) ___*D*___     6) ___*Pass*___

7) ♠ Q 9 3       8) ♠ A J 9 2     9) ♠ J 4
 *10* ♥ Q J 8       ♥ 8 3      *13* ♥ A J 10
    ♦ J 8 7 4 3      ♦ A 8 5 4     *16* ♦ Q J 10 8 3
    ♣ A 7           ♣ A 6 5        ♣ A Q J

7) ___*Pass*___     8) ___*Double*___     9) ___*1 NT*___

---

## Answers to Exercise

## Exercise Seven — Review of Competitive Bidding

    1) 1♠        2) Double      3) 2♦

    4) 1NT      5) Double      6) Pass

    7) Pass      8) Double      9) 1NT

**Exercise Eight** — Watching Your Entries

How many sure entries to the dummy can you get from each of the following suits (a)? How many entries might you get if the missing cards are favorably placed (b)?

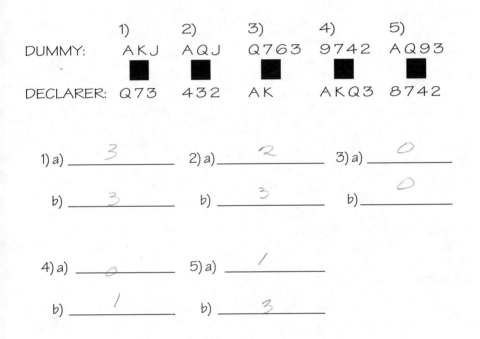

|  | 1) | 2) | 3) | 4) | 5) |
|---|---|---|---|---|---|
| DUMMY: | A K J | A Q J | Q 7 6 3 | 9 7 4 2 | A Q 9 3 |
| DECLARER: | Q 7 3 | 4 3 2 | A K | A K Q 3 | 8 7 4 2 |

1) a) _____3_____   2) a) _____2_____   3) a) _____0_____

   b) _____3_____      b) _____3_____      b) _____0_____

4) a) _____0_____   5) a) _____1_____

   b) _____1_____      b) _____3_____

---

**Answers to Exercise**

**Exercise Eight** — Watching Your Entries

1) a) 3      2) a) 2      3) a) 0      4) a) 0      5) a) 1

   b) 3         b) 3         b) 0         b) 1         b) 3

## Exercise Nine — Taking Tricks
### (E-Z Deal Cards: #6, Hand 1 — Dealer, North)

Turn up the cards from the first pre-dealt deal. Put each hand dummy-style at the edge of the table in front of each player.

### The Bidding

What would North open the bidding? How can East compete in the auction? South passes. West knows that partner has approximately the values for an opening bid to overcall at the two level. At what level does the partnership belong? What Golden Game does West bid? How does the auction proceed from there? Who is the declarer?

Dealer:   ♠ K 10 7 5 3   *13*
North   ♥ J 6 4
        ♦ K Q 9
        ♣ A 8

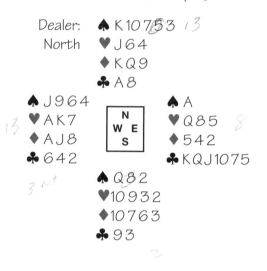

♠ J 9 6 4           ♠ A
♥ A K 7            ♥ Q 8 5   *8*
♦ A J 8            ♦ 5 4 2
♣ 6 4 2           ♣ K Q J 10 7 5

*13*

♠ Q 8 2
♥ 10 9 3 2
♦ 10 7 6 3
♣ 9 3

*3 N+*

### The Defense

Which player makes the opening lead? What would the opening lead be? Which card would South play on the first trick? Why? How will this help North?

### The Play

Review the steps in declarer's PLAN. How does declarer plan to make the contract?

## Exercise Nine — Taking Tricks

### The Bidding

- North would open the bidding 1♠.
- East overcalls 2♣.
- West knows the partnership belongs in a game and bids 3NT.
- All players pass. West is the declarer in 3NT.

### The Defense

- North makes the opening lead of the ♠5.
- South plays the ♠8 to give an encouraging signal.
- When regaining the lead, North can lead a low spade to South's ♠Q.

### The Play

- Declarer needs nine tricks and has five sure winners. More than enough tricks can be developed in the club suit through promotion — if the opponents don't take too many spade tricks before declarer has a chance to develop these tricks.

# Exercise Ten — Maintaining Communications
## (E-Z Deal Cards: #6, Hand 2 — Dealer, East)

Turn up the cards from the second pre-dealt deal. Put each hand dummy-style at the edge of the table in front of each player.

### The Bidding

East and South pass. What would West open the bidding? How can North describe this hand? East passes. What does South respond to partner's overcall? How does the bidding proceed? What is the contract? Who is the declarer?

### The Defense

Which player makes the opening lead? What would the opening lead be? Which diamonds does West know that partner doesn't hold? Which card would West play? Why?

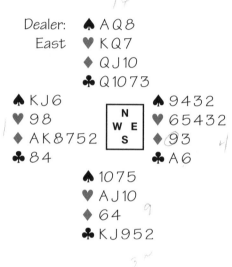

Dealer:  ♠ A Q 8
East     ♥ K Q 7
         ♦ Q J 10
         ♣ Q 10 7 3

♠ K J 6              ♠ 9 4 3 2
♥ 9 8                ♥ 6 5 4 3 2
♦ A K 8 7 5 2        ♦ 9 3
♣ 8 4                ♣ A 6

         ♠ 10 7 5
         ♥ A J 10
         ♦ 6 4
         ♣ K J 9 5 2

### The Play

Review the steps in declarer's PLAN. How does declarer plan to make the contract?

**Exercise Ten** — Maintaining Communications

## The Bidding

- West opens the bidding 1♦.

- North overcalls 1NT.

- South knows there is enough for game and responds 3NT to partner's overcall.

- The final contract is 3NT and North is the declarer.

## The Defense

- East makes the opening lead of the ♦9, top of a doubleton in partner's suit.

- West knows partner does not hold the ♦Q, the ♦J or the ♦10 because East leads the top card with a doubleton and a low card with three or more.

- West plays the ♦8, ducking the trick, in order to keep an entry to the winners in hand in case East later wins a trick. West also wants to encourage so that East will lead the suit again if East gets the lead.

## The Play

- Declarer needs nine tricks and has four sure tricks. Declarer can try to develop four winners in clubs and a trick in spades, and can even try to promote a winner in the diamonds. All of this is dependent upon the opponents not being able to take too many diamond winners when they get the lead with the ♣A.

# Exercise Eleven — Partnership Cooperation

## (E-Z Deal Cards: #6, Hand 3 — Dealer, South)

Turn up the cards from the third pre-dealt deal. Put each hand dummy-style at the edge of the table in front of each player.

## The Bidding

What is South's opening bid? With no five-card suit to overcall but with support for all of the unbid suits, how does West compete? What does North do? How many points does East have? At what level does the partnership belong? What does East bid? How does the bidding proceed from there? What is the contract? Who is the declarer?

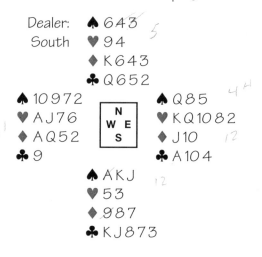

Dealer:  ♠ 6 4 3
South    ♥ 9 4
         ♦ K 6 4 3
         ♣ Q 6 5 2

♠ 10 9 7 2          ♠ Q 8 5
♥ A J 7 6    N      ♥ K Q 10 8 2
♦ A Q 5 2  W   E    ♦ J 10
♣ 9          S      ♣ A 10 4

         ♠ A K J
         ♥ 5 3
         ♦ 9 8 7
         ♣ K J 8 7 3

## The Defense

Which player makes the opening lead? What would the opening lead be? Which card does North play on the first trick? Why? What does South lead next? If North wins a trick, which suit should North lead next? Why?

## The Play

Review the steps in declarer's PLAN. How does declarer plan to make the contract?

**Exercise Eleven** — Partnership Cooperation

## The Bidding

- South opens 1♣.
- West competes by making a takeout double.
- North passes (although raising to 2♣ is a possibility).
- 13. East knows the partnership belongs in game and bids 4♥.
- All pass and East is the declarer in 4♥.

## The Defense

- South leads the ♠A, top of touching high cards.
- North plays the ♠3 to give a discouraging signal.
- South switches to another suit, leading a diamond through the strength in dummy.
- If North wins a trick, North should lead spades since it looks as if South can't lead the suit without giving up a trick.

## The Play

- Declarer can afford three losers and has six. Two club losers can be ruffed in the dummy and the diamond loser could be eliminated with the help of a successful finesse.

# Exercise Twelve — Putting Signals to Work
## (E-Z Deal Cards: #6, Hand 4 — Dealer, West)

Turn up the cards from the fourth pre-dealt deal. Put each hand dummy-style at the edge of the table in front of each player.

## The Bidding

What is West's opening bid? Can North complete in the auction? How? What does East respond to partner's opening bid? Does South have to bid? Should South bid? What does South do? How does the auction proceed from there? What is the contract? Who is the declarer?

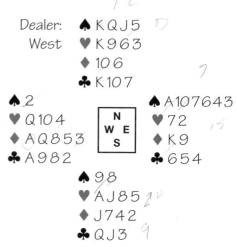

Dealer: ♠ K Q J 5
West    ♥ K 9 6 3
        ♦ 10 6
        ♣ K 10 7

♠ 2                 ♠ A 10 7 6 4 3
♥ Q 10 4          ♥ 7 2
♦ A Q 8 5 3      ♦ K 9
♣ A 9 8 2        ♣ 6 5 4

        ♠ 9 8
        ♥ A J 8 5
        ♦ J 7 4 2
        ♣ Q J 3

## The Defense

Which player makes the opening lead? What would the opening lead be? Why? How does East know partner's lead is a singleton? After winning the first trick, which card does East play to the second trick? Why? What does West do next?

## The Play

Review the steps in declarer's PLAN. How does declarer plan to make the contract?

## Exercise Twelve — Putting Signals to Work

### The Bidding

- West opens 1 ♦.
- North competes in the auction by making a takeout double.
- East responds 1♠ to West's opening bid.
- South doesn't have to bid but doesn't want to let the opponents buy the contract too easily. South, therefore, bids 2 ♥.
- All players pass and South is the declarer in 2 ♥.

### The Defense

- West leads the ♠2, a singleton in partner's suit.
- East suspects that this a singleton since the ♠2 is the lowest missing card and partner would play the top card from a doubleton.
- East wins the trick with the ♠A and returns the ♠10, showing a preference for diamonds rather than clubs.
- West ruffs the next spade and plays the ♦A and another diamond based on partner's suit-preference signal.

### The Play

- Declarer can afford five losers and has six, one too many. Declarer may be able to avoid a trump loser with a successful finesse if the suit divides 3–2. Declarer may choose to play the ♥A and the ♥K, hoping the ♥Q is a doubleton since declarer suspects the finesse will lose. Two of declarer's diamond losers could be ruffed in the dummy or one ruffed in the dummy and one discarded on the extra spade winner after the ♠A is driven out.

# CHAPTER 7
## *Interfering with Declarer*

In the previous chapter, we saw how the defenders work together to take the tricks to which they are entitled. The defenders must also work together to try to prevent declarer from taking any tricks declarer isn't entitled to. In this chapter, we will look at techniques the defenders use to make it difficult for declarer to make the contract.

## DEFENDING AGAINST SUIT ESTABLISHMENT

Declarer often needs to establish tricks in long suits to make a contract. Declarer uses a combination of promotion (driving out the defenders' higher-ranking cards) and length (leading the suit until the defenders have no cards left in the suit). Once winners have been established in a suit, declarer will need an entry to get to them. The defenders can't do anything about the cards declarer has been dealt, but they can make it as difficult as possible for declarer to establish winners and then get to them.

### The Defensive Holdup Play

In previous chapters, we have looked at how the defenders can hold up their winner in a suit in order to strand declarer's winners. For example, consider this layout:

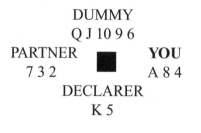

| | DUMMY | |
| --- | --- | --- |
| | Q J 10 9 6 | |
| PARTNER | | YOU |
| 7 3 2 | | A 8 4 |
| | DECLARER | |
| | K 5 | |

Declarer plans to promote four winners in this suit by driving out the defenders' ace. Declarer starts by leading the king, high card from the short side. If you take the first trick with the ace, declarer has four established winners in the dummy and can use the 5 as an entry to dummy's winners after regaining the lead. To make things difficult for declarer, you can use the *defensive holdup,* refusing to take your ace until declarer doesn't have any cards left in the suit. Since you can't see how many cards there are in declarer's hand, your partner must cooperate by giving you a count signal so that you know how long to hold up.

On the layout shown, partner plays the 2 on the first trick, the start of a low-high signal to show an odd number. When you refuse to win the first trick, declarer leads the 5 to one of dummy's high cards. On this trick, partner plays the 3 (or 7), confirming an odd number of cards. Since partner can't have started with five cards in the suit, you can deduce that partner has three, leaving declarer with only two. This information tells you that it is safe to win the second trick with your ace. Declarer doesn't have any small cards left as an entry to the winners. If partner had played high-low to show an even number, declarer would have started with three cards and you would need to wait until the third round to take your ace.

Of course, your holdup play will not prevent declarer from reaching dummy's winners if there is an entry in another suit, but it may cause some inconvenience. Declarer may not have an entry in another suit or may have to use up an entry that declarer would rather save for other purposes. A holdup play can be quite effective, especially in a notrump contract, even when declarer does have an easy outside entry to dummy. Suppose we change the layout slightly:

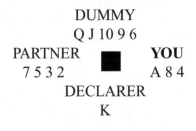

DUMMY
Q J 10 9 6
PARTNER        YOU
7 5 3 2        A 8 4
DECLARER
K

If declarer leads the king and you win the first trick with the ace, declarer can use an outside entry to get to dummy's winners and take four tricks in the suit. If you hold up the ace, declarer can use an outside entry to get to dummy and lead the suit a second time. But when you now win the trick with your ace, declarer would need a second entry to dummy to get back to the established winners. If there was only one outside entry to dummy, your holdup play restricts declarer to one trick in the suit.

With the above layout, it may appear dangerous to hold up the ace in a suit contract since declarer may end up with no losers in the suit. When declarer goes to dummy with an outside entry and then leads the suit a second time, your ace can be trumped when you play it. If there is only one entry to dummy, however, sacrificing your ace may be worthwhile. If you won the ace on the first round, declarer might be able to discard up to four losers on dummy's established winners. It costs you a trick in the short run but may gain you more than one trick in the long run. You will have to judge more carefully in a suit contract whether or not to hold up your winners.

Even when declarer has an outside entry to dummy, you may be able to prevent a suit becoming established by holding up when you have two winners in the suit. Consider this layout:

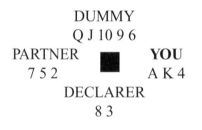

DUMMY
Q J 10 9 6
PARTNER          YOU
7 5 2            A K 4
DECLARER
8 3

Suppose declarer leads the suit and you win the first trick with the king. When declarer regains the lead, there is still a low card left to lead to dummy to drive out your ace. It won't do any good to hold up now since declarer has an outside entry to dummy to get to the winners once they are established. Look at the difference if you hold up both the ace and the king on the first trick, waiting until the second trick to win with your king. Now when declarer regains the lead, there aren't any low cards left. Declarer would have to use the only entry to dummy in order to lead the suit again and drive out your ace. Then there would be no entry left in dummy to get to the established winners. By letting declarer win the first trick, you prevent declarer from ever establishing any more winners in the suit.

Here is a complete deal to illustrate the possibilities for defeating a contract by holding up with two winners in a suit:

Contract: 3NT
Lead: ♠Q

DUMMY
♠ 7 5
♥ A 8 3
♦ K J 9 8 5
♣ 7 6 3

PARTNER
♠ Q J 10 9
♥ J 7
♦ 7 4 2
♣ Q 10 8 5

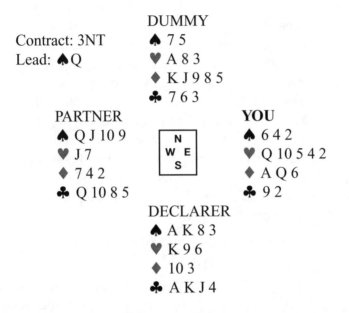

YOU
♠ 6 4 2
♥ Q 10 5 4 2
♦ A Q 6
♣ 9 2

DECLARER
♠ A K 8 3
♥ K 9 6
♦ 10 3
♣ A K J 4

Against 3NT, partner leads the ♠Q. Declarer has two spade tricks, two heart tricks, and two club tricks. One extra trick can come from a successful club finesse or a 3–3 division of the missing clubs, but the most promising suit is diamonds. Declarer can take a finesse, hoping your partner has the ♦Q. Even if this doesn't work, however, declarer can promote three tricks in the suit by driving out the ♦Q and the ♦A. So declarer wins the first trick with the ♠K and leads the ♦10, playing a low diamond from dummy. This is your chance to put the holdup play to work by refusing to win the first trick with the ♦Q, even though it is tempting to do so.

Let's take a look at what happens if you win the first diamond trick with the ♦Q. You lead back a spade to drive out declarer's remaining ♠A (declarer could also win any other return in hand). Declarer leads another diamond to dummy to drive out your ♦A. It's too late to hold up.

Dummy still has the ♥A as an entry. Declarer ends up with three diamond tricks to go with the other six sure tricks, enough to make the contract.

Instead, let declarer win the first diamond trick. Declarer will lead another diamond to dummy's ♦J (or ♦9 or ♦8), hoping to repeat the successful finesse. Now you win this second diamond trick with the ♦Q and lead back a spade. Declarer is helpless. Declarer can win the spade trick and use dummy's ♥A as an entry to lead another diamond and drive out your ♦A, but there won't be any entries left to get to dummy's established winners. Declarer's only chance is to use dummy's ♥A as an entry to try the club finesse, hoping that you have the ♣Q and the suit divides 3–3. When this fails, declarer is defeated and ends up with only two spade tricks, two heart tricks, the initial diamond trick, and two club tricks. You defeat the contract by two tricks.

There are many opportunities to make declarer's life difficult by holding up your winners. Here is a typical layout:

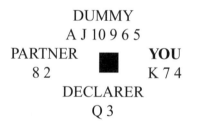

DUMMY
A J 10 9 6 5
PARTNER                    YOU
8 2                        K 7 4
DECLARER
Q 3

Trying to establish winners in this suit, declarer leads the queen and plays a low card from dummy. This would be successful if your partner held the king since declarer's queen would win the trick and declarer could repeat the finesse. It would also be successful if you won the first trick with the king since the remaining cards in dummy would be winners, and declarer would have a low card left to get to them. If there aren't any outside entries to the dummy, you can limit declarer to one or two winners by holding up the king. When the queen wins the first trick and another low card is led toward dummy, declarer will be faced with a dilemma. A trick can be won with dummy's ace to guarantee two tricks in the suit. If, however, your partner holds the king, declarer can finesse dummy's jack (or 10 or 9), and if partner's king next falls under the ace, declarer ends up with six tricks.

In the actual layout, if declarer takes a finesse, you can now win the king. Since the winners are stranded provided there is no outside entry, declarer won't get any more tricks.

Notice that partner clarifies the layout of the suit for you by giving a count signal when the queen is led. Partner plays the 8, starting a high-low, to show an even number. The situation becomes a little more exciting if this is the complete layout:

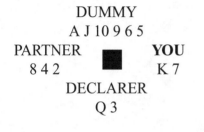

DUMMY
A J 10 9 6 5
PARTNER     YOU
8 4 2        K 7
DECLARER
Q 3

When declarer plays the queen, partner signals with the 2, to show an odd number. Assuming partner has three cards, that leaves declarer with two. Do you hold up on the first trick? If it takes you too long to decide, you're better off winning the first trick with the king. Otherwise, declarer may figure out that you're thinking about whether or not to hold up your king and may play dummy's ace on the second round of the suit, ending up with all of the tricks! If your nerves are strong and you don't take too long to think about it, you can risk playing a low card. If declarer repeats the finesse, confident that your partner has the king, your holdup play will be successful and will limit declarer to one trick in the suit. What if declarer goes up with the ace on the second round of the suit? You win some and you lose some — this time you would lose.

## Attacking Entries

Another way for the defenders to make life difficult for declarer is by driving out entries before declarer is ready to use them. Take a look at this deal:

```
                        DUMMY
Contract: 3NT           ♠ A 5
Lead: ♥ J               ♥ 7 4 2
                        ♦ J 5 4
                        ♣ K J 10 9 3
      PARTNER                          YOU
      ♠ 10 6 4          ┌─────┐        ♠ K Q 9 3
      ♥ J 10 9 8        │  N  │        ♥ A 5
      ♦ 9 6 3           │W   E│        ♦ 10 8 7 2
      ♣ 8 6 2           │  S  │        ♣ A 7 5
                        └─────┘
                        DECLARER
                        ♠ J 8 7 2
                        ♥ K Q 6 3
                        ♦ A K Q
                        ♣ Q 4
```

Partner leads the ♥ J against 3NT. You play the ♥ A, third hand high, since you know that declarer holds the ♥ Q. Declarer may or may not hold the ♥ K, depending on whether partner has led from the top of a sequence or from an interior sequence. Before automatically returning partner's suit, however, you need to consider the whole picture. Looking at dummy, you can see that declarer will probably try to establish the club suit by driving out your ♣ A and use the ♠ A as an entry to the established winners. You can foil this plan by leading the ♠ K (or ♠ Q) to remove dummy's entry before declarer is ready to use it. Declarer can win with dummy's ♠ A and lead a club to the ♣ Q and the ♣ 4 back to one of dummy's high clubs. You hold up your ♣ A, watching partner's count signal to see on which round you should win the trick. When partner shows three clubs, you win the second round and declarer is held to one club trick rather than the four tricks that would be available if you left the ♠A as an entry to dummy.

Leading back the ♠K wasn't too difficult when you were looking at the ♠Q as well and could see that you were also promoting a trick for yourself. Let's look at the layout of the spade suit by itself:

| | DUMMY | |
|---|---|---|
| | ♠A 5 | |
| PARTNER | | YOU |
| ♠10 6 4 | ■ | ♠K Q 9 3 |
| | DECLARER | |
| | ♠J 8 7 2 | |

The lead of the ♠K actually costs a trick since declarer can win dummy's ♠A and lead toward the ♠J for a second trick. The sacrifice of one trick is worthwhile, however, since you prevent declarer from getting four club tricks. Suppose declarer holds the ♠Q:

| | DUMMY | |
|---|---|---|
| | ♠A 5 | |
| PARTNER | | YOU |
| ♠10 6 4 | ■ | ♠K 9 8 3 |
| | DECLARER | |
| | ♠Q J 7 2 | |

It would still be worthwhile to lead the ♠K to drive out dummy's ♠A, even though declarer gets tricks with both the ♠Q and the ♠J. Notice that the halfhearted attempt of leading a low spade wouldn't work. Declarer could win with the ♠Q or the ♠J, keeping the ♠A in dummy. By lead-ing the ♠K, you are certain of driv-ing out dummy's ♠A. Of course, you may not hold the ♠K. In that case, you would have to lead a low spade, hoping that partner can drive out dummy's entry. For example:

| | DUMMY | |
|---|---|---|
| | ♠A 5 | |
| PARTNER | | YOU |
| ♠K 10 6 | ■ | ♠9 8 4 3 |
| | DECLARER | |
| | ♠Q J 7 2 | |

When you lead back a low spade, de-clarer can't prevent your partner from driving out dummy's ♠A.

In addition to driving out declarer's entries, the defenders can sometimes prevent declarer from creating an entry. Consider this layout:

DUMMY
♠Q 6 5

PARTNER 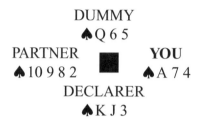 YOU
♠10 9 8 2          ♠A 7 4

DECLARER
♠K J 3

If it's necessary to create an entry to dummy, declarer might try leading the king, and then the jack. If you win either the first trick or the second trick with your ace, dummy's queen will become an entry. By refusing to win either the first or the second trick, declarer can't get to dummy in this suit. Partner should be helping you out by playing high-low to give you a count signal. If partner has four cards, declarer has three and you must wait until the third round to win the trick.

Here is a more complicated example combining the holdup play with denying declarer an entry:

Contract: 3NT
Lead: ♠J

DUMMY
♠ A 7 5
♥ J 5 2
♦ 8
♣ Q J 9 7 5 2

PARTNER
♠ J 10 9 8
♥ 8 4
♦ J 10 7 4
♣ A 8 4

```
    N
 W     E
    S
```

YOU
♠ 4 3 2
♥ A 10 9 6
♦ Q 9 5 2
♣ K 6

DECLARER
♠ K Q 6
♥ K Q 7 3
♦ A K 6 3
♣ 10 3

Partner leads the ♠J and the defenders will have to cooperate carefully to defeat the contract. Declarer wins the first trick with the ♠Q, keeping the ♠A in the dummy, and leads the ♣10, planning to establish the extra tricks needed in the club suit. Partner must cooperate by playing low, holding up the ♣A. Since declarer has an entry to dummy, you can't afford to win the first club trick, either, but must let declarer win. It may seem difficult to leave yourself with the singleton ♣K, but it's unlikely that declarer has the ♣A since declarer probably would have played it earlier. Declarer leads another club and partner must play low again, letting you win the trick with the ♣K, otherwise your side's ♣A and ♣K would fall on the same trick! When you win the ♣K, you return a spade, partner's suit. It doesn't do declarer any good to win in hand, since there aren't any clubs left to play. Suppose declarer wins dummy's ♠A and leads another club to establish the suit. Partner wins with the ♣A and leads another spade to drive out declarer's remaining ♠K. Declarer now leads the ♥Q. If you win the ♥A, dummy's ♥J will become an entry. You must allow declarer's ♥Q to win the trick. If declarer continues by leading the ♥K, you must also let this trick win. If instead declarer leads a low heart toward dummy's ♥J, you must win this trick to prevent declarer from ever reaching the stranded clubs in the dummy. With careful cooperation between the defenders, declarer ends up with only three spade tricks, two heart tricks, two diamond tricks, and one club trick — one trick short of making the contract.

# DEFENDING AGAINST DECLARER'S LOW CARDS

Declarer can get tricks from a long suit by continuing to play it until the defenders don't have any cards left in the suit. The defenders must be careful not to make declarer's task any easier by throwing away the cards that would prevent declarer from establishing the suit.

## Discarding

You are often faced with the problem of which suit to discard when you can't follow suit to the current trick. In choosing your discard, you must be careful not to present declarer with a trick to which declarer isn't entitled. Any time declarer has a long suit in hand or in the dummy, there's the possibility that a low card in that suit will become a winner. The defenders have to guard against this by making sure that at least one member of the partnership keeps the same number of cards in the suit as declarer. Since you aren't able to see into partner's or declarer's hand, it won't always be apparent which suit you must guard against. In some situations, however, it's obvious that you can't afford to discard from a particular suit since partner can't protect it. Consider this layout:

DUMMY

A K Q 10

**YOU**

J 4 3 2

Whatever cards partner holds, only you can prevent declarer from getting four tricks in this suit. If you discard one of your cards, declarer can play the ace, the king, and the queen and the 10 will become a trick.

    The situation can be less obvious if we change the layout to something like this:

DUMMY

A Q 6 5

**YOU**

7 4 3 2

It doesn't look as though your four small cards are of much use, but discarding one of them would give declarer a trick if this is the complete layout of the suit:

DUMMY

A Q 6 5

PARTNER          **YOU**

J 10 8          7 4 3 2

DECLARER

K 9

If you discard a card in the suit, declarer will play the king and then the 9 to dummy's ace and queen. Dummy's remaining 6 will have become a winner. You must tenaciously hold on to all four of your cards in the suit to prevent declarer from getting an extra trick.

You need to keep the same number of cards as dummy. If declarer discards one of dummy's cards in the suit, then you can safely discard one of your cards. The situation can be even more difficult when it's declarer who holds the length in the suit, since you can't see the hidden cards. For example, suppose this is the layout:

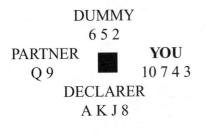

|              | DUMMY      |            |
| ------------ | ---------- | ---------- |
|              | 6 5 2      |            |
| PARTNER      |            | **YOU**    |
| Q 9          |            | 10 7 4 3   |
|              | DECLARER   |            |
|              | A K J 8    |            |

Looking at three low cards in dummy, it may not seem that there's much to guard against. Discarding a low card, however, is doubly dangerous. First, it will cost a trick even if declarer chooses to finesse the jack, losing to partner's queen. When declarer later takes the ace and the king, your 10 will fall and declarer's 8 will become a trick. Worse, declarer may assume from your discard that you don't have the queen to protect and may play the ace and the king, rather than taking the finesse, ending up with all four tricks in the suit!

Without seeing declarer's hand, how are you to know that you must hold on to all of your cards in a suit such as this? One place from which you get information about declarer's hand is through the bidding. Suppose the auction proceeds as follows:

| NORTH (DUMMY) | EAST (YOU) | SOUTH (DECLARER) | WEST (PARTNER) |
| ------------- | ---------- | ---------------- | -------------- |
|               |            | 1 ♠              | Pass           |
| 2 ♣           | Pass       | 2 ♦              | Pass           |
| 3 ♠           | Pass       | 4 ♠              | Pass           |
| Pass          | Pass       |                  |                |

Partner leads the ♥ J, and you see the following cards when dummy arrives:

DUMMY

Contract: 4♠       ♠ A 8 3
Lead: ♥ J          ♥ Q 7 3
                   ♦ 6 4 3
                   ♣ A J 4 2

PARTNER                          YOU
                                 ♠ 9 2
      ♥ J          | N  |        ♥ A K 4
                   | W  E |      ♦ 10 7 5 2
                   | S  |        ♣ K Q 10 3

Declarer plays a small heart from dummy, and you let partner's ♥ J win the trick. Partner leads another heart, and you take the ♥ K and the ♥ A as declarer follows suit both times. Needing only one more trick to defeat the contract, you lead the ♣ K. Declarer plays the ♣ 7, partner plays the ♣ 9, and declarer wins the trick with dummy's ♣ A. Declarer then plays three rounds of trumps, the ♠ A, the ♠ K, and the ♠ Q. On the third round of trumps, you discard a small club. Declarer leads two more spades. Partner discards the ♣ 5 and the ♣ 6 while declarer discards a small club and a small diamond from dummy. You can afford to discard your ♣ 10 on the fourth round of spades, but what do you discard on the fifth round? These are the remaining cards:

DUMMY
   ♦ 6 4
   ♣ J 4
           YOU
   ⬛       ♦ 10 7 5 2
           ♣ Q

One of your cards must go. Which one? If you recall the bidding, declarer bid diamonds on the second round of the auction. It looks as if declarer's last four cards are diamonds, so you must discard the ♣ Q, even though it's a winner. Declarer can't have any clubs left. If you discard a diamond, declarer makes the contract since the complete deal looks like this:

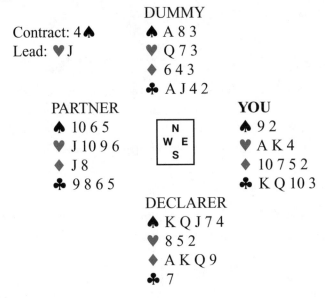

Contract: 4♠
Lead: ♥ J

DUMMY
♠ A 8 3
♥ Q 7 3
♦ 6 4 3
♣ A J 4 2

PARTNER
♠ 10 6 5
♥ J 10 9 6
♦ J 8
♣ 9 8 6 5

YOU
♠ 9 2
♥ A K 4
♦ 10 7 5 2
♣ K Q 10 3

DECLARER
♠ K Q J 7 4
♥ 8 5 2
♦ A K Q 9
♣ 7

If you ever discard a diamond, declarer takes four diamond tricks to go along with the five spade tricks and the ♣A. The key clues came from the auction and partner's play to the club suit. Declarer opened the bidding 1♠, showing a five-card suit, and later bid diamonds to show four of them. Once declarer shows up with three hearts, there is room left for only one club. You must grimly hold on to all four of your diamonds, since partner will be unable to guard the suit.

Where else do your clues come from? Sometimes you can tell a lot from the way declarer is playing. At other times, partner can help you out. Did you notice that partner played high-low in the club suit on the above deal? This couldn't be attitude, since you can see all of the high club cards. It must be a count signal to show an even number of clubs. This confirms the fact that partner started with four clubs while declarer started with only one.

You have to keep both your ears and eyes open when trying to determine which suit you can safely discard from. You can't afford to be left holding on to your high cards in one suit while declarer is taking tricks with small cards in the suit which you discarded.

# DEFENDING AGAINST FINESSES

Another way declarer takes tricks is by using the finesse. You can make it difficult for the declarer by not disclosing the location of the cards that declarer is looking for unless you have to. Remember that declarer can't see the cards in your hand or your partner's hand.

## Ducking

In the chapter on second hand low, you have already seen how playing a low card, rather than your high card, can create a problem for declarer. For example:

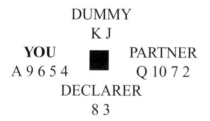

If declarer leads a low card toward dummy, you must play a low card to leave declarer with a guess. When you duck, declarer doesn't know whether to play dummy's king or jack in order to get one trick from the suit.

Similarly, you should usually play low when declarer leads a low card in this situation:

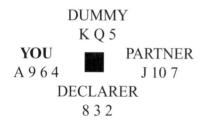

Declarer can win the first trick with dummy's queen (or king) but may have difficulty finding an entry back in order to repeat the finesse.

You can also make things difficult for declarer by not taking your trick when declarer's finesse is actually going to lose. Let's change the above layout slightly, putting you on the other side:

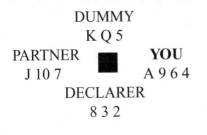

When declarer leads a low card to dummy's queen, you shouldn't be in any hurry to win the first trick with your ace. If you play a low card, declarer may think your partner has the ace and use up an entry to come back to lead toward dummy again. The second time, declarer's finesse will be unsuccessful because you'll take dummy's king with your ace. If you had won the trick the first time, revealing the situation, declarer might have found a  better use for that entry.

If we change the layout slightly, giving dummy the 10, it's even more important that you let declarer win the first trick:

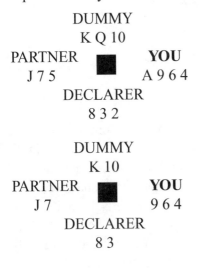

If declarer starts this suit by playing a low card to dummy's queen and you win the trick with the ace, the remaining cards look like this:

If two tricks are needed from this suit, declarer will lead toward dummy the next time and finesse the 10, trapping your partner's jack. You will have forced declarer to find the winning play. If you duck your ace the first time, declarer will be faced with a problem when crossing back to play another low card toward dummy. When partner follows with a second low card, declarer will have to guess whether to play dummy's king (correct if partner started with the ace) or dummy's 10 (correct if you started with the ace).

Here is a complete deal showing how declarer can be led astray when you don't let it be known that a finesse is going to lose:

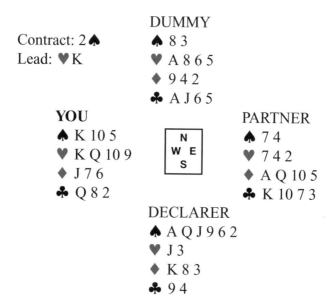

Contract: 2 ♠
Lead: ♥ K

DUMMY
♠ 8 3
♥ A 8 6 5
♦ 9 4 2
♣ A J 6 5

YOU
♠ K 10 5
♥ K Q 10 9
♦ J 7 6
♣ Q 8 2

PARTNER
♠ 7 4
♥ 7 4 2
♦ A Q 10 5
♣ K 10 7 3

DECLARER
♠ A Q J 9 6 2
♥ J 3
♦ K 8 3
♣ 9 4

You lead the ♥ K against 2 ♠. Declarer wins with dummy's ♥ A and sees that there is a spade loser, a heart loser, three diamond losers, and a club loser. The contract can be made if either the spade or the diamond finesse works. Suppose declarer starts by playing a small spade from the dummy, finessing the ♠ J, hoping that your partner holds the ♠ K. If you win this trick with the ♠ K, declarer is left with little choice. Declarer will have to use the other entry to dummy, the ♣ A, to lead toward the ♦ K. This play will be successful and the contract will be made.

Look at the difference if you let the ♠ J win the first trick. It will look to declarer as if the spade finesse is working. Declarer may use the remaining entry to dummy to lead another spade toward the ♠ Q, repeating the finesse. This time, you win the trick with the ♠ K. Now declarer doesn't have an entry left to get to the dummy and lead toward the ♦ K. Provided you and your partner are careful not to give declarer a free finesse by leading diamonds, they will have to be led from declarer's hand and all three diamond tricks will be lost. Declarer will go down one trick in a contract that could have been made. Next time, declarer might be a little more wary when the first finesse seems to have worked.

## Covering

You generally wait to cover the last honor led from dummy when declarer is finessing. There are times, however, when you can give declarer a more difficult time by covering. First, look at this layout:

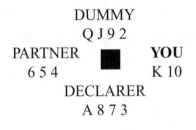

DUMMY
Q J 9 2
PARTNER     YOU
6 5 4       K 10
DECLARER
A 8 7 3

If declarer leads the queen from dummy, planning to finesse, you make it easy if you play the 10. The queen will win the trick, and now that the 10 has appeared, declarer can repeat the finesse, losing no tricks in the suit. If you cover the queen with the king, declarer is faced with a problem. These are the remaining cards:

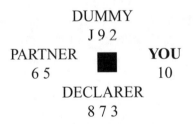

DUMMY
J 9 2
PARTNER     YOU
6 5        10
DECLARER
8 7 3

You can see that declarer should play dummy's jack next, dropping your 10, but it's not so obvious for declarer. If declarer thinks your partner has the 10, declarer may finesse dummy's 9, and lose a trick to your 10.

You have to visualize the problem you will create for declarer by covering. Here is a different type of opportunity:

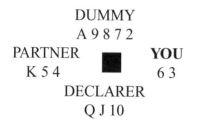

| DUMMY |
|---|
| A 9 8 7 2 |

PARTNER      YOU
K 5 4        6 3

| DECLARER |
|---|
| Q J 10 |

Normally, you don't cover if there is nothing to promote in the partnership hands. In this situation, if there isn't an outside entry to the dummy, you can block the suit by covering on the first or second round. If declarer wins with dummy's ace, the side will take only three tricks in the suit. If you waited to play your king until the third round of the suit, declarer can take all five tricks with no problem.

## DEFENDING AGAINST DECLARER'S TRUMPS

In a trump contract, declarer expects to take advantage of the trump suit by ruffing your winners. The defenders have to try to counter declarer's plans, using the trump suit to their advantage whenever possible.

### Leading Trumps

In the chapter on opening leads against suit contracts, you saw examples where the auction indicated that an initial trump lead might prevent declarer from ruffing losers in the dummy. The auction is not always so informative, but it still may not be too late to lead trumps once the opening lead has been made. Consider this deal:

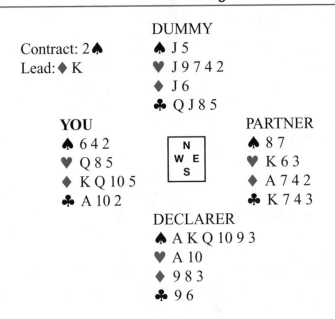

Contract: 2♠
Lead: ♦ K

DUMMY
♠ J 5
♥ J 9 7 4 2
♦ J 6
♣ Q J 8 5

YOU
♠ 6 4 2
♥ Q 8 5
♦ K Q 10 5
♣ A 10 2

PARTNER
♠ 8 7
♥ K 6 3
♦ A 7 4 2
♣ K 7 4 3

DECLARER
♠ A K Q 10 9 3
♥ A 10
♦ 9 8 3
♣ 9 6

The contract is 2♠ and you start by leading the ♦ K. Partner plays an encouraging ♦ 7, to show the ♦ A, and it's time to pause. With only two diamonds in dummy, your side won't be able to take more than two diamond tricks unless you eliminate dummy's trumps. Declarer is unlikely to help you out by drawing trumps when holding more than two diamonds. Instead, declarer will probably want to ruff a loser in the dummy. It's up to you to prevent this by shifting to a trump. When you lead a spade, declarer can win and lead a diamond to make dummy void, but you can win and lead another trump. There are no trumps left in dummy and declarer will end up losing three diamond tricks, two club tricks, and one heart trick. You started leading trumps just in time.

## Overruffing

One way to stop declarer from ruffing losers in the dummy is by ruffing higher than the dummy. Look at this deal:

```
                         DUMMY
Contract: 4 ♥            ♠ 10 8 3 2
Lead: ♠A                 ♥ 9 7 6
                         ♦ 9 2
                         ♣ A K 6 3
         PARTNER                        YOU
         ♠ A K Q J 5     ┌─────┐        ♠ 9 6
         ♥ 4 2           │  N  │        ♥ 10 8 3
         ♦ Q 10 7 3      │W   E│        ♦ J 6 5
         ♣ Q 10          │  S  │        ♣ 9 8 7 4 2
                         └─────┘
                         DECLARER
                         ♠ 7 4
                         ♥ A K Q J 5
                         ♦ A K 8 4
                         ♣ J 5
```

Your partner leads the ♠A, the ♠K, and the ♠Q to the first three tricks. You follow suit on the first two rounds but must find a discard on the next round. It doesn't look as though you need all of your small clubs, and it seems straightforward to discard one, but look what happens. Declarer ruffs the third round of spades and, with diamond losers in the hand, plays the ♦A and the ♦K, leads another diamond, and ruffs in dummy. Declarer can then draw trumps and make the contract, losing only two spade tricks and one diamond trick.

To prevent this result, discard a diamond, not a club, on the third round of spades. When declarer tries to ruff a diamond loser in dummy, you can overruff. Declarer loses that trick and still has to lose a diamond trick. Notice how partner helped you out by leading the third round of spades, allowing you to discard a diamond. Partner had to visualize the possible advantage of leading another high spade.

## The Uppercut

Sometimes the defenders can cooperate to create a trump trick out of thin air. Here's an example:

Contract: 4♠
Lead: ♦ A

DUMMY
♠ 10 8 6 4
♥ A K
♦ J 8 7
♣ A K Q J

YOU
♠ J 5
♥ 10 6 4 2
♦ A K Q 5
♣ 9 4 2

PARTNER
♠ Q
♥ J 9 8 3
♦ 9 4 3
♣ 10 8 7 5 3

DECLARER
♠ A K 9 7 3 2
♥ Q 7 5
♦ 10 6 2
♣ 6

You take the first three diamond tricks against 4♠ as everyone follows suit. At this point, the situation looks hopeless for the defense. Declarer doesn't have any losers left in hearts, diamonds, or clubs, and it doesn't look as though there are any trump tricks to lose. All is not quite over, however, if the defenders cooperate. With nothing better to do, you can lead your last diamond, even though all of the other players are void in the suit. Declarer plans to ruff with one of the small spades in hand and then draw trumps, but this is where partner can cooperate. Partner can see no real use for the ♠Q, unless it can help promote a trump trick for your side. Partner ruffs with the ♠Q, knowing that declarer can overruff. Look at the devastating result for declarer who has to overruff with the ♠K to win the trick. When declarer plays the ♠A next, you play your ♠5 and your ♠J has been promoted into the setting trick. Because this play is like hitting declarer on the jaw, it is often called an uppercut. Again, the defenders have cooperated to use the trump suit against declarer.

# BIDDING REVIEW

There are large bonuses in the scoring for bidding and making slam contracts. To bid a slam, you and your partner need to have enough combined strength and must find a suitable denomination in which to play the contract.

## The Strength Required for a Slam

As when deciding whether the partnership belongs in part-game or game, one partner must add the points promised by the other partner to those in the hand to determine if there is enough combined strength, using the following guideline:

**STRENGTH REQUIRED FOR SLAM**

- Small Slam (12 tricks): 33 or more points.
- Grand Slam (13 tricks): 37 or more points.

## The Denomination for Slam

Since the same number of tricks are required for a slam in any denomination, the partnership should generally look for a Golden Fit of eight or more cards in any suit. If a suitable trump fit can't be found, then the partnership should play in notrump.

If there is enough combined strength and a suitable fit has been found, then a slam can be bid directly (more sophisticated methods will be discussed in the next two books in this series).

Here are some examples. Suppose your partner opens the bidding 1NT (16 to 18 points):

♠ —
♥ A 9 3
♦ K Q 10 8 6 5 2
♣ A J 3

With 14 HCPs plus 3 points for the seven-card suit, there should be at least 33 combined points (16+17= 33). Partner must have at least two diamonds, so there is a Golden Fit. Respond 6 ♦.

♠ K 9 3
♥ A 10 8
♦ A K 7 5
♣ A 10 7

With 18 HCPs, there is a minimum of 34 points (16+18) and a maximum of 36 points (18+18) in the combined hands. You don't have any method of finding out if partner has four or more diamonds, so simply bid the most likely slam, 6NT.

♠ A J 8 3
♥ K J 7 5
♦ A 9 4
♣ A 7

You have 17 HCPs, enough for a small slam. There may be a Golden Fit in either hearts or spades, and you can find out by using the Stayman convention. Bid 2♣. If partner rebids 2♥ or 2♠, you can bid slam in that suit. If partner rebids 2♦, denying a four-card major suit, you can bid 6NT.

## Inviting Slam

When you know the denomination you want to play in but are not sure if there is enough combined strength for slam, you invite partner to bid slam by bidding one level beyond game. Partner will accept when at the top of the range but pass with minimum values.

For example, suppose partner opens 2NT (22 to 24):

♠ K 10 9
♥ Q 9 3
♦ J 10 9 5
♣ A 6 4

With 10 HCPs, there may not be enough for slam if opener has only 22 points (10+22=32), but there will be enough if opener has a maximum (10+24=34). Invite partner to slam by bidding one level beyond game, 4NT.

♠ A J 9 7 4 2
♥ Q 3
♦ J 9 5
♣ 7 4

With 8 HCPs plus 2 points for the six-card suit, you have enough to invite slam. Since there must be a Golden Fit in spades, invite slam by bidding one level beyond game, 5♠.

# PLAY OF THE HAND REVIEW

As we have seen, while declarer is trying to develop the extra winners needed to make the contract, the defenders are doing their best to stop declarer from succeeding. When puting together a PLAN, declarer has to watch out for the opponents.

## The Holdup Play

Just as the defenders hold up to try to strand declarer's winners, declarer must hold up to disrupt the defenders' communications. This is the classic example:

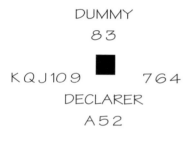

DUMMY
83

K Q J 10 9          7 6 4

DECLARER
A 5 2

West leads the king against your notrump contract. If you must let the opponents win one or more tricks while developing the winners you need, you must hold up your ace twice so that East has no cards left in the suit. If West doesn't have an outside entry, then it's safe to let East win a trick. On the other hand, it's still dangerous to let West win a trick. West has become the dangerous opponent.

In one sense, you have an easier time than the defenders when holding up since you can see both of your hands. You don't need signals to tell you how many cards are in partner's hand. On the other hand, you don't know how the missing cards are divided. If they are divided 5–3, as in the above layout, then East has no cards left. If they are divided 4–4, East will still have a card left. The only time you can be certain is when one defender shows out of the suit. The defenders' bidding and signals will sometimes give you the clues you need to decide how long you need to hold up.

## Avoiding the Dangerous Opponent

When one opponent is dangerous and the other is not, you want to avoid giving up the lead to the dangerous opponent. An opponent who can take enough winners to defeat your contract is dangerous. An opponent who is in a position to trap one of your high cards is also dangerous.

For example, consider this layout:

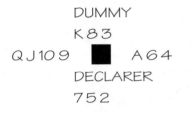

DUMMY
K 8 3
Q J 10 9    A 6 4
DECLARER
7 5 2

West is the dangerous opponent, since West is in the position to lead the queen, trapping dummy's king. East is not dangerous since East can't lead the suit without giving you a trick with dummy's king.

When one opponent is dangerous and the other is not, you want to try to lose a trick to the non-dangerous opponent if one must be lost. For example, suppose West is the dangerous opponent and you need to develop an extra trick from this layout:

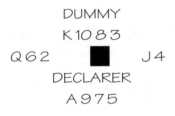

DUMMY
K 10 8 3
Q 6 2    J 4
DECLARER
A 9 7 5

It won't do any good to play the ace, the king, and then give up a trick. West, the dangerous opponent, will win the third round. Instead, lead a low card toward dummy. It won't do West any good to play the queen, since you can win dummy's king and take all of the tricks. When West plays a low card, play dummy's 8 or 10, letting East win the trick. When you regain the lead, you'll get three tricks from the suit without having to give up the lead to West.

# SUMMARY

The defenders want to develop their own tricks, but whenever possible they also want to prevent declarer from developing tricks. The defenders must watch to see what declarer is trying to do and look for ways to thwart those plans.

When declarer is trying to develop tricks in a long suit, the defenders can make use of the holdup play, refusing to take their winner(s) until declarer's winners are stranded. The defenders can also attack declarer's entries to try to drive them out before declarer is ready to use them.

When discarding, the defenders must be careful to prevent declarer from winning undeserved tricks with low cards. In general, the defenders must work together so that at least one of them keeps enough cards in each suit to prevent declarer's low cards from becoming established. The defenders will have to share the responsibility, with one defender guarding a suit that the other defender can't protect. Since declarer's cards are hidden, the defenders must listen to the bidding and watch each other's signals for clues as to which cards to keep.

When declarer is taking finesses, the defenders should avoid taking their winners before they have to, keeping declarer in doubt as to the location of the missing cards.

When defending trump contracts, the defenders must look for ways to prevent declarer from ruffing losers in dummy, either by leading trumps or by being in a position to overruff the dummy. The defenders should also look for opportunities to promote tricks for their side whenever possible.

## Exercise One — The Defensive Holdup

In each of the following layouts, declarer doesn't have any entries to the dummy other than the cards in the suit. To limit declarer to the minimum number of tricks, which cards would you and partner play on the first trick if declarer leads the 10 (a)? Which cards would you play on the second trick if declarer leads a low card to dummy's queen (b)?

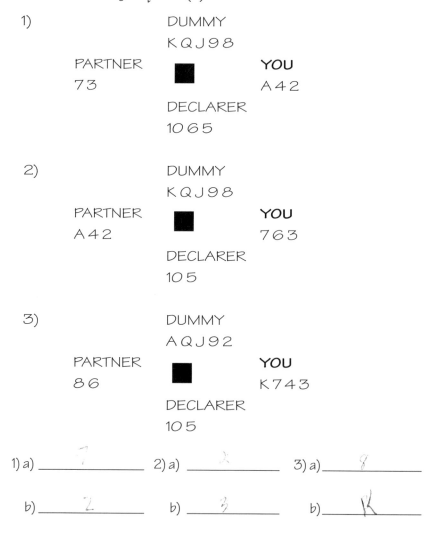

1)
    DUMMY
    K Q J 9 8

PARTNER              YOU
7 3                  A 4 2

    DECLARER
    10 6 5

2)
    DUMMY
    K Q J 9 8

PARTNER              YOU
A 4 2                7 6 3

    DECLARER
    10 5

3)
    DUMMY
    A Q J 9 2

PARTNER              YOU
8 6                  K 7 4 3

    DECLARER
    10 5

1) a) _____ 7 _____     2) a) _____ 2 _____     3) a) _____ 8 _____

   b) _____ 2 _____        b) _____ 3 _____        b) _____ K _____

**Exercise One** — The Defensive Holdup

1) a) On the first trick, partner plays the 7 to show an even number; you hold up and play a low card.

   b) On the second round of the suit, partner plays the 3 and again you hold up, playing a low card.


2) a) On the first round, partner plays the 2, and you play the 3 to start to show an odd number of cards in the suit.

   b) On the second round of the suit, partner could play the ace knowing from your signal that declarer has only two cards in the suit.


3) a) On the first round, partner plays the 8 to start to show two cards in the suit. You play a low card.

   b) The second time the suit is played, partner plays the 6 and you play the king.

## Exercise Two — Attacking Entries

In each of the following layouts, you are on lead. Which card would you lead to prevent declarer from using this suit later as an entry to the dummy?

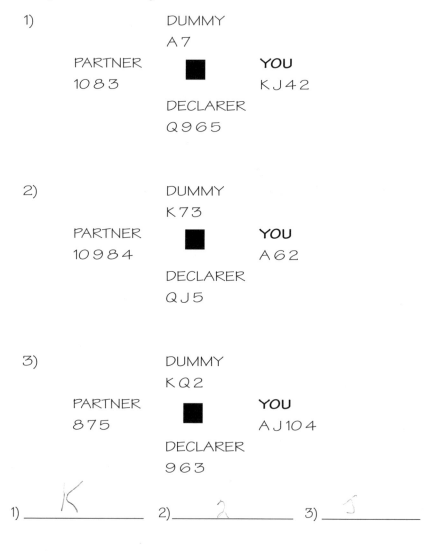

1)                          DUMMY
                            A 7
         PARTNER            ■            YOU
         10 8 3                          K J 4 2
                            DECLARER
                            Q 9 6 5


2)                          DUMMY
                            K 7 3
         PARTNER            ■            YOU
         10 9 8 4                        A 6 2
                            DECLARER
                            Q J 5


3)                          DUMMY
                            K Q 2
         PARTNER            ■            YOU
         8 7 5                           A J 10 4
                            DECLARER
                            9 6 3


1) _____K_____     2)_____2_____     3) _____J_____

**Exercise Two** — Attacking Entries

    1) King      2) Low     3) Jack (or 10)

## Exercise Three — Watching Your Discards

In each of the following layouts, how many tricks does declarer get if you discard a low card in the suit (a)? How many tricks does declarer get if you don't discard any cards in the suit (b)?

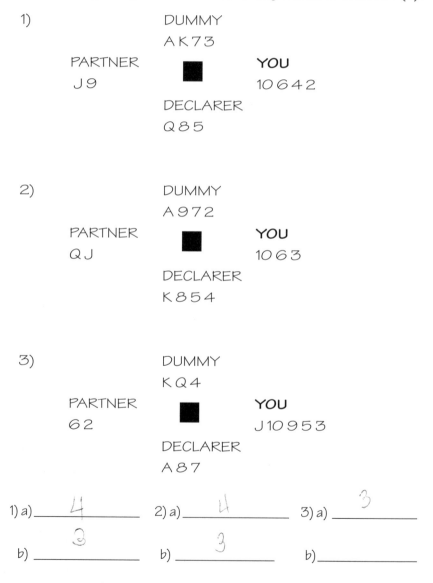

1)

DUMMY
A K 7 3

PARTNER      YOU
J 9          10 6 4 2

DECLARER
Q 8 5

2)

DUMMY
A 9 7 2

PARTNER      YOU
Q J          10 6 3

DECLARER
K 8 5 4

3)

DUMMY
K Q 4

PARTNER      YOU
6 2          J 10 9 5 3

DECLARER
A 8 7

1) a) _____4_____    2) a) _____4_____    3) a) _____3_____

b) _____3_____         b) _____3_____         b) _____

**Exercise Three** — Watching Your Discards

1) a)     If you discard a low card, declarer gets four tricks.

   b)     If you don't discard any cards, declarer gets only three tricks.

2) a)     Declarer gets four tricks if you discard a card.

   b)     If you don't discard any cards, declarer gets only three tricks.

3) a) & b) Whether you discard or not, declarer is entitled to only three tricks in this suit.

## **Exercise Four** — Practicing Counting

Suppose you can see the following cards in the dummy and your own hand:

DUMMY
♠ 10 7 5 3
♥ A 6 2
♦ K 9 6 2
♣ 7 5

YOU
♠ K 8 6
♥ J 8 7 3
♦ 10 3
♣ Q 9 6 2

1) How many spades does declarer have if partner shows out (discards) on the second round?

2) If partner is known to have one spade, five hearts, and four diamonds, how many clubs does partner hold?

3) Given partner's distribution as above, what is declarer's exact distribution?

4) Given the above information, from which suit should you be careful not to discard?

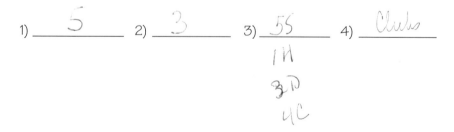

1) _____5_____  2) _____3_____  3) ___55___  4) ___Clubs___
                                    1H
                                    3D
                                    4C

**Exercise Four** — Practicing Counting

1) Five    2) Three    3) 5-1-3-4    4) Clubs

## Exercise Five — Defending against Finesses

In each of the following layouts, you are defending a notrump contract and declarer leads a low card toward dummy's jack. Which card should partner play and which card should you play to give declarer the most difficulty in the suit?

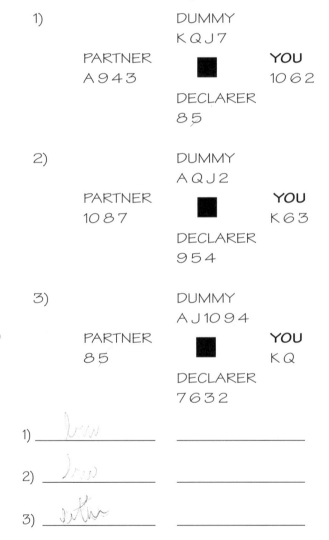

1)
DUMMY
K Q J 7

PARTNER          YOU
A 9 4 3          10 6 2

DECLARER
8 5

2)
DUMMY
A Q J 2

PARTNER          YOU
10 8 7           K 6 3

DECLARER
9 5 4

3)
DUMMY
A J 10 9 4

PARTNER          YOU
8 5              K Q

DECLARER
7 6 3 2

1) _____     _____

2) _____     _____

3) _____     _____

**Exercise Five** — Defending against Finesses

1) Declarer gets three tricks without any entry problems if your partner plays the ace on the first round. Both of the defenders should play low.

2) Partner should play low on the first trick, and you should also play low. This way declarer gets only two tricks in the suit.

3) Partner plays the 5 and you play the king or the queen.

## Exercise Six — Defending against Trump Suits

On the following deal, how can the defenders defeat declarer's 2♠ contract after West leads the ♥Q?

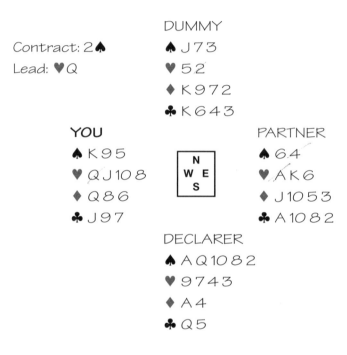

DUMMY

Contract: 2♠
Lead: ♥Q

♠ J 7 3
♥ 5 2
♦ K 9 7 2
♣ K 6 4 3

YOU

♠ K 9 5
♥ Q J 10 8
♦ Q 8 6
♣ J 9 7

N
W E
S

PARTNER

♠ 6 4
♥ A K 6
♦ J 10 5 3
♣ A 10 8 2

DECLARER

♠ A Q 10 8 2
♥ 9 7 4 3
♦ A 4
♣ Q 5

## Exercise Six — Defending against Trump Suits

Declarer has one too many losers and may hope to ruff a heart loser in the dummy. The defenders can prevent this by leading a trump at the first opportunity. East has to lead the trump so that West wins a trick with the ♠K. East will have to overtake the first heart and lead a spade. After gaining the lead, West has to play another spade. This is very delicate for the defenders. If declarer wins the second spade in the dummy and leads the remaining heart, East would have to play low and let West win the trick so that West could lead another trump.

## Exercise Seven — Review of Slam Bidding

Your partner opens the bidding 2NT showing a balanced hand of 22 to 24 points. What do you respond with each of the following hands?

1) ♠ 8 6 2
♥ K J 3
♦ A 8 4 2
♣ 9 6 2

2) ♠ Q 10 8
♥ 9 6 2
♦ K 6 3
♣ K Q 7 5

3) ♠ A 4 2
♥ J 7 3
♦ J 10 6 3
♣ A Q 5

1) _3NT_   2) _4NT_   3) _6NT_

4) ♠ A J 3
♥ K Q 5
♦ Q J 9
♣ K 10 9 2

5) ♠ 7 6 3
♥ Q
♦ A J 9 7 5 2
♣ K 9 7

6) ♠ K 10 9 8 6 3 2
♥ 10 9
♦ 5 2
♣ A 5

4) _7NT_   5) _2D_   6) _5S_

7) ♠ K Q 9 3
♥ J 8
♦ J 8 7 4
♣ A 7 3

8) ♠ 9 2
♥ A Q J 4 3
♦ A 8 5
♣ 7 6 5

9) ♠ K J 8 4
♥ A J 10 3
♦ J 8 3
♣ 7 2

7) _3C_   8) _3H_   9) _3C_

---

## Answers to Exercise

## Exercise Seven — Review of Slam Bidding

1) 3NT   2) 4NT   3) 6NT
4) 7NT   5) 6♦   6) 5♠
7) 3♣ (Stayman)   8) 3♥   9) 3♣ (Stayman)

## Exercise Eight — Watching out for the Opponents

You are declarer on the following deal in a contract of 3NT. West leads the ♥5 and East plays the ♥K on the first trick. Where are your extra tricks going to come from? What's the danger? Which card do you play on the first trick? Why?

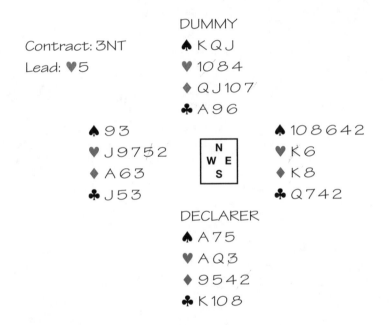

Contract: 3NT
Lead: ♥5

DUMMY
♠ K Q J
♥ 10 8 4
♦ Q J 10 7
♣ A 9 6

♠ 9 3
♥ J 9 7 5 2
♦ A 6 3
♣ J 5 3

N
W E
S

♠ 10 8 6 4 2
♥ K 6
♦ K 8
♣ Q 7 4 2

DECLARER
♠ A 7 5
♥ A Q 3
♦ 9 5 4 2
♣ K 10 8

## Answers to Exercise

### Exercise Eight — Watching out for the Opponents

The extra tricks that declarer needs can come from the diamond suit. The danger is that you have to let the opponents in twice while promoting your diamond winners. Play the ♥8 on the first trick and let East win with the ♥K. You're holding up your winners in the suit to try to strand West's winners.

## Exercise Nine — The Defensive Holdup
### (E-Z Deal Cards: #7, Hand 1 — Dealer, North)

Turn up the cards from the first pre-dealt deal. Put each hand dummy-style at the edge of the table in front of each player.

### The Bidding

What would North open the bidding? East and West pass throughout. At what level does South know the partnership belongs? Is there a Golden Fit in a major suit? What does South respond? How does the auction proceed? Who is the declarer?

Dealer:　♠ J62
North　♥ AK75
　　　　♦ Q4
　　　　♣ AK63

♠ Q95　　　　　♠ K1074
♥ Q94　　N　　♥ J832
♦ K65　W　E　♦ 83
♣ Q1082　S　　♣ J75

♠ A83
♥ 106
♦ AJ10972
♣ 94

### The Defense

Which player makes the opening lead? What would the opening lead be? Which card would West play on the first trick if a low card is played from dummy? What would West do next? Which card would West play if the first trick is won in dummy? Which suit must the defenders try to stop declarer from establishing? How can the defenders stop declarer from establishing that suit?

### The Play

Review the steps in declarer's PLAN. How does declarer plan to make the contract?

## Exercise Nine — The Defensive Holdup

### The Bidding

- North opens the bidding 1NT.
- South knows the partnership belongs in game and responds 3NT.
- All pass and North is the declarer in 3NT.

### The Defense

- East leads the ♠4, fourth highest.
- West plays the ♠Q, third hand high.
- West returns the ♠9, top of the remaining doubleton in partner's suit.
- If the first trick is won in dummy, West would encourage with the ♠9.
- The defenders want to try to prevent declarer from establishing diamonds.
- West can refuse to win the ♦K when declarer finesses the ♦Q. Since the ♠A is gone, the diamond tricks will be stranded if West wins the ♦K on the second diamond lead.

### The Play

- Declarer needs three more tricks to make the contract and is going to try to get them from the diamond suit. Declarer plans to lead the ♦Q, taking a finesse. Declarer should duck the first spade trick, holding up to try to prevent the defenders from taking too many spades. The second problem for the declarer is that the diamonds could be stranded.

## Exercise Ten — Discarding Carefully
### (E-Z Deal Cards: #7, Hand 2 — Dealer, East)

Turn up the cards from the second pre-dealt deal. Put each hand dummy-style at the edge of the table in front of each player.

### The Bidding

What would East open the bidding? North and South pass throughout. What does West know about the minimum combined strength of the partnership hands? At what level does the partnership belong? Is there any known Golden Fit? What does West respond? How does the auction proceed from there? What is the contract? Who is the declarer?

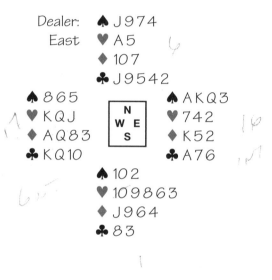

Dealer: ♠ J 9 7 4
East    ♥ A 5
        ♦ 10 7
        ♣ J 9 5 4 2

♠ 8 6 5            ♠ A K Q 3
♥ K Q J    N      ♥ 7 4 2
♦ A Q 8 3   W   E   ♦ K 5 2
♣ K Q 10    S      ♣ A 7 6

        ♠ 10 2
        ♥ 10 9 8 6 3
        ♦ J 9 6 4
        ♣ 8 3

### The Defense

Which player makes the opening lead? What would the opening lead be? Which suit must South guard? Which suits can North guard? How can North get clues as to which cards to discard and which cards to keep?

### The Play

Review the steps in declarer's PLAN. How does declarer plan to make the contract?

## Exercise Ten — Discarding Carefully

### The Bidding

- East opens the bidding 1NT.

- West knows that there are at least 33 combined points and that the partnership belongs in slam.

- Without a known Golden Fit, West responds 6NT.

- All pass. The final contract is 6NT, and East is the declarer.

### The Defense

- South leads the ♥10.

- South guards the diamonds and North guards the spades and clubs.

- North gets clues as to which cards to discard and which to keep by watching the cards partner and declarer play.

### The Play

- After the ♥A is driven out, declarer has three sure spade tricks, two heart tricks, three diamond tricks, and three club tricks. The last trick can come from either the spade suit or the diamond suit, if either suit divides 3–3 or if the defense errs while discarding.

## Exercise Eleven — Making Declarer Guess

### (E-Z Deal Cards: #7, Hand 3 — Dealer, South)

Turn up the cards from the third pre-dealt deal. Put each hand dummy-style at the edge of the table in front of each player.

### The Bidding

What is South's opening bid? East and West pass throughout. How many points does North have in support of South's suit? At what level does the partnership belong? In which denomination does the partnership belong? What does North respond? How does the bidding proceed from there? What is the contract? Who is the declarer?

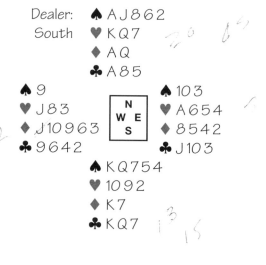

Dealer: ♠ A J 8 6 2
South ♥ K Q 7
♦ A Q
♣ A 8 5

♠ 9
♥ J 8 3
♦ J 10 9 6 3
♣ 9 6 4 2

♠ 10 3
♥ A 6 5 4
♦ 8 5 4 2
♣ J 10 3

♠ K Q 7 5 4
♥ 10 9 2
♦ K 7
♣ K Q 7

### The Defense

Which player makes the opening lead? What would the opening lead be? What possibilities can East see for a second defensive trick? What does East plan to do if a heart is led toward dummy? Why? Which suit must West avoid discarding?

### The Play

Review the steps in declarer's PLAN. How does declarer plan to make the contract?

## Exercise Eleven — Making Declarer Guess

### The Bidding

- South opens the bidding 1♠.
- North has 21 points in support of spades.
- The partnership belongs in slam in spades.
- North responds 6♠.
- All pass. The final contract is 6♠ and South is the declarer.

### The Defense

- West leads the ♦J.
- East sees that West might have a heart or a club trick.
- If a heart is led to dummy, East ducks hoping that declarer might have a guess in the heart suit.
- West has to avoid discarding hearts to keep the ♥J guarded.

### The Play

- Declarer can only afford one loser. There are two possible losers in the heart suit. Declarer plans to lead up to dummy's hearts, hoping that West has the ♥A.
- If East has the ♥A, declarer can hope West has the ♥J and lead the ♥10 for a finesse.

# Exercise Twelve — A Trump in Time

## (E-Z Deal Cards: #7, Hand 4 — Dealer, West)

Turn up the cards from the fourth pre-dealt deal. Put each hand dummy-style at the edge of the table in front of each player.

## The Bidding

What is West's opening bid? North and South pass throughout. Can East support partner's suit? What does East respond? How does the auction proceed from there? What is the contract? Who is the declarer?

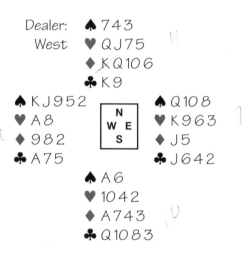

Dealer: ♠ 7 4 3
West ♥ Q J 7 5
♦ K Q 10 6
♣ K 9

♠ K J 9 5 2        ♠ Q 10 8
♥ A 8              ♥ K 9 6 3
♦ 9 8 2            ♦ J 5
♣ A 7 5            ♣ J 6 4 2

N
W E
S

♠ A 6
♥ 10 4 2
♦ A 7 4 3
♣ Q 10 8 3

## The Defense

Which player makes the opening lead? What would the opening lead be? Which card would South play on the first trick? Why? After seeing the dummy, what does North lead next? Why? How can South cooperate? What must South be careful to do if declarer leads a second diamond from dummy? Why?

## The Play

Review the steps in declarer's PLAN. How does declarer plan to make the contract?

## Exercise Twelve — A Trump in Time

### The Bidding

- West opens the bidding with 1♠.
- East can support partner's suit and bids 2♠.
- All pass. The final contract is 2♠ and West is the declarer.

### The Defense

- North leads the ♦K, top of touching high cards.
- South would play the ♦7 on the first trick to encourage.
- North leads a trump to try to stop declarer from ruffing a diamond in the dummy.
- South cooperates by winning the ♠A and leading another spade.
- If declarer leads a second diamond from dummy, South has to play low, not the ♦A.
- South wants North to be able to win the trick and lead another trump.

### The Play

- Declarer can afford five losers and has one too many. Declarer may be able to eliminate a diamond loser by ruffing one in the dummy. Declarer plans to give up two diamond tricks before drawing trumps.

# CHAPTER 8
## *Making a Plan*

In the previous chapters, we've looked at the various techniques the defenders have available. We've explored how they can work together to take tricks and to prevent declarer from taking tricks. A number of guidelines have been developed to help the defenders handle situations where they're not sure of the best play. Now it's time to put it all together and see how the defenders go about making a plan to defeat the declarer. Having a plan will help the defenders decide when to apply a guideline such as "return partner's lead" and when to step outside of it to try something different.

## THE DEFENDERS' PLAN

Ideally, the defenders want to make their plan in the same fashion as declarer. They have to go through the same four steps:

> 1. **P**ause to consider your objective
> 2. **L**ook at your winners and losers
> 3. **A**nalyze your alternatives
> 4. **N**ow put it all together

The disadvantage the defenders have is that they can't see each other's hands. Nonetheless, the idea of making a plan is still important. The defenders have to be more flexible than declarer, modifying their plan as the play goes along and they get more information about their combined holdings. Let's start by going through the basic planning steps and by seeing how they can be applied.

### Step One — The Objective

The defenders' basic objective is to defeat the contract whenever possible. The objective can be put into concrete terms in the same fashion that declarer determines how many winners are needed in a notrump contract or how many losers declarer can afford in a suit contract. The defenders consider how many tricks they need to defeat the contract. For example, when the contract is 2♠, declarer can afford five losers. The defenders need to find six tricks to come out on top.

Determining your objective may seem like a trivial task, but you shouldn't ignore it in favor of considering the best way to handle an individual suit.

## Step Two — Counting Tricks

The next step for declarer is to count winners or losers in order to see what is needed to achieve declarer's objective. Declarer does this by looking at the combined holdings in each suit. The defenders, unable to see each other's holdings, don't have it so easy. Suppose these are the defenders' hands:

| YOU | PARTNER |
|---|---|
| ♠ A K 6 4 | ♠ Q J 7 3 |
| ♥ A Q | ♥ 5 4 |
| ♦ J 8 5 4 | ♦ 10 9 2 |
| ♣ 9 6 2 | ♣ 8 7 5 3 |

If you're defending a notrump contract, you can see immediately that you have two spade winners and a heart winner. You wouldn't be able to tell right away that your side also has two more sure tricks in spades. Hopefully as the play progresses, you will be able to find that out. For example, partner may be able to make an encouraging signal in spades.

If you're defending a heart contract, it's less obvious how many tricks you have. The only trick you're sure to get is the ♥ A. The number of spade tricks depends on how the missing spades are divided. Looking at the combined hands, the best you could hope for is that the missing spades are divided 3–2, and you can take two tricks before declarer is able to trump in hand or in the dummy. If the missing spades are divided 4–1, you'll get only one trick, and if they're divided 5–0, there're no sure tricks for the defense.

If you're unable to see partner's hand, how would you know you can expect to take no more than two spade tricks? Often the auction will give you the clues you need. If your side has bid and raised a suit, you can generally expect that you have at least eight of them between you and partner and are unlikely to take more than two tricks against a suit contract, even when your side has all of the top cards in the suit. The fewer cards your side has in a suit, the more likely it is that your high cards will take tricks.

The best you can do before seeing the dummy is estimate the number of tricks you are likely to have. With the above hand, you know you'll get at least one heart trick if hearts is the trump suit. However, if the opponent on your right bid hearts first, you might expect RHO to have the ♥K. In that case, you'll get tricks with both the ♥A and the ♥Q. You won't know for sure when you make the opening lead, but you'll be waiting anxiously to see dummy. If the ♥K doesn't appear in the dummy, you can be confident about taking two heart tricks.

As a defender, you must be patient when trying to count your tricks. You can come up with an initial estimate but may have to adjust your estimate when dummy appears and as the play progresses.

## Step Three — The Alternatives

Once it has been determined how many winners declarer requires and how many declarer has, or the number of losers declarer can afford and the number declarer has, the next step is to look at the alternatives available for establishing extra winners or eliminating excess losers. Declarer looks at each combined suit in turn and analyzes the possibilities. The defenders want to take the same approach, looking to see where they can develop additional tricks.

As you have seen in earlier chapters, the defenders use exactly the same techniques as declarer for developing tricks. They can promote winners, establish long suits, take finesses, and ruff their losers. Again, they are hampered by the inability to see their combined holdings in a suit. That's why they often have to fall back on general guidelines: leading the fourth highest of their longest and strongest suit against notrump contracts; leading the top of touching high cards against suit contracts; playing second hand low and third hand high; covering an honor with an honor; leading through strength.

Once dummy appears, however, the defenders gain the advantage of seeing the location of half of declarer's cards. By visualizing the layout of the missing cards, a defender can often see possibilities for developing tricks. As play progresses, more information comes to light. The defenders can signal each other, and the line of play chosen by declarer will provide clues to the location of the missing cards.

Once more, the defenders must be patient about analyzing their alternatives. They'll have to revise their earlier thoughts as each card is played. For example, suppose you start off on opening lead with this hand, defending against a spade contract:

♠ 9 6 3    It looks as though you have one sure trick, the ♦ A.
♥ Q J 10   Where can other tricks come from? The heart suit
♦ A Q 6    offers the possibility of promotion. If declarer holds
♣ Q 9 5 2  the ♥ A and the ♥ K, you may be able to drive them
           out and promote a winner for your side. If partner
has the ♥ K, the promotion idea will work that much more quickly. There's also the possibility that partner has the ♥ A, and you'll be able to trap the ♥ K if it turns up in dummy. The diamond suit has the possibility of providing two tricks, especially if declarer has the ♦ K, provided you don't lead the ♦ A initially. You'll have to wait until partner or declarer leads the suit. On the other hand, if partner has the ♦ K, you may want to lead the suit as soon as you get the opportunity. You will want to take your winners before declarer is able to discard the diamond losers on another suit. The club suit offers some potential as well. If partner has some strength in the suit, you may be able to establish one or more winners by leading that suit.

Often the auction will have provided some clues. If partner has bid clubs, you might expect to be able to take or establish winners in that suit by leading a club. If declarer has bid diamonds, you would expect declarer to have the ♦ K and would want to wait to trap it. With no information to go on, you would probably choose to lead the ♥ Q and wait to see what further information you can get. Suppose this dummy comes down:

DUMMY
♠ K 8 5
♥ K 9 3
♦ 7 4 2
♣ A 8 6 3

**YOU**
♠ 9 6 3
♥ Q J 10
♦ A Q 6
♣ Q 9 5 2

Having led the ♥ Q, you're about to get additional information. If declarer wins the first trick with the ♥ A, you know that your only possibility to promote a trick in the suit is by driving out dummy's ♥ K. On the other hand, if declarer plays a low heart from dummy and your ♥ Q wins the first trick, it would be reasonable to assume that partner has the ♥ A and dummy's ♥ K is trapped. By continuing to lead hearts, you may be able to get one or two more tricks for the defense, depending on how many hearts declarer started with. You still don't know where the ♦ K is, but at least you know it's not in dummy. Perhaps partner will be able to clarify the situation later, either by giving an encouraging or discouraging signal, or by leading the suit. The possibilities in the club suit are also not clear, but you can see that partner can't have both the ♣ A and the ♣ K. You'll have to watch as the play develops to see whether this suit represents a potential source of tricks for the defense or for declarer.

## Step Four — Putting It All Together

The final step in declarer's plan is to choose from among the alternatives the one most likely to succeed and put everything together into an integrated plan. Declarer must be careful to watch the entries, using them wisely, and to watch out for the opponents, anticipating the damage they might do if they gain the lead.

The defenders need to put their plan together in a similar fashion. For example, to develop tricks in a suit, the suit may have to be led from a particular side. The defenders have to use their entries wisely. They also have to be aware of what declarer may do when in the lead, such as discarding or ruffing losers. The defenders have to coordinate their efforts, since there are two of them, each with an idea of what the plan should be. This is both a disadvantage and an advantage. Sometimes two heads are better than one!

You've already seen examples of how the defenders cooperate when executing their plan. A guideline such as *return partner's suit* helps point you in the right direction, even when you can't be sure of exactly what partner has in mind. A guideline such as *lead through strength* helps to get a suit led from the appropriate side. The defenders hope, as the play develops, that the individual plans made by the defenders will merge into a single unified plan, with both defenders focusing their efforts in the same direction.

As the defensive plan takes shape, you need to rely less on the guidelines. The overall plan has priority, and you may find that you need to override a particular guideline when the situation warrants it. Returning partner's suit may not be the way to defeat the contract, you may have to play second hand high or third hand low to give the defense its best chance.

# BEFORE THE OPENING LEAD

While it's difficult to make a complete plan before you have even seen the dummy, going through the steps is still worthwhile. It'll help you pick out the situations where the standard guidelines may not apply.

## Defending a Notrump Contract

Suppose the auction proceeds as follows:

| NORTH (DUMMY) | EAST (PARTNER) | SOUTH (DECLARER) | WEST (YOU) |
|---|---|---|---|
|  |  | 1NT | Pass |
| 3NT | Pass | Pass | Pass |

The bidding hasn't given you much information, and you have to find an opening lead from the following hand:

♠ K J 9 5 3
♥ A 8
♦ A 6
♣ Q 10 8 5

Knowing the guideline *fourth highest from your longest and strongest,* you might lead the ♠5. It's good practice, however, to go through the planning steps first. This first step is to consider your objective. To defeat three notrump, you need to take five tricks. The next step is to see how many tricks you have. There are two sure tricks, the ♥A and the ♦A, so you'll need to find three more to reach your objective. The third step is to consider the alternatives for developing the extra tricks you need. Any of the suits might provide the tricks you require and, without seeing partner's hand or the dummy, you can't be sure which suit will work out best. You do know that a good source of tricks is often the longest combined suit in the combined partnership hands. With no other information to go on, that makes spades an attractive possibility. You may change your mind later if, for example, partner turns up with a singleton spade, but you can't see a better alternative. The last step is to put everything together. You plan to lead a low spade, hoping partner will have some help in the suit. You also plan to use the ♥A and the ♦A as entries to help you establish the suit and then take your winners. So your plan leads you back to the conclusion that your opening lead should be the ♠5.

Here is the complete deal:

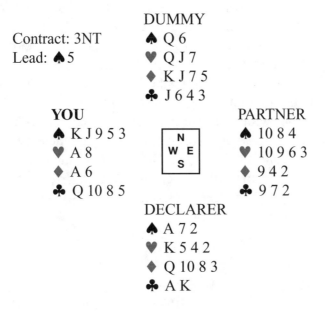

Contract: 3NT
Lead: ♠5

DUMMY
♠ Q 6
♥ Q J 7
♦ K J 7 5
♣ J 6 4 3

YOU
♠ K J 9 5 3
♥ A 8
♦ A 6
♣ Q 10 8 5

PARTNER
♠ 10 8 4
♥ 10 9 6 3
♦ 9 4 2
♣ 9 7 2

DECLARER
♠ A 7 2
♥ K 5 4 2
♦ Q 10 8 3
♣ A K

Declarer wins the first trick with dummy's ♠Q and, needing to develop some extra winners, leads a small diamond to the ♦Q. Having seen the dummy, there's nothing to make you revise your original plan. You win the ♦A and continue to establish your spade suit, leading the ♠K (or ♠J) to drive out declarer's ♠A. Declarer has only two spade tricks, three diamond tricks, and two club tricks to take, so declarer will have to lead a heart to try to establish the other winners needed to make the contract. You win the ♥A, your second entry, and take three spade tricks to defeat the contract.

Even though you don't have much to guide you before making your opening lead, you can see that it's possible to visualize how the play is likely to go and make a plan. This deal turned out much the way you expected. Now, suppose the auction goes exactly the same way, but we move a couple of cards around in your hand:

♠ 9 8 5 4 3      You go about making your plan in the same manner.
♥ A 8            You need five tricks to defeat the contract, and you
♦ A 6            start with the same two sure tricks. Where can the
♣ K Q J 10       additional tricks come from? Spades is your longest
                 suit and you may be able to establish the tricks you
need in that suit. You must look at all of the alternatives, however, and
this draws your attention to the club suit. By leading the ♣K, you'll be
able to drive out the ♣A and promote three winners in the suit. Putting
those tricks together with your two aces will give you enough tricks to
reach your objective. Leading a spade may or may not achieve your objective. Leading a club is a sure thing. By making a plan before making
the opening lead, you come to the conclusion that the ♣K is a better lead
than your fourth highest spade, even though spades is your longest suit.

Let's look at the complete deal:

```
                        DUMMY
Contract: 3NT        ♠ A J
Lead: ♣K             ♥ K J 7
                     ♦ J 10 7 3 2
                     ♣ 9 4 3

      YOU                              PARTNER
   ♠ 9 8 5 4 3                       ♠ 7 6
   ♥ A 8                             ♥ 9 5 4 2
   ♦ A 6              ┌─────┐        ♦ 9 5 4
   ♣ K Q J 10         │  N  │        ♣ 7 6 5 2
                      │W   E│
                      │  S  │
                      └─────┘
                     DECLARER
                     ♠ K Q 10 2
                     ♥ Q 10 6 3
                     ♦ K Q 8
                     ♣ A 8
```

When you lead the ♣K, declarer has no chance. After winning the ♣A, it will be necessary to lead a diamond to establish the tricks needed to make the contract. You win the ♦A and take your club winners and the ♥A. If you lead a spade originally, declarer will win dummy's ♠A and lead a diamond to drive out your ♦A. Now it will be too late to lead a club. Declarer has four spade tricks, four diamond tricks, and the ♣A, enough to make the contract.

## Defending a Suit Contract

Making a plan before making the opening lead can be equally effective against a suit contract. Suppose the auction proceeds as follows:

| NORTH (DUMMY) | EAST (PARTNER) | SOUTH (DECLARER) | WEST (YOU) |
|---|---|---|---|
| | 1♥ | 1♠ | Pass |
| 3♠ | Pass | 4♠ | Pass |
| Pass | Pass | | |

You have to make the opening lead with the following hand:

♠ 7 5
♥ J 10 7
♦ 8 6 4
♣ 10 9 7 5 2

*Lead partner's suit* jumps out as the guideline to apply, but first go through the planning steps. You'll need four tricks to defeat the contract. You don't appear to have any, so it looks as though they will have to come from partner. What are the possibilities? Partner is likely to have some strength in hearts, since partner bid the suit. You may be able to help partner establish some tricks in the suit by leading a heart. Nothing else looks more appealing, so you lead the ♥J, top of touching cards in partner's suit.

Here is the complete deal:

```
                        DUMMY
Contract: 4♠            ♠ K 10 9 2
Lead: ♥J                ♥ K 9
                        ♦ J 10 9 3 2
                        ♣ Q J
YOU                                      PARTNER
♠ 7 5                   ┌─────┐          ♠ 6 4
♥ J 10 7               │  N  │          ♥ A Q 8 4 2
♦ 8 6 4                │W  E │          ♦ A 7 5
♣ 10 9 7 5 2           │  S  │          ♣ A 8 3
                        └─────┘
                        DECLARER
                        ♠ A Q J 8 3
                        ♥ 6 5 3
                        ♦ K Q
                        ♣ K 6 4
```

Your lead of the ♥J easily defeats the contract. Dummy's ♥K is trapped. Partner gets two heart tricks and the ♦A and the ♣A, enough to defeat the contract. If you had led another suit, declarer would have made the contract. Partner would be unable to trap dummy's ♥K by leading into dummy's strength and would get only the three aces. Declarer would be able to discard the other heart losers. Leading partner's suit turned out to be the winning defense. Now, let's have the auction go the same way, but change your hand slightly:

♠ 7 5            Again your objective is to take four tricks and you
♥ J 10 7 6 5     don't have any sure tricks in your hand. Since part-
♦ 8              ner opened the bidding 1 ♥, the heart suit is again a
♣ 10 9 7 5 2     possible source of tricks. This time, however, you
                 have five of them. Partner is also showing at least
a five-card suit. The opponents have at most three between them, so one
opponent can have no more than a singleton heart. At best, your side will

get one trick from the suit. Are there any alternatives? You have a singleton diamond. If you lead it, partner may be able to win the trick and lead one back for you to ruff. If you can get back to partner's hand, you may even be able to get a second ruff. That looks like a more promising plan than leading the ♥ J.

You lead the ♦ 8 and this is the complete deal:

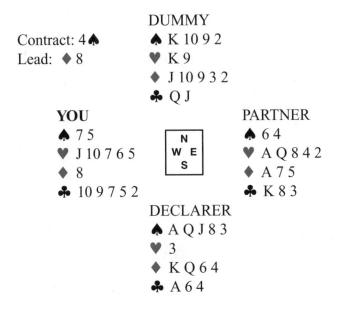

DUMMY
Contract: 4♠          ♠ K 10 9 2
Lead: ♦ 8              ♥ K 9
                      ♦ J 10 9 3 2
                      ♣ Q J

YOU                                    PARTNER
♠ 7 5                                  ♠ 6 4
♥ J 10 7 6 5      N                    ♥ A Q 8 4 2
♦ 8             W   E                  ♦ A 7 5
♣ 10 9 7 5 2        S                  ♣ K 8 3

DECLARER
♠ A Q J 8 3
♥ 3
♦ K Q 6 4
♣ A 6 4

Partner will need to cooperate, but your unusual lead of a diamond, rather than partner's suit, should be a tip-off to the winning defense. Partner wins the first trick with the ♦ A and leads a diamond back for you to ruff. Partner should return the ♦ 7, a suit-preference signal for the higher-ranking suit. Now you return a heart. Partner must be careful to win this trick and lead the last diamond for you to ruff, rather than trying to take a second heart trick. With careful cooperation, the partnership has found the only defense to defeat the contract. If you hadn't taken the time to make a plan beforehand, you might have been lulled into following the general guideline to lead partner's suit.

# AFTER THE OPENING LEAD

After the opening lead has been made, both defenders can see the dummy and adjust their plan accordingly. The further the play progresses, the more information they'll have and the more accurate their plan will become. Here are some examples.

## A Shift in Time

You are East and the auction goes as follows:

| NORTH | EAST | SOUTH | WEST |
|-------|------|-------|------|
| (DUMMY) | (YOU) | (DECLARER) | (PARTNER) |
| | | 1♠ | Pass |
| 2♣ | Pass | 2♠ | Pass |
| 4♠ | Pass | Pass | Pass |

Partner leads the ♦5 and this is the complete deal:

Contract: 4♠
Lead: ♦5

DUMMY
♠ Q 9 8
♥ Q 6 2
♦ A Q 3
♣ Q J 10 7

PARTNER
♠ 6 5
♥ A 9 5
♦ K 10 8 5 2
♣ 8 4 2

YOU
♠ 10 4
♥ K J 8 4
♦ J 9 6
♣ A 9 6 3

DECLARER
♠ A K J 7 3 2
♥ 10 7 3
♦ 7 4
♣ K 5

Declarer wins the first trick with dummy's ♦Q, draws trump by playing the ♠A and the ♠K and then leads the ♣K, on which your partner plays the ♣2. Since partner obviously doesn't need to show attitude toward clubs, the ♣2 must be a count signal, showing an odd number, likely three. Declarer started with only two clubs, but there's not much point in holding up your ♣A, since there are plenty of entries to dummy. After winning the ♣A, it may be tempting to lead back a diamond, following the guideline to "return partner's suit." You should've been busy revising your plan, however.

You need four tricks to defeat the contract and can see only one for sure, the ♣A. Where are the others to come from? You might be able to establish a trick in diamonds by driving out dummy's ♦A but, even if declarer started with a diamond loser, it can probably be discarded on one of dummy's established club winners. The only hope is in the heart suit. Can you visualize a layout of the suit which will let you take three tricks?

If partner has the ♥A, you can lead a low heart. Partner will win with the ♥A and lead a heart back, trapping dummy's ♥Q. Since that's your only hope, you win the ♣A and return the ♥4, forgetting about partner's original suit. Hopefully, partner is busy planning too and can see that the only way to defeat the contract is to take three heart tricks quickly. After winning the ♥A, partner leads back the ♥9 and declarer is defeated. If you'd returned partner's suit after winning the ♣A, declarer would have discarded two heart losers on dummy's extra club winners and ended up making an overtrick.

Shifting from one suit to another in order to take your winners before declarer can discard losers is an important consideration in your plan. Let's put you back on opening lead after the auction has gone as follows:

| NORTH (DUMMY) | EAST (PARTNER) | SOUTH (DECLARER) | WEST (YOU) |
|---|---|---|---|
| | Pass | 1♠ | Pass |
| 2♣ | Pass | 2♠ | Pass |
| 4♠ | Pass | Pass | Pass |

You lead the ♥A, and this is the complete layout:

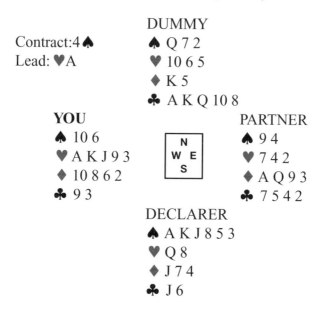

                              DUMMY
        Contract:4♠          ♠ Q 7 2
        Lead: ♥A             ♥ 10 6 5
                             ♦ K 5
                             ♣ A K Q 10 8
        YOU                                    PARTNER
        ♠ 10 6                                 ♠ 9 4
        ♥ A K J 9 3                            ♥ 7 4 2
        ♦ 10 8 6 2                             ♦ A Q 9 3
        ♣ 9 3                                  ♣ 7 5 4 2
                              DECLARER
                             ♠ A K J 8 5 3
                             ♥ Q 8
                             ♦ J 7 4
                             ♣ J 6

You need four tricks. It's not clear how many heart tricks you can take, but after seeing the dummy and partner's first card, the picture becomes clearer. Partner plays the ♥2 on the first trick, a discouraging card, apparently denying having the ♥Q. Partner is unlikely to have exactly two hearts since partner might have encouraged, hoping to get a ruff, with that holding. Partner could also have a singleton heart, so you continue with the ♥K. When declarer's ♥Q appears, the layout of the heart suit becomes evident. You could continue by leading the ♥J, making declarer ruff, but you must first consider your plan. You've taken two tricks and two more are needed to defeat the contract. Partner may have a trump trick, but partner will get that without your help.

The only other possibility appears to be diamonds. If partner has tricks in diamonds, they may disappear if you don't lead one now. Declarer may be able to discard the diamond losers on dummy's extra club winners after drawing trumps. In order to achieve your objective of defeating the contract, you must shift to a diamond. On the actual deal, partner is able to take two diamond tricks, trapping dummy's ♦K, and you defeat the contract. If you led anything else, declarer would draw trumps and take the rest of the tricks. You may have been lucky to find partner with the ♦A and the ♦Q, but if you hadn't thought about your plan, even that fortunate holding would not have been enough.

## Giving the Right Signal

Making a plan will often help you choose the appropriate signal to give partner when you have the opportunity. Consider this deal:

```
                        DUMMY
Contract: 2♠            ♠Q 7
Lead: ♥A                ♥10 8 7
                        ♦A Q 8
                        ♣K Q J 8 4

        PARTNER                    YOU
        ♠J 6 5          ┌───┐      ♠9 3
        ♥A K J 6        │ N │      ♥Q 9 2
        ♦7 4 3        W │   │ E    ♦K J 9 5
        ♣9 6 3          │ S │      ♣A 7 5 2
                        └───┘
                        DECLARER
                        ♠A K 10 8 4 2
                        ♥5 4 3
                        ♦10 6 2
                        ♣10
```

Partner leads the ♥A after the bidding has gone:

| NORTH | EAST | SOUTH | WEST |
|-------|------|-------|------|
| (DUMMY) | (YOU) | (DECLARER) | (PARTNER) |
| 1♣ | Pass | 1♠ | Pass |
| 1NT | Pass | 2♠ | Pass |
| Pass | Pass | | |

Looking at the ♥Q in your hand, it would seem natural to make an encouraging signal with the ♥9, but first you must consider your plan. To defeat 2♠, you need to take six tricks. It looks as though you may be able to get three heart tricks to go along with your ♣A, but where are the other tricks going to come from? Looking at your diamond holding, there's the possibility of two diamond tricks, provided the suit is led from partner's side, through dummy's strength. How can you get partner to lead a diamond? Not by encouraging in the heart suit! Instead, play the ♥2, a discouraging signal. On seeing this card, partner may not be certain what to do, but it doesn't look as though leading a club will help the defense establish tricks. You hope partner will also realize that the defenders will need some tricks from the diamond suit and use this opportunity to lead one through dummy's strength to help you out.

If partner leads a diamond, the defenders can prevail. If declarer plays dummy's ♦A and leads the ♣K to drive out your ♣A, you can lead a heart to partner and partner can lead another diamond through, trapping dummy's ♦Q. You end up with three heart tricks, two diamond tricks, and one club trick. It doesn't do declarer any good to finesse dummy's ♦Q. You win the ♦K, lead a heart to partner, and partner leads another diamond, establishing your ♦J as a trick. It also doesn't do any good for declarer to play the ♦8 when your partner leads one. You win the trick with the ♦J, lead back a heart, and partner leads another diamond to set up the second diamond trick for the defense.

If you played an encouraging heart on the first trick, partner would take the ♥K and lead another heart to your ♥Q. Now it's too late to lead diamonds. Declarer will drive out your ♣A and discard the diamond losers on dummy's ♣Q and ♣J, making an overtrick.

Sometimes, you have to do the exact opposite to the above example. You may need to play an encouraging card when you don't have any interest in the suit partner has led. Suppose the auction goes this way:

| NORTH | EAST | SOUTH | WEST |
|-------|------|-------|------|
| (DUMMY) | **(YOU)** | (DECLARER) | (PARTNER) |
| | | 1 ♠ | Pass |
| 3 ♠ | Pass | 4 ♠ | Pass |
| Pass | Pass | | |

Partner leads the ♥ J and this is the complete deal:

Contract: 4 ♠
Lead: ♥ J

DUMMY
♠ 9 7 4 2
♥ A K 5
♦ A 7 3
♣ A 8 6

PARTNER
♠ A Q J
♥ J 10 9 4
♦ Q 6 4
♣ Q 9 5

YOU
♠ 5
♥ 8 7 2
♦ 10 9 5 2
♣ 10 7 4 3 2

DECLARER
♠ K 10 8 6 3
♥ Q 6 3
♦ K J 8
♣ K J

Declarer wins dummy's ♥ A and leads a spade toward the ♠ K. After winning the first spade trick, what does partner do next? Partner can see that there are three spade tricks and that one more trick is needed to defeat the contract. If you gave a discouraging signal on the first heart trick by playing the ♥ 2, partner will know the extra trick will have to come from either diamonds or clubs. Partner may lead one of these suits, hoping that you have the king, or at least the jack, so that a trick can be established before all of the trumps are gone, and declarer can discard any loser in the suit.

Looking at the actual deal, your side will not defeat the contract if partner leads either a diamond or a club. If partner leads a diamond, declarer will get a trick with the ♦ J. If partner leads a club, declarer will get a trick with the ♣J and later discard a diamond loser on dummy's ♣A. The only safe defense is for partner to take the spade winners and lead another heart. Declarer will eventually have to lose another trick due to the unfavorable lie of the missing queens. Partner may conclude that this is the way to defend, but you can help out. Instead of playing a discouraging card on the first trick, play an encouraging card, the ♥8 (or ♥7). It's not that you like hearts so much, it's that your plan doesn't indicate anything better for partner to lead.

## Working Together

Although each partner's plan may be vague to start with, the direction will become clearer as the play progresses. Eventually, the two separate plans should merge into one. Take a look at this deal:

| NORTH (DUMMY) | EAST (PARTNER) | SOUTH (DECLARER) | WEST (YOU) |
|---|---|---|---|
| | | | Pass |
| | | 1 ♥ | Pass |
| 2 ♥ | Pass | Pass | Pass |

Contract: 2 ♥
Lead: ♦10

DUMMY
♠ 7 6 3
♥ J 10 6 2
♦ K J 7
♣ K Q 8

YOU
♠ A Q 8 4
♥ 9 8
♦ 10 9 8 6
♣ J 9 3

PARTNER
♠ 10 9 2
♥ K 4
♦ A Q 5
♣ 10 7 6 4 2

DECLARER
♠ K J 5
♥ A Q 7 5 3
♦ 4 3 2
♣ A 5

You don't have much to go on before you make the opening lead. You know you need six tricks to defeat 2 ♥, but it's hard to see where they will come from. One possibility is the ♠A and the ♠Q. You probably can get two tricks if either partner or declarer has the ♠K. If declarer has it, you'll have to wait for partner or declarer to lead the suit. In the meantime, you start off by leading the ♦10, top of your sequence, hoping partner has some help in the suit so you can establish some tricks.

You and your partner are in a similar position before dummy comes down — uncertain where all of the tricks will come from. Once partner sees the dummy and your opening lead, however, things pick up. Partner can see that your lead has trapped dummy's ♦K and ♦J, since partner holds the ♦A and the ♦Q. If declarer doesn't have a singleton or doubleton diamond, it may be possible to get three tricks from that suit. What possibilities are there for more tricks? Partner may think you have a trump trick or the ♣A. Those you are likely to get anyway. Looking at the spade weakness in dummy, however, there is the possibility of trapping high cards in declarer's hand, provided partner leads the suit through the assumed strength.

Suppose declarer puts dummy's ♦J on your ♦10 and partner wins the trick with the ♦Q. Now partner leads back the ♠10, leading through strength and up to the weakness in dummy. Declarer plays the ♠J, and you win the trick with the ♠Q. Things come into focus, and the defense is shifting into high gear. You can lead back the ♦9, trapping dummy's ♦K. After winning the ♦A, partner leads back another spade, trapping declarer's ♠K. The defense ends up taking the first six tricks, three diamond tricks and three spade tricks. After the opening lead, the opportunities for the defenders became clearer and clearer.

On the above deal, both defenders followed the guideline of *leading through strength*. Sometimes your defensive plan will show that it's time to lead right into strength.

Suppose the auction goes like this:

| NORTH | EAST | SOUTH | WEST |
|-------|------|-------|------|
| (DUMMY) | **(YOU)** | (DECLARER) | (PARTNER) |
| 1 ♥ | Pass | 1NT | Pass |
| Pass | Pass | | |

Partner makes the opening lead of the ♠J, and this is the full deal:

```
                      DUMMY
   Contract: 1NT      ♠ K Q 6
   Lead: ♠ J          ♥ J 10 9 8 5
                      ♦ K J 10
                      ♣ K 8
   PARTNER                         YOU
   ♠ J 10 9 4          N           ♠ 8 3 2
   ♥ A 7 6 4       W       E       ♥ K 3
   ♦ 8 6               S           ♦ A Q 7 4 2
   ♣ A J 5                         ♣ 10 7 2
                      DECLARER
                      ♠ A 7 5
                      ♥ Q 2
                      ♦ 9 5 3
                      ♣ Q 9 6 4 3
```

Declarer wins the first trick with the ♠A and leads the ♥Q. Partner and dummy play low hearts and it's up to you. You consider holding up the first round, but there appears to be enough entries to dummy for declarer to establish the suit, so you win the ♥K. What next? Your plan says you need seven tricks. Where will they come from? You may be able to establish some tricks in spades, the suit partner led, depending on how many partner holds. It looks as though partner has the ♥A, and declarer is planning to drive it out to establish winners in the suit. Partner may come up with a trick or two in clubs, but by that time, declarer will probably have enough winners to make the contract.

It looks as if you need some tricks from the diamond suit. Holding the ♦ A and the ♦ Q, usually you would want partner to lead the suit through dummy's strength, but you have no time to wait. Lead back a small diamond, into dummy's strength, letting dummy win a trick with the ♦ 10. Declarer will lead another heart to drive out partner's ♥ A and establish three winners in the suit. Now it's up to partner who must assume that you have a good reason for leading back a diamond, rather than a spade. Cooperating with your plan, even though partner can't see your hand, partner leads back a diamond, enabling you to take four diamond tricks. Together with the two heart tricks and partner's ♣ A, you just manage to defeat the contract.

## Giving the Defensive Plan Priority

Here is an example of ignoring the principle of *second hand low*. South opens 1NT and is raised to 3NT by North. Partner leads the ♥ Q, and this is the complete layout:

```
                     DUMMY
Contract: 3NT        ♠ K 6 4
Lead: ♥ Q            ♥ K 7 3
                     ♦ 9 6 4
                     ♣ A 9 5 2

      PARTNER                      YOU
      ♠ J 5            ┌───────┐   ♠ Q 10 9 7 2
      ♥ Q J 10 8 5     │  N    │   ♥ 6 4
      ♦ K 3            │ W  E  │   ♦ A 8 5
      ♣ Q 7 4 3        │  S    │   ♣ 10 8 6
                       └───────┘
                     DECLARER
                     ♠ A 8 3
                     ♥ A 9 2
                     ♦ Q J 10 7 2
                     ♣ K J
```

Declarer wins the first trick with dummy's ♥ K and leads a diamond from dummy. If you instinctively follow by playing the ♦ 5, second hand low, declarer makes the contract. How do you know that this is the time to play *second hand high*? You have to be busy making your plan. You can see only one sure trick for the defense, the ♦ A. Partner's lead of the ♥ Q, however, gives you valuable information. It looks as though partner has led from a long suit headed by a sequence. This should be a good potential source of tricks for the defense, you hope enough to defeat the contract. When putting your plan together, is there any problem? Just as declarer has to be careful to watch entries when making a plan, so must the defenders. While partner may be able to establish the heart suit when partner next gets the lead, there may not be any entries left. It won't do any good if you get the lead — partner's winners will be stranded.

To prevent this, you need to use your entry first to establish partner's winners. Partner's entry is used later to take the heart winners. Play the ♦ A right away and lead another heart, establishing the suit. When declarer tries to establish the winners needed in the diamond suit, partner will get a trick with the ♦ K and will be able to take the heart tricks, defeating the contract.

If you play a low diamond on the first trick, declarer will play a high diamond, driving out partner's ♦ K. Partner can lead another heart to drive out declarer's ♥ A, but it won't do any good. Declarer can drive out your ♦ A, and you won't have any hearts left to lead. Declarer ends up with two spade tricks, two heart tricks, three diamond tricks, and two club tricks, making the contract.

Normally, you don't want to let declarer ruff losers in the dummy. Here's a deal to show that there are times when you must actually force declarer to ruff in the dummy in order to defeat the contract. Here's the complete deal:

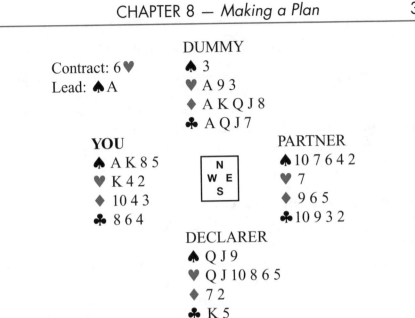

Contract: 6 ♥
Lead: ♠ A

DUMMY
♠ 3
♥ A 9 3
♦ A K Q J 8
♣ A Q J 7

YOU
♠ A K 8 5
♥ K 4 2
♦ 10 4 3
♣ 8 6 4

PARTNER
♠ 10 7 6 4 2
♥ 7
♦ 9 6 5
♣ 10 9 3 2

DECLARER
♠ Q J 9
♥ Q J 10 8 6 5
♦ 7 2
♣ K 5

The opponents have a long auction to 6 ♥. Holding the ♠A and the ♠K, as well as the ♥K, you might think of doubling the contract. If you do, you had better be careful while defending it. You start off by leading the ♠A, hoping to take two quick spade tricks, but the sight of dummy forces you to abandon your original plan. The singleton spade in dummy implies that you aren't going to get a second trick in that suit. In addition, the ♥A has shown up in dummy, leaving your ♥K in danger of being trapped. Is there anything you can do to find the second trick you need?

The answer is to lead your ♠K, even though declarer can ruff it in dummy. The advantage of this play is that declarer will be left with only two hearts in dummy and will no longer be able to trap your ♥K. When declarer leads the ♥Q, you'll refuse to cover, and eventually you'll take the setting trick with the ♥K. It's always a good feeling to defeat an opponent's slam contract.

# BIDDING REVIEW

When both sides are in the auction, it isn't always possible to make the ideal bid. The opponents' bidding often takes away the room you and your partner need to describe your hands. In such situations, you may have to make the best bid possible, rather than the best possible bid. Competition gives an added element of excitement to the auction.

## When an Opponent Overcalls

Suppose your partner opens the bidding 1♦, and you hold the following hand:

♠ K 10 6 3
♥ J 6 4
♦ 10 8
♣ A 9 6 3

With 8 HCPs, you plan to respond 1♠, bidding a new suit at the one level. If the opponent on your right overcalls 1♥, no harm has been done. You can still respond 1♠. The opponent's bid hasn't interfered with your natural response. On the other hand, if the opponent overcalls 1♠, rather than 1♥, you can't make your normal response. On this hand, however, you have a suitable alternative. You can respond 1NT, showing partner that you have 6 to 10 points. Things are more difficult if the opponent overcalls 2♣. You don't have enough strength to bid at the two level. Instead, you'll have to pass. This is not ideal, because partner doesn't know you have some strength. The auction isn't over, however. Partner still has another chance to bid if holding more than a minimum hand — you may still get an opportunity to describe your hand.

## The Penalty Double

One bid that becomes available when the opponents interfere with your auction is the penalty double. A double is for takeout only if your partner hasn't already made a bid in the auction. For example, suppose your partner opens the bidding 1♥, and you have the following hand:

♠ A J 8 3
♥ 8
♦ K J 10 6 4
♣ Q 10 3

If the opponent on your right overcalls 2♦, this is a good hand on which to make a penalty double. With partner having the strength for an opening bid, it's very unlikely that the opponents can make a contract of 2♦. Your double tells partner you would like to defend the hand for penalties. You're not concerned about warning the opponents that they are in trouble. It doesn't look as though they have any better place to play the contract.

## When an Opponent Makes a Takeout Double

If an opponent doubles your partner's bid for takeout, it doesn't take up any room in the auction. The easiest thing to do is to continue making your natural bids as though nothing happened. In later books in the series, we'll look at the use of the redouble after an opponent has doubled. For now, bidding naturally will suffice.

## Competing for Partscore

When both sides are bidding and the strength is fairly evenly divided, you'll often be faced with having to choose between the following actions:

• Pass, planning to defend against the opponents' contract.

• Bid higher, hoping to buy the contract or to push the opponents even higher.

For example, suppose partner opens the bidding 1♥ and you hold the following hand:

♠ 7 4
♥ A 9 6 3
♦ K 10 8 6 5
♣ 9 5

If the opponent on your right overcalls 1♠, you would raise to 2♥, hoping to play there if partner has a minimum hand. If the opponent on your left bids 2♠, however, and partner and the overcaller both pass, you're faced with a decision. You can pass and defend 2♠, hoping to defeat that contract, or you can bid on to 3♥, hoping to make that contract or push the opponents up to 3♠. With good support for your partner and little defense against a spade contract, you should bid 3♥ on the actual hand. Partner will know that you're just competing. You limited your hand to 6 to 10 points when you raised to 2♥ originally.

# PLAY OF THE HAND REVIEW

When declarer is putting together a plan in a suit contract, one of the key considerations is how to handle the trump suit. Declarer must decide whether to draw trumps right away or to delay drawing trumps while dealing with other priorities.

## Drawing Trumps

In general, you want to draw trumps as soon as possible to avoid having the opponents ruff any of your winners. If you don't need your trumps for any other purpose, you should draw trumps when:

- You don't have more losers than you can afford.
- You have more losers than you can afford but can draw trumps without giving up the lead to the opponents.
- You have more losers than you can afford but there aren't too many quick losers if you have to give up the lead while drawing trumps.

For example, consider the following deal. You are playing in a 4♠ contract and the opening lead is the ♦J:

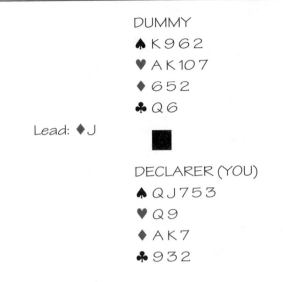

DUMMY

♠ K 9 6 2

♥ A K 10 7

♦ 6 5 2

♣ Q 6

Lead: ♦ J

DECLARER (YOU)

♠ Q J 7 5 3

♥ Q 9

♦ A K 7

♣ 9 3 2

You have a spade loser, a diamond loser, and three club losers. You'll have to give up the lead to draw trumps because the opponents have the ♠A. You have only three quick losers, however — the ♠A and two club tricks. It's safe to start drawing trumps. Once the opponents' trumps are gone, you plan to discard a diamond loser on dummy's extra heart winner and ruff a club loser in the dummy. If you tried to discard your diamond loser before drawing trumps, an opponent might ruff one of your heart tricks. Now you could no longer make the contract.

## Delaying Drawing Trumps

You'll have to delay drawing trumps when:

- You may have to give up the lead and have too many quick losers.
- You need the trumps for other purposes, such as ruffing losers or for entries.
- You need to get to the other hand so that you can take a finesse in the trump suit to avoid a loser.

Consider the following deal in a contract of 4♠ with the opening lead of a club:

DUMMY

♠ K 9 3

♥ A K 7 5

♦ 10 5

♣ K 8 4 2

Lead: ♣J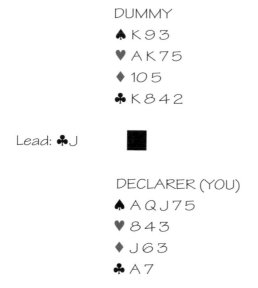

DECLARER (YOU)

♠ A Q J 7 5

♥ 8 4 3

♦ J 6 3

♣ A 7

There's a heart loser and three diamond losers. You can eliminate one of the diamond losers by ruffing in dummy. You need only
one trump to ruff your loser, but you can't afford to draw even
one round. You'll have to give up the lead twice to make dummy
void in diamonds so that you can ruff your loser. The opponents
may try to foil your plan by leading trumps when they get in. You
must therefore lead a diamond immediately after winning the first
club trick. The opponents can lead trumps twice, but you'll still
have one left in dummy to ruff your loser.

## SUMMARY

Each defender makes a plan, going through the same steps as declarer:

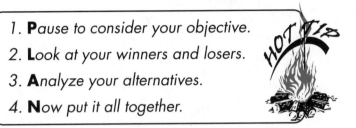

> 1. **P**ause to consider your objective.
> 2. **L**ook at your winners and losers.
> 3. **A**nalyze your alternatives.
> 4. **N**ow put it all together.

Since the defenders can't see their combined holding in each suit, it's sometimes difficult to determine where their tricks will come from. Nonetheless, making a plan will often point them in the right direction and, as the hand progresses, the plan will become more concrete. The defenders try to work together, giving each other information through their signals and trying to visualize how they can help each other. They both want to end up working on the same plan.

## Exercise One — Before Dummy Comes Down

You (West) are on lead with the following hand:

♠ 10 9 8 3
♥ K 5
♦ A Q 3
♣ J 6 4 2

The auction has gone:

| NORTH (DUMMY) | EAST (PARTNER) | SOUTH (DECLARER) | WEST (YOU) |
|---|---|---|---|
|  |  | 1♥ | Pass |
| 2♣ | Pass | 2♦ | Pass |
| 2♥ | Pass | 4♥ | Pass |
| Pass | Pass |  |  |

How do you plan to defeat the contract? What's your opening lead?

## Answers to Exercise

## Exercise One — Before Dummy Comes Down

First pause to consider your objective. You need four tricks to defeat declarer's 4♥ contract. Next look at the tricks you have. It's likely that you have a trick with the ♦A and perhaps the ♥K. You might get a trick with the ♦Q. Although you aren't sure where all of your tricks will come from, your best lead is probably a spade. You hope partner has a trick in that suit and will be able to lead a diamond to trap declarer's ♦K. Together with the ♥K, the prospects aren't too bad. You'll lead the ♠10, top of touching high cards, and wait to see dummy.

## Exercise Two — After Dummy Comes Down

You (East) are defending a contract of 4♠ after the bidding has gone:

| NORTH | EAST | SOUTH | WEST |
|---|---|---|---|
| (DUMMY) | (YOU) | (DECLARER) | (PARTNER) |
| 1♦ | Pass | 1♠ | Pass |
| 1NT | Pass | 4♠ | Pass |
| Pass | Pass | | |

Partner leads the ♥2 and dummy is put down:

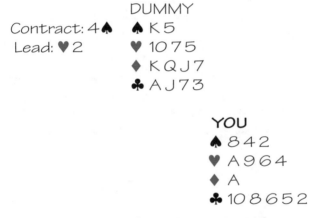

Contract: 4♠
Lead: ♥2

DUMMY
♠ K 5
♥ 10 7 5
♦ K Q J 7
♣ A J 7 3

YOU
♠ 8 4 2
♥ A 9 6 4
♦ A
♣ 10 8 6 5 2

How do you plan to defeat the contract?

## Answers to Exercise

### Exercise Two — After Dummy Comes Dow

Partner leads the ♥2, and you're third hand to play. Before automatically playing third hand high, consider your plan. You need four tricks. You have two aces. You have the potential for a trump trick by getting a ruff in the diamond suit. Take the first trick with the ♥A. Now, instead of returning partner's suit, play the ♦A. Then return partner's suit by playing the ♥4, and wait for partner to get the lead and return a diamond.

## Exercise Three — Competitive Bidding

Your partner opens the bidding 1♥, and the opponent on your right overcalls 2♣. What do you bid on each of the following hands?

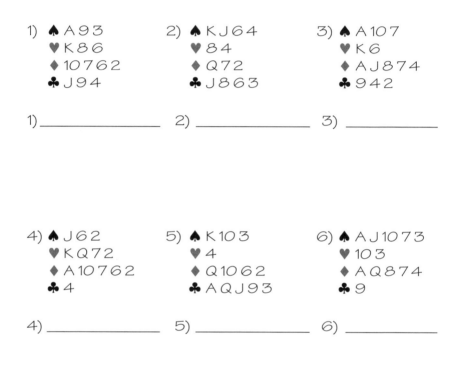

1) ♠ A 9 3
♥ K 8 6
♦ 10 7 6 2
♣ J 9 4

2) ♠ K J 6 4
♥ 8 4
♦ Q 7 2
♣ J 8 6 3

3) ♠ A 10 7
♥ K 6
♦ A J 8 7 4
♣ 9 4 2

1) _____  2) _____  3) _____

4) ♠ J 6 2
♥ K Q 7 2
♦ A 10 7 6 2
♣ 4

5) ♠ K 10 3
♥ 4
♦ Q 10 6 2
♣ A Q J 9 3

6) ♠ A J 10 7 3
♥ 10 3
♦ A Q 8 7 4
♣ 9

4) _____  5) _____  6) _____

## Answers to Exercise

### Exercise Three — Competitive Bidding

1) 2♥        2) Pass        3) 2♦

4) 3♥ or 4♥    5) Double    6) 2♠

## Exercise Four — Drawing Trumps

How do you plan to play in a contract of 6♣ after an opening lead of the ♥K?

DUMMY
♠ K 9
♥ A 9 6 4
♦ A Q 7
♣ 10 9 6 3

Lead: ♥K

DECLARER (**YOU**)
♠ A Q J 5
♥ J 7
♦ 8
♣ K Q J 8 5 2

## Answers to Exercise

## Exercise Four — Drawing Trumps

You need 12 tricks and can afford only one loser. You start with a heart loser and a trump loser, one too many. Since you can't do anything about the trump loser, you'll have to get rid of the heart loser. You can create an extra diamond winner if the finesse in diamonds works. This is a chance you have to take if you're going to make your slam.

## Exercise Five — *Making a Plan*

### (E-Z Deal Cards: #8, Hand 1 — Dealer, North)

Turn up the cards from the first pre-dealt deal. Put each hand dummy-style at the edge of the table in front of each player.

### The Bidding

North and South pass throughout the auction. What would East open the bidding? How does West plan to show support for partner's major with 12 dummy points? How does the auction proceed? What is the contract? Who is the declarer?

Dealer:  ♠ 8
North   ♥ J 10 9 2
        ♦ A 8 6 2
        ♣ A 10 4 3

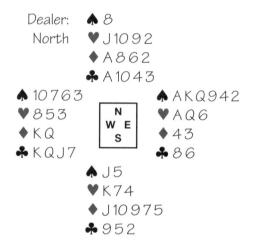

♠ 10 7 6 3                ♠ A K Q 9 4 2
♥ 8 5 3                    ♥ A Q 6
♦ K Q                        ♦ 4 3
♣ K Q J 7                ♣ 8 6

                ♠ J 5
                ♥ K 7 4
                ♦ J 10 9 7 5
                ♣ 9 5 2

### The Defense

Which player makes the opening lead? What would the opening lead be? After seeing the dummy, how does North plan to defeat the contract?

### The Play

Review the steps in declarer's PLAN. How does declarer plan to make the contract?

## Exercise Five — Making a Plan

### The Bidding

- East opens 1♠.
- West makes a limit raise and bids 3♠.
- East rebids 4♠.
- All pass and East is the declarer in 4♠.

### The Defense

- South leads the ♦J.
- The defenders need four tricks. North has two tricks. The other tricks will have to come with partner's help. Neither diamonds nor clubs look promising. The heart suit is the best possibility. North plans to lead back a heart rather than return partner's suit.

### The Play

- Declarer has one too many losers. Declarer could try to eliminate a heart loser by discarding it on dummy's extra club winners after the ♣A has been driven out. Another possibility is to take a finesse in hearts.

## Exercise Six — Finding a Shift

### (E-Z Deal Cards: #8, Hand 2 — Dealer, East)

Turn up the cards from the second pre-dealt deal. Put each hand dummy-style at the edge of the table in front of each player.

### The Bidding

What would East open the bidding? North and South pass throughout. What does West respond? How does East describe the hand on the rebid? What level does West know the partnership belongs in? Is there a Golden Fit? What does West rebid? What is the contract? Who is the declarer?

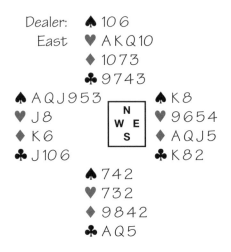

Dealer:   ♠ 10 6
East    ♥ A K Q 10
     ♦ 10 7 3
     ♣ 9 7 4 3

♠ A Q J 9 5 3         ♠ K 8
♥ J 8              ♥ 9 6 5 4
♦ K 6             ♦ A Q J 5
♣ J 10 6          ♣ K 8 2

     ♠ 7 4 2
     ♥ 7 3 2
     ♦ 9 8 4 2
     ♣ A Q 5

### The Defense

Which player makes the opening lead? What would the opening lead be? What is North's original plan. What further information does North have after the first trick? After the second trick? Which cards might partner hold to defeat the contract?

### The Play

Review the steps in declarer's PLAN. How does declarer plan to make the contract?

## Exercise Six — Finding a Shift

### The Bidding

- East opens the bidding 1♦, and West responds 1♠.
- East rebids 1NT to show a balanced minimum hand.
- West knows the partnership belongs in game in a known Golden Fit and bids 4♠.

### The Defense

- North leads the ♥A and plans to take as many hearts as possible.
- After the first two tricks, North knows that partner has three hearts and that declarer has only two.
- Partner might hold the ♣Q and the ♣A or the ♦K and the ♣A.

### The Play

- Declarer has two heart losers and two potential club losers.
- Declarer hopes to discard the club losers on dummy's extra diamond winners.

## Exercise Seven — Making Use of Signals

### (E-Z Deal Cards: #8, Hand 3 — Dealer, South)

Turn up the cards from the third pre-dealt deal. Put each hand dummy-style at the edge of the table in front of each player.

### The Bidding

South and West pass. Why can't North open 1NT? What does North bid? East passes. Without support for opener's suit and no suit to bid at the one level, what does South respond? West passes. How does North show maximum strength and balanced distribution? How does the bidding proceed from there? What is the contract? Who is the declarer?

Dealer:   ♠ A K
South     ♥ K J 10 6 5
          ♦ Q 10 3
          ♣ K Q J

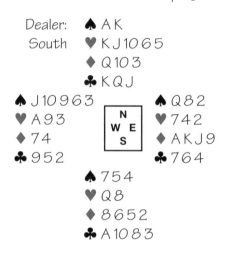

♠ J 10 9 6 3          ♠ Q 8 2
♥ A 9 3             ♥ 7 4 2
♦ 7 4               ♦ A K J 9
♣ 9 5 2            ♣ 7 6 4

            ♠ 7 5 4
            ♥ Q 8
            ♦ 8 6 5 2
            ♣ A 10 8 3

### The Defense

Which player makes the opening lead? What would the opening lead be? Does East like the suit partner led? How does East plan to defeat the contract? What signal does East give on the first trick?

### The Play

Review the steps in declarer's PLAN. How does declarer plan to make the contract?

## Exercise Seven — Making Use of Signals

### The Bidding

- North, having too much to start with 1NT, bids 1♥.
- South responds 1NT.
- North bids 3NT.
- All pass and South is the declarer in 3NT.

### The Defense

- West leads the ♠J.
- Although East likes partner's suit, there's a better chance for the defense in the diamond suit.
- East, therefore, discourages with the ♠2.

### The Play

- With two sure tricks in spades and four in clubs, declarer plans to promote tricks in the heart suit in order to make the contract.

## Exercise Eight — The Lesser of Evils
### (E-Z Deal Cards: #8, Hand 4 — Dealer, West)

Turn up the cards from the fourth pre-dealt deal. Put each hand dummy-style at the edge of the table in front of each player.

### The Bidding

West passes. What is North's opening bid? East passes. How does South show support for partner's major and the strength of the hand? West passes. What does North rebid? How does the auction proceed from there? What is the contract? What is the contract? Who is the declarer?

Dealer: ♠ K 6
West ♥ A 9 5 4 2
♦ A 4 3
♣ K 6 4

♠ J 9 7 4 2          ♠ A 10 3
♥ 6                         ♥ K 7 3
♦ J 7 2                   ♦ 10 9 8 6
♣ J 10 9 3             ♣ A 8 5

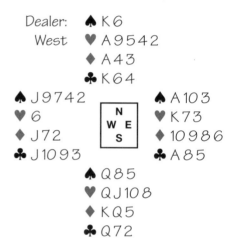

♠ Q 8 5
♥ Q J 10 8
♦ K Q 5
♣ Q 7 2

### The Defense

Which player makes the opening lead? What is East's plan? What would the opening lead be? Does West like the suit partner has led? Does West prefer another suit? Which card would West play on the first trick? Why? After regaining the lead, how does West plan to defend? Why?

### The Play

Review the steps in declarer's PLAN. How does declarer plan to make the contract?

## Exercise Eight — The Lesser of Evils

### The Bidding

- North opens the bidding 1 ♥.
- South responds 3 ♥.
- North bids 4 ♥.
- All pass and North is the declarer in 4 ♥.

### The Defense

- East leads the ♦10.
- Although West doesn't particularly like diamonds, there doesn't appear to be a better suit, so West encourages East to continue in diamonds.

### The Play

- Declarer has a spade loser, a heart loser, and two club losers. The main hope is that the heart finesse will work. If not, declarer may have to find an opponent with a doubleton ♣A. Declarer will lead toward one of the club honors in dummy and then play low from both hands on the second trick.

## Exercise Nine — Third Hand not so High
### (E-Z Deal Cards: #8, Hand 5 — Dealer, North)

Turn up the cards from the fifth pre-dealt deal. Put each hand dummy-style at the edge of the table in front of each player.

### The Bidding

North and South pass. What would East open the bidding? At what level does West know the partnership belongs? Is there a Golden Fit in a major suit? How can West find out? What does East rebid? What does West rebid? How does the auction proceed from there? What is the contract? Who is the declarer?

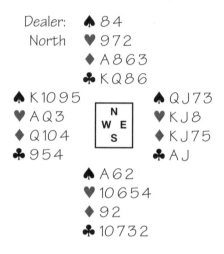

Dealer: ♠ 8 4
North ♥ 9 7 2
♦ A 8 6 3
♣ K Q 8 6

♠ K 10 9 5　　　　♠ Q J 7 3
♥ A Q 3　　　　　 ♥ K J 8
♦ Q 10 4　　　　　♦ K J 7 5
♣ 9 5 4　　　　　 ♣ A J

♠ A 6 2
♥ 10 6 5 4
♦ 9 2
♣ 10 7 3 2

### The Defense

Which player makes the opening lead? How might South plan to get a second trick from the trump suit? What would the opening lead be? How does North know that partner is unlikely to have a singleton diamond? How does North plan to defeat the contract? Which card would North play on the first trick? Why?

### The Play

Review the steps in declarer's PLAN. How does declarer plan to make the contract?

## Exercise Nine — Third Hand not so High

### The Bidding

- East opens 1NT.
- The partnership belongs in game.
- West uses the Stayman Convention and bids 2♣ to see if there is a Golden Fit.
- East shows a four-card spade suit by bidding 2♠.
- West bids 4♠ and all pass. East is the declarer.

### The Defense

- South makes the opening lead.
- South hopes to ruff a diamond.
- The opening lead is the ♦ 9.
- East would probably not have five diamonds and four spades and open 1NT.
- The next time South gets the lead, South can return a diamond.
- North can take the ♦ A and give South a ruff.
- North would play the ♦ 8 on the first trick.
- North wants to give South an encouraging signal.

### The Play

- Declarer has only three losers and will have to draw trumps as quickly as possible to make sure the defenders don't get an extra trick by ruffing one of declarer's winners.

## Exercise Ten — *Working Together*

### (E-Z Deal Cards: #8, Hand 6 — Dealer, East)

Turn up the cards from the sixth pre-dealt deal. Put each hand dummy-style at the edge of the table in front of each player.

### The Bidding

East and West pass throughout. What does South open the bidding? What does North respond? How does the auction proceed from there? What is the contract? Who is the declarer?

Dealer: ♠ Q J 10
East ♥ K 3 2
♦ Q 10 7 5
♣ K 9 4

♠ K 8 6 5 2        ♠ A 9 3
♥ 10 6 4    N      ♥ 9 8 5
♦ 8 3    W   E     ♦ A 6 2
♣ J 8 6      S     ♣ 10 5 3 2

♠ 7 4
♥ A Q J 7
♦ K J 9 4
♣ A Q 7

### The Defense

Which player makes the opening lead? How does West plan to defeat the contract? What would the opening lead be? Which card does East play to the first trick? How does East plan to defeat the contract? Which card does East return? Which card does West play? Why? Does East plan to hold up if declarer leads diamonds?

### The Play

Review the steps in declarer's PLAN. How does declarer plan to make the contract?

## Exercise Ten — *Working Together*

### The Bidding

- South opens 1NT.

- North responds 3NT.

- All pass and South is the declarer in 3NT.

### The Defense

- West leads the ♠5. East wins the trick with the ♠A and returns a spade.

- West ducks to keep an entry once the spades are established.

- East doesn't plan to hold up the ♦A.

### The Play

- The declarer plans to get the necessary extra tricks by promoting diamond winners.

# Exercise Eleven — Trump Promotion
## (E-Z Deal Cards: #8, Hand 7 — Dealer, South)

Turn up the cards from the seventh pre-dealt deal. Put each hand dummy-style at the edge of the table in front of each player.

### The Bidding

What is South's opening bid? East and West pass throughout. Does North know if there is a Golden Fit? At what level does the partnership belong? What does North respond? How does the bidding proceed from there? What is the contract? Who is the declarer?

Dealer: ♠ 10 9 8 6 5 2
South ♥ 6 4 2
♦ K Q
♣ K Q

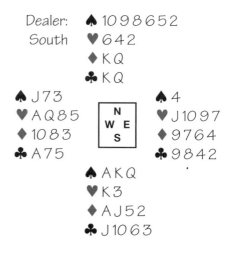

♠ J 7 3      ♠ 4
♥ A Q 8 5      ♥ J 10 9 7
♦ 10 8 3      ♦ 9 7 6 4
♣ A 7 5      ♣ 9 8 4 2

♠ A K Q
♥ K 3
♦ A J 5 2
♣ J 10 6 3

### The Defense

Which player makes the opening lead? What would the opening lead be? How many defensive tricks can West see? What possibilities are there for defeating the contract? What is West's plan?

### The Play

Review the steps in declarer's PLAN. How does declarer plan to make the contract?

## Exercise Eleven — Trump Promotion

### The Bidding

- South opens 1NT.
- North knows there is a Golden Fit and that the partnership belongs in game.
- North responds 4♠.
- All pass and North is the declarer in 4♠.

### The Defense

- East leads the ♥ J.
- After taking the ♥ A, the ♥ Q and the ♣A, West returns another heart, hoping that declarer will have to ruff in the dummy to promote West's ♠J.

### The Play

- Declarer has four potential losers and hopes that either the ♥ A is in the right place for the ♥ K to take a trick or that there aren't any losers in the trump suit.

## Exercise Twelve — *Second Hand High*

### (E-Z Deal Cards: #8, Hand 8 — Dealer, West)

Turn up the cards from the eighth pre-dealt deal. Put each hand dummy-style at the edge of the table in front of each player.

### The Bidding

What is West's opening bid? North and South pass throughout the auction. What does East respond? How does the auction proceed from there? What is the contract? Who is the declarer?

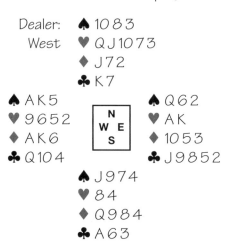

Dealer:   ♠ 10 8 3
West      ♥ Q J 10 7 3
          ♦ J 7 2
          ♣ K 7

♠ A K 5              ♠ Q 6 2
♥ 9 6 5 2            ♥ A K
♦ A K 6             ♦ 10 5 3
♣ Q 10 4            ♣ J 9 8 5 2

          ♠ J 9 7 4
          ♥ 8 4
          ♦ Q 9 8 4
          ♣ A 6 3

### The Defense

Which player makes the opening lead? What would the opening lead be? How does South plan to defeat the contract? What does South plan to do after regaining the lead? If declarer leads a club, which card should South play? Why?

### The Play

Review the steps in declarer's PLAN. How does declarer plan to make the contract?

## Exercise Twelve — Second Hand High

### The Bidding

- West opens 1NT.

- East responds 3 NT.

- All pass and the final contract is 3NT. West is the declarer.

### The Defense

- North leads the ♥ Q.

- South hopes the defense has enough heart tricks to defeat the contract.

- South plans to lead hearts at every opportunity. If declarer leads a club, South will take the ♣A immediately and return a heart.

### The Play

- Declarer hopes to get the extra tricks needed from promotion in the club suit once the ♣A and the ♣K have been driven out.

# APPENDIX

Glossary of Terms

# GLOSSARY OF TERMS

**Attitude Signal** — An attitude signal gives your partner advice on whether or not to lead or continue playing a particular suit. It's partner's option to follow this advice as seems fit.

**Blocked** — A situation in which entry problems within a particular suit make it difficult or impossible to take winners or possible winners in that suit.

**Broken Sequence** — A sequence in which the top two cards are touching (solid), but a card is missing before the next highest card (K–Q–10 or Q–J–9, for example).

**Captain** — The partner who knows more about the combined hands and is responsible for directing the partnership to its final contract. Usually the responder is the captain.

**Combined Hands** — The cards making up both hands belonging to one partnership.

**Combined Points** — The total number of points belonging to a partnership.

**Convention** — A bid that conveys a meaning other than that which would normally be attributed to it.

**Count Signal** — A method of following suit or discarding that tells partner how many cards you have in a suit.

**Dangerous Opponent** — A defender is dangerous when able to lead a card that will set your contract.

**Defensive Signals** — Specific cards played by the defenders in certain situations by which each defender can paint a picture to give partner the information needed to make an appropriate decision.

**Discarding a Loser** — Getting rid of a card in a player's hand that could lose a trick to the opponents.

**Distribution** — The number of cards held in each suit by a particular player or by a partnership; the number of cards held in a particular suit by a partnership.

**Drawing Trumps** — The playing of trumps until there are none in the opponents' hands.

**Duck** — To play a low card and surrender a trick which could be won, with the object of preserving an entry or of shutting out an opponent's suit.

**Entry** — A card that provides a means of winning a trick in a particular hand.

**Equals (Play from)** — When holding cards of equal rank in a suit, it is often important which card is chosen to be played to a particular trick. A defender's card may provide partner with important information, or it may deceive the declarer.

**Finesse** — An attempt to win a trick with a card that does not rank as high as one held by the opponents.

**Forcing (Bid)** — A bid that requires partner to bid again.

**Fourth Highest** — The fourth highest card of a long suit, starting at the top and counting down (e.g., K–5–4–**3**–2).

**High-Low (Signal)** — The order of playing cards so that a higher card is played first followed by a lower card (the 5 followed by the 3, for example) expressing the desire for partner to continue playing the suit or suggesting an interest in that suit being played when partner obtains the lead. It may also suggest that the player started with an even number of cards in the suit.

**Holdup (Play)** — Refusing to take a winner at your first opportunity with the intention of removing link cards in that suit from an opponent.

**High Card Points (HCPs)** — The points assigned to the four honor cards. Ace — 4; King — 3; Queen — 2; Jack — 1.

**Interior Sequence** — A sequence in which the top card is not contiguous with the solid (touching) portion of the sequence (K–J–10 or A–10–9, for example).

**Invitational (Bid)** — A bid that invites partner to bid again.

**Link** — A card which can be led to a winner (entry) in the opposite hand.

**Long Suit** — A suit which contains four or more cards.

**Lose Control** — A situation in which declarer has no trumps left to prevent the defenders from taking their winners.

**Loser** — A card in a player's hand that could lose a trick to the opponents.

**Low-High (Signal)** — A low card followed by a higher card (the 3 followed by the 5, for example), indicating an odd number of cards in the suit or a lack of interest in the suit.

**MUD** — A lead convention in which the original lead from three small cards is the middle one, followed in play by the higher. The name comes from the first letters of middle, up, down, the order in which the cards are played.

**Natural Trump Trick** — Trick in a trump suit which will eventually be a winner. For example, a defender's holding of Q–J–10–9 in the trump suit is two natural trump tricks when declarer holds the ace and king.

**Opening Lead** — The card led by declarer's left-hand opponent after the auction has ended.

**Opponents' Suit** — A suit held or bid by one or both of the opponents.

**Overruff** — To ruff higher than the opponent on one's right after a non-trump suit has been led.

**Overtake** — To play a higher card than the one already played by partner.

**Partner's Suit** — The suit bid or rebid by your partner.

**Passive Lead** — An opening lead which is unlikely to hurt the defending side, but is not expected to have a positive value. In certain situations, a trump lead may be passive.

**Preemptive (Bid)** — A bid made to interfere with the opponents' auction. It usually is made with a long suit and a weak hand.

**Quick Loser** — A quick loser is one that will be lost as soon as you give up the lead.

**Redouble** — A call made after the opponents have doubled. Originally it was used to increase the scoring value of overtricks or undertricks. In modern bidding methods, it is often used for other purposes.

**Ruff** — Playing a trump on a trick when you are void in the suit led.

**Sacrifice** — A bid made without the intention of fulfilling the contract but of preventing the opponents from playing and making their contract. The assumption is that you will lose fewer points by going down in your bid than the opponents would have received for making their contract.

**Second Hand** — The second player to play to a trick after the lead is made.

**Shift** — To lead a suit other than that previously led.

**Short Suit** — In an original hand of 13 cards, a suit containing three cards or fewer.

**Signoff (Bid)** — A bid that asks partner to pass.

**Splitting Honors** — Playing one of two honors which are in sequence. Playing the king or queen from a holding of the K–Q–6, for example.

**Spot (Cards)** — Cards ranking below the 10 . . . from the 9 to the 2.

**Stranded** — Winners that cannot be taken because there is no entry to them.

**Stayman (Convention)** — An artificial response of 2♣ to an opening bid of 1NT (or 3♣ in response to a 2 NT opening), asking opener to bid a four-card major suit when holding one, and otherwise to bid 2♦ or 3♦ after a 2 NT opening.

**Stronger Suit** — A suit which has equal length to another suit but has more high-card strength.

**Suit Preference (Signal)** — A device in defensive play whereby a player may indicate a desire to have partner lead one suit rather than another, when partner has a choice.

**Sure Trick** — A trick that can be taken without giving up the lead to the opponents.

**Third Hand** — The partner of the leader to a trick.

**Top of Nothing** — The highest ranking card of three or more low cards.

**Top of a Sequence** — The highest ranking card in a sequence.

**Touching Honors** — Two or more honors in sequence. In a holding of Q–J–10–7, e.g., the first three are touching honors.

**Trapping** — Finessing.

**Unbid Suit(s)** — A suit or suits not bid by a partnership during the auction.

**Unblocking** — Playing or discarding a high card during the play in order to get rid of it to allow the opposite hand to take tricks in the suit.

**Uppercut** — A ruff, usually by a defender, aimed at promoting a trump trick for partner.

**ACBL has what you need to brush up or polish your skills and techniques, or even learn new ones!**
**We can help you with great gift ideas for any occasion!**

### Your "Source" for information

- ✔ Playing cards
- ✔ Duplicate boards
- ✔ Bidding boxes
- ✔ Convention cards and holders
- ✔ Movement cards
- ✔ Bridge games
- ✔ Tote bags
- ✔ Bridge books with coded cards for practice
- ✔ Videos

- ✔ Bridge software, including CD ROM
- ✔ Tablecloths
- ✔ Windbreakers, shirts, aprons
- ✔ Dangle earrings and LM jewelry
- ✔ More than 100 bridge books by great authors
- ✔ Bridge Bucks and other prizes

Call, write, e-mail, or fax your request for a free catalog today!

Your friendly Sales Representative will be happy to help you with your order.

Orders are shipped the next day.

Same day service is available if you order early.

Browse our web page, **www.acbl.org** and shop our new, secure catalog at your convenience.

**CREDIT CARD ORDERS:** (toll-free)
1 (800) 264-2743 (U.S.) • 1 (800) 264-8786 (Canada)
or Fax (901) 398-7754 E-mail: Sales@acbl.org

# ARE YOU A MEMBER?

The American Contract Bridge League (ACBL) is dedicated to the playing, teaching, and promotion of contract bridge.

The membership of 170,000 includes a wide range of players — from the thousands who are just learning the joy of bridge to the most proficient players in North America. The ACBL has long been the center of North American bridge activity. In 1997, the organization celebrated its 60th Anniversary. ACBL invites you to join in the excitement of organized bridge play.

ACBL offers sanctioned games at local clubs, tournaments, on cruise ships, and on the Internet! The ACBL is a service-oriented membership organization offering considerable benefits to its members including reduced playing fees at tournaments!

If you are not a member of the ACBL, join today to take advantage of the reduced rates for first-time members and to receive one of our outstanding bridge magazines — *The Bridge Bulletin* (monthly) or *Play Bridge* (bi-monthly)! You will receive an ACBL player number and any masterpoints (the measure of achievement for all bridge players) you win at ACBL clubs and tournaments will be automatically recorded to your account!

You can enjoy the fun, friendship, and competition of bridge with an ACBL membership. Join today by visiting our web site **www.acbl.org** or by calling ACBL Headquarters in Memphis, TN (901) 332–5586, ext. 259. ACBL is a Great Deal!

American Contract Bridge League
2990 Airways Blvd.
Memphis, TN 38116
(901) 332–5586 • www.acbl.org